UNCONDITIONAL SURRENDER

God's Program for Victory

Other books by Gary North—

Marx's Religion of Revolution, 1968
An Introduction to Christian Economics, 1973
None Dare Call It Witchcraft, 1976
How You Can Profit from the Coming Price Controls, 1977
The Dominion Covenant: Genesis, 1981
Successful Investing in an Age of Envy, 1981

UNCONDITIONAL SURRENDER

God's Program for Victory

Gary North

Geneva Press

ISBN 0-939404-00-1

Geneva Press is part of the ministry of Geneva Divinity School.
Address: 708 Hamvassy, Tyler, TX 75701.

This book is dedicated to
James Robison
who has already begun an
important program for victory.

iii

TABLE OF CONTENTS

PREFACE vii

Part One: FOUNDATIONS 1

   Introduction to Part One 3

   1. God 9

   2. Man 23

   3. Law 55

   Summary of Part One 83

Part Two: INSTITUTIONS 87

   Introduction to Part Two 89

   4. Family 91

   5. Church 105

   6. State 129

   7. Economy 145

   Summary of Part Two 169

Part Three: EXPECTATIONS 173

   Introduction to Part Three 175

   8. The Kingdom of God 179

   9. A Strategy for Dominion 215

   Summary of Part Three 229

CONCLUSION 231

BIBLIOGRAPHY 237

SCRIPTURE INDEX 249

GENERAL INDEX 256

ORDER BLANKS 265

PREFACE

This book was born of necessity. I publish a bi-weekly economic newsletter, *Remnant Review*, which is sent to people who are interested in ways of preserving and increasing their capital. In my June 6, 1980 issue, I wrote about the "Four G's" in investing: gold, groceries, guns, and God. I had plenty of recommendations on the first three, but when I came to the fourth, I got stuck. I wanted to recommend a good introductory book on the significance of Christianity for the modern world, and I couldn't think of one. There are books of many kinds, all dealing with one aspect or another of Christian faith and worship, but I couldn't think of one that was general, theologically accurate, comprehensive, and readable.

This began to bother me. I publish seven newsletters, and I write four of them, so my time is extremely scarce. Furthermore, I run the Institute for Christian Economics, and one of my continuing projects is writing a complete economic commentary on the Bible. I spend a minimum of ten hours a week, fifty weeks per year, on this project. So I knew I didn't have much time to write a book. At the same time, I became convinced that an introductory volume was needed.

To get the job done without ruining my schedule, I decided to write this book, but with a time limit. That limit was two weeks. I began on July 2, 1980, and I finished the first draft on July 14. In fact, I even had half a day to spare, since I finished in the afternoon.

I had James Jordan read the manuscript, and he made some important suggestions. I have included most of them in the final version. Still, the book is basically the product of two weeks of writing. The entire project took one month: from beginning to final draft.

I wanted it to be readable. Complexity makes books unreadable, so I wrote it rapidly: no notes, no outline, and with only the chapter headings in mind. But I had been studying the Bible for over 20 years before I began this project. (I used the King James Version for citations, since most readers own this translation.) I made major revisions only in the chapter on man, with James Jordan's help, in the section dealing with salvation. I am least happy with this section, since it's more complex than I had hoped, but I have been unable to figure out a way to make it shorter or easier. I wanted it to be accurate.

I simply didn't have time to be more thorough. I hope that my approach has at least made the book readable. Anyone who wants to pursue some of these topics in greater detail can follow through by reading the books in the bibliography section. No single handbook can serve as a final source on the meaning and implications of Christianity.

I decided orginally to call the book, *Christianity: What Difference Does It Make?* Some of my associates wanted me to call it, *Sheer Christianity*, a title reminiscent of C. S. Lewis' *Mere Christianity*. But I have stuck with *Unconditional Surrender*, since I think it comes closer to the major themes of this book.

What I wanted to produce was a handbook that could serve as an introduction to the basics of Christianity, but also as a study guide for people who are already Christians, but who have never spent much time considering the social, political, and economic implications of Christianity. It might be thought of as a fat tract. It might be thought of as a Christian manifesto. My hope is that it will at least be thought of.

The book is divided into three sections. The first section, "Foundations," covers the fundamentals of orthodox Christianity. These are the religious principles that set Christianity apart from all other religions. The second section, "Institutions," covers the implications of Christianity for the major institutions of human life. We should expect to find a very different approach in each major institution from what we would expect to find in non-Christian cultures. Finally, there is the third section on "Expectations." What should we expect in the future? How will we implement the principles we found in section one? Do we have time to develop the institutional base of section two? What is the proper plan of action? What are we required by God to do?

This book will inevitably offend everybody. It breaks with most of what we know as "establishment Christianity." There are a lot of establishment Christians who think they aren't part of a religious establishment, but they are. When they read this book, and if they think about what they are reading, they will either have to reject much of what I conclude in this book or else they will have to begin to labor long and hard to rethink the religious principles they have been taught for many years.

Any time a reader doesn't like what he's reading, he should check his premises. Then he should check out the documentation I provide. Errors in any human book are inevitable, but it's a question of reducing errors to a minimum. This book breaks with many of the traditional slogans of Christian churches, yet it was written in terms of this presupposition: **the Bible is the inspired Word of God**. It was perfect in the original manuscripts (autographs). It is because I believe the Bible is inspired, with respect to both its historical data and its theological judgments, that I decided to write this book. I am convinced that much of what passes for conservative Christianity in the late 20th century is neither conservative nor Christian.

What I recommend to the reader is simple to state, but difficult to achieve: **respect for what the Bible says**. Something isn't Christian because I say it is, but because the Bible says it is. At the same time, something isn't Christian just because some pastor or some paperback book says it is. Just because you haven't heard anything like the message this book presents doesn't means it isn't an accurate message. You have to make up your own mind. Tradition is no substitute for personal responsibility. Slogans you learned in Sunday school may not be what the Bible really teaches. Just because you may have an outline at the foot of each page in your Bible doesn't guarantee that the text of the Bible teaches what's in those footnotes. **You** have to decide, not in terms of what men say, but what the Bible says.

PART I

FOUNDATIONS

INTRODUCTION TO PART I

For about as long as I can remember, I've heard people tell me that such and such a church or group or belief "isn't a religion; it's a way of life." Have you ever heard that slogan? Think about it. Have you ever heard of a religion that isn't a way of life? Furthermore, have you ever heard of a way of life that wasn't basically a sort of religion? Every time I hear someone say that "Christianity is just another religion, but I'm looking for a way of life," I begin to wonder just how much that person knows about either Christianity or ways of life.

Christianity is a religion. No doubt about **that** fact! It has church buildings, and ministers, and church socials, and missionaries, and collection plates. It has youth groups, Bible studies, summer camps, hymnals, seminaries, and mortgages. It has marriages, baptisms, and funerals. It's a religion.

But Christianity is also a way of life. It has a moral code. It has a system of church courts. It has creeds, doctrines, and catechisms. It has members who share similar views on the meaning of life and death, good and bad, history and the future, men and women, God and man. And because Christians think about these subjects in ways different from the ways that Moslems, Buddhists, Hindus, and atheists think about them, the kinds of societies Christians have built, or have influenced, look a lot different from other societies. In other words, **it really makes a difference what people believe**. Their ideas have consequences.

People usually don't think deeply about the way they live. They take most things for granted. There's not enough time in a day to think everything through. We can't question everything all the time. But once in a while a person sits down and asks himself: "What kind of a world am I living in? Why is it the way it is? Is it going to change some day? Is it going to change for the better?" And then he may ask himself: "Who am I? What am I doing here?

3

What should I be doing? Where am I going?''

And then, if he's a typical 20th century man, he opens a can of beer, turns on the television set, and forgets all his questions.

The Bible talks about the person who does this sort of thing. ''But be ye doers of the word, and not hearers only, deceiving your own selves. For if any be a hearer of the word, and not a doer, he is like unto a man beholding his natural face in a glass [mirror], for he beholdeth himself, and goeth his way, and straightway forgetteth what manner of man he was'' (James 1:22-24). A man asks himself some very good questions, and then he doesn't do anything to get some good answers.

What good are questions if you never get any decent answers? Not much good at all.

Maybe you've started asking yourself some good questions. Maybe you think that a little book like this can help get you started in finding answers to good questions. Whatever your reason for reading this far, I'm going to try to give you a hand. No book of this size will give you all the answers. Life isn't that easy. But it will help you get **some** answers, and maybe you'll even pick up a few ideas about how you can get a lot more answers. And when you get answers, you can start taking action.

But first you need some questions. Let me suggest a few. When I taught college a few years ago, I told my students a little trick they could use to help them ''get a handle'' on history, government, sociology, and economics courses. I told them they could ask themselves three questions about any society known to man, and if they could get even short answers to these three questions, they could probably pass the course. Here are the three questions.

1. What does a society believe about **God**?
2. What does a society believe about **man**?
3. What does a society believe about **law**?

It looks easy enough, doesn't it? Well, looks are deceiving. A serious scholar could spend a lifetime taking one society and studying just one of these questions. But you don't have a lifetime to spend this way, and neither do I. So the best we can do is look at a few books or articles, and then hope that the writers knew what they were writing about.

We all know that people don't agree with each other about everything, not even people in a very small community. In fact, sometimes it seems that people don't agree about much of anything. But once in a while, we can find out what people do agree about. One of the best times to find out what people really believe is when they face a life-and-death crisis. "When the chips are down," if I may use a gambling term, we find out what people think is really important.

Sometimes men have to die for their beliefs. Maybe there's a war, or a revolution, or some sort of major crisis. What is a man willing to die for? What are a lot of men in a society willing to die for? God, country, and family? Fame and fortune? Honor? When we pin men down and ask them what really matters to them, we get some idea of who they are and what they are. We get some idea of who they think they would like to become. We find out what they want out of life when they face a situation that threatens their lives. **There's** a man's religion.

Think about it yourself. Is there something in your life that you would really be willing to die for? Most parents would say that they'd be willing to die for their children. But what about an idea or a belief? If an enemy were holding a gun to your head, and he told you that he was going to pull the trigger unless you were willing publicly to renounce some idea, is there any idea so precious to you that you'd say, "Shoot." Now you're getting close to **your** religion.

About 1800 years ago, there were people in the Roman Empire who told the Emperor and his officials, "Shoot." Of course, they didn't have guns back then. But they had lions and arenas. They had chopping blocks for human heads. They had all sorts of tortures available. The Roman Empire waged war on the early Christians, and a significant number of them absolutely refused to toss a bit of incense on an altar to the Emperor. Was that such a big deal? They thought so. They resisted, they died, and after three hundred years of on-and-off persecution, they won. From about the year 363, all the Emperors of the Roman Empire professed faith in Jesus Christ as the living God who controls history. Anyone who refused to make this profession didn't become Emperor. Maybe they all didn't believe in Christ, but they said they did.

The early Christians believed that it makes a difference what you believe about God. They were willing to die for their belief. They believed the words of Jesus: "For whosoever will save his life shall lose it: and whosoever will lose his life for my sake shall find it. For what is a man profited, if he shall gain the whole world, and lose his own soul? Or what shall a man give in exchange for his soul?'' (Matthew 16:25-26). They believed that you can't buy your way out of hell and into heaven.

Is there anything on earth so important to you that you'd die in order to preserve it, or to assert your commitment to it? If so, then that's probably your highest goal, your most cherished possession. We might even say it's your God. One thing is for sure: it's about as close as you can come to locating your God. If you'd give your life for it, it must be pretty important to you.

Some people believe the slogan, concerning Communism, "Better dead than red." Others disagree: "Better red than dead," since you can always fight another day, or at least you may have time to see Communism collapse. But the two positions are opposed to each other. You can't work out a compromise here.

Yet other people want a third alternative: "Neither red nor dead." They want a **positive** alternative. They don't want the lesser of two evils. They know what they want, and they're willing to work hard to achieve their goal.

That's my position. I want a positive alternative. My motto in life is this: **You can't fight something with nothing**. If you don't like what's going on around you, then get out and try to change it. If you don't like something, offer something else that's better. That's why I took the time to write this book. I didn't like the others.

I'm concerned about the state of the world today. I'm convinced that Western Civilization is at a turning point. I don't want the leaders and citizens of the Free World to make decisions that will spell the doom of our way of life. Yet there are a lot of things about our way of life that I'd like to see changed. In fact, I'm convinced that if they're not changed, we're going to lose the positive aspects of our way of life for a long, long time. I don't want to have to make the choice between "Better red than dead" or "Better dead than red." While there's still time, I'd like the third alternative: **neither!**

But you can't fight something with nothing. That's why I'd like it if you'd give some time and effort to thinking about some basic problems. Is the world facing a crisis of monumental proportions? Is there anything we can do to solve the problems we're facing? Can we find where we went wrong, and then do something about it? Is there anything we can do that will make a difference?

That's what this book is about: **doing something**—many things, in fact—that will unquestionably make a **lot** of difference. But we can't know which things will make a difference if we don't understand the nature of our world, ourselves, and our resources. That's what I want you to think about.

Perhaps you aren't very familiar with the history of Christianity over the last century or so. One of the continuing debates concerns the legitimacy of social action. Those who have tended to reject the basic doctrines of the faith—the infallibility of the Bible, the deity of Christ, the reality of the virgin birth, the second coming of Christ in judgment, etc.—have been the proponents of social action by Christians, especially political action. On the other hand, those who have defended the traditional doctrines have tended to drop out of politics. They have concentrated on preaching, evangelism, foreign missions, Bible conferences, study groups, and so forth. They have concerned themselves with bringing the message of personal salvation—a message which has deemphasized or even denied the possibility of Christian social reconstruction.

One slogan which pretty well summarizes the division is this: "The liberals have believed in history but not in God, while the conservatives have believed in God but not in history." What this book stresses is the reality of both God and history. Individuals are saved, but if they bear spiritual fruit, they will also bear cultural fruit. God speaks to this world, for He made this world. He calls people to repentance, but repentance from specific sins, specific ways of life, specific attitudes, specific philosophies, and specific economic doctrines. God speaks to the whole man, and therefore He speaks to the whole world. We must therefore preach the **whole counsel of God,** just as the prophets of the Old Testament did.

Religions, if they are truly religions, have implications for this world. A true religion is a way of life. Any version of Christianity which is not **applied** Christianity isn't Christianity. Action for action's sake isn't Christianity, but action for God's sake, and according to God's revealed guidelines, is Christianity. So now the question to be answered is: What **is** Christianity?

Remember my three questions? The questions we can use to discover the most important features of any society? What kind of **God** do Christians believe in? What is their view of **man**? And finally, what is their view of **law**?

Can Christianity make a difference? The Bible says it can. History says that it has in the past. But **will** it make a difference? **That's** the question!

What is Christianity, anyway? What is it really all about? Does it make much sense to ask whether Christianity can make a difference if we don't know what it is in the first place?

Let's look at our three questions: God, man, and law. What does the Bible say about these three topics? Until we know the answers, we sure can't apply them to ourselves, our world, and our futures.

Chapter 1

GOD

What does the Bible have to say about God? A whole lot, as you probably guessed. It says that God is **light**. "This then is the message which we have heard of him, and declare unto you, that God is light, and in him is no darkness at all" (I John 1:5). (If you're wondering what "I John 1:5" means, I'll tell you. In the New Testament, as in the Old Testament, we have the various books marked off by chapters and verses. These divisions were made over a thousand years after the books of the New Testament were written. "I John 1:5" refers to the first epistle of John, chapter one, verse five. If you've figured out that there must be a "II John," you're on target. In fact, there's even a "III John." It's only one chapter long, however, so we write "III John 3." The "3" refers in this case to the verse, not the chapter).

The Bible also tells us that God is **love**. "He that loveth not knoweth not God; for God is love" (I John 4:8). If a man loves nothing or no one, then he obviously can't be a follower of God, John said, since God is love.

The trouble is, there are many religions that tell us that God is light and love. The words don't tell us that much about God. You can put almost any interpretation on "light" and "love." We need to know more about God than this.

Why not start at the beginning? Why not start with the opening words of the Book of Genesis, the first book in the Bible? "In the beginning God created the heaven and the earth." Above all else, God is the **Creator**.

Now we're getting somewhere. The concept of God as the absolute Creator is unique to Christianity and Judaism. There are other religions that speak of God as the molder of the world, or the original being, but no religions other than Christianity and Judaism speak of God as the absolute, sovereign, "no help needed"

9

Creator. The first chapter of Genesis says that He created the whole universe by the power of His word. No pre-existing matter, no spare parts lying around the back yard, not even a back yard for spare parts to be lying around in. Nothing.

God created all things **out of nothing**. Now that's a hard doctrine to believe. Men just don't want to believe it. They'll go to incredible lengths to avoid believing this. They create myths, like the myth of the cosmic egg. Or maybe they choose to believe in an eternal ocean, and out of the watery ocean all things, including gods, have sprung. Modern scientists follow the lead of Greek philosophers who lived 2500 years ago, and conclude: 1) that the universe has always existed just about the way it exists now (the "steady-state" theory); or 2) that the universe started when there was a huge explosion in some eternal matter-energy (the "Big Bang" theory). Of course, modern scientists dress up the theories with a lot of mathematics and fancy words, but they really haven't come up with any new outlines.

Creation out of nothing is what the Bible teaches. It doesn't teach that God dropped a part of Himself down into space, and that this spark of divinity turned into the world. It doesn't teach that He molded pre-existing matter into what we see today. It doesn't say that the world of matter somehow imitated God, who is nothing more than "thought thinking itself." (This suggestion was made by Aristotle in his book, *Physics*, chapter 8, which he wrote around 330 B.C.). What the Bible teaches is that God said, "Let there be light," and there was light (Genesis 1:3). One after another, God said, "Let there be. . ." and immediately there **was**. The firmament, water, dry land, grass, sun, moon, stars, animals, and finally, man: God said, "Let there be. . ." and there was.

He did all this in six days. Hebrew grammar can't tell us whether these were 24-hour days. A lot of modern Christians have argued that they weren't. But when you think about it, why not? I mean, if God created everything out of nothing, which is one of the most difficult things in the world to believe in, why not accept the Bible's words at face value? The ancient Hebrews certainly believed that the six days were really days. Each day had a morning and evening. Adding up the days produced the 7-day week, with a day of rest every seventh day. Besides, what good is the theory of billion-year days, assuming you take seriously the Genesis account of creation? The sun, moon, and stars were created on the fourth day. But the herb-yielding seeds and fruit trees were created on the third day (Genesis 1:11-12). What scientist will accept the idea that the plants of the earth were created before the sun was created? Not an evolutionist. Not even if we try to argue that the word "day" could mean a billion years. The modern scientist cannot possibly accept the idea of God's creation out of nothing, so redefining "day" to mean a longer period of time solves nothing.

What we learn in the first chapter of Genesis is one of the most important doctrines of Christianity: God created the world out of nothing. He is totally separate from the world. He is totally sovereign over the world. The *Oxford English Dictionary* defines "sovereign" in this way: "One who has supremacy or rank above, or authority over, others; a superior; a ruler, governor, lord, or master. . ." Yet even these words are insufficient to convey to us the Bible's doctrine of the sovereignty of God over His creation. **God is the absolute controller of everything that happens. He controls the universe because He made the universe.** It has no independence from God because it was made by God. It is **presently sustained** by God. The **providence of God** means simply God's active sustaining and ordering of His universe.

The Bible doesn't teach that the universe is a huge clock or machine that God made a long time ago, when He first wound up the spring, and now it ticks away, completely independent of God. The universe is God's **property**, and He guards it jealously. In the Psalms, those inspired poems and hymns of the Old Testament, we read: "The earth is the Lord's, and the fulness thereof; the world, and they that dwell therein. For he founded it upon the seas, and established it upon the floods" (Psalm 24:1-2). The earth is filled with living things, including you and me. All living creatures belong to God, including you and me.

The Creator-Creature Distinction

We can call this doctrine of creation the **Creator-creature distinction**. There is a basic difference between God and the universe, between God and man. Man is a created being. No man stands alone. No man stands independent of God. No man merges into God, either. God tells us very specifically that "my thoughts are not your thoughts, neither are your ways my ways" (Isaiah 55:8). Why not? "For as the heavens are higher than the earth, so are my ways higher than your ways, and my thoughts than your thoughts'' (Isaiah 55:9).

This doesn't mean that God is so far removed from us that He cares nothing for us. On the contrary: "For thus saith the high and lofty One that inhabiteth eternity, whose name is Holy; I dwell in the high and holy place, with him also that is of a contrite and humble spirit, to revive the spirit of the humble, and to revive the heart of the contrite ones" (Isaiah 57:15). Does this mean that God's people, who have contrite and humble hearts in front of God's holiness, really dwell with Him in those high places? **In principle, His people dwell with Him in spirit,** for He reaches down and touches them, heals their wounds, and lifts their spirits up. We are like people who have residences elsewhere, so we put down our home address, even when we're far away from home. The Apostle Paul wrote: "For our conversation [the old English word for **citizenship**] is in heaven; from whence also we look for the Saviour, the Lord Jesus Christ" (Philippians 3:20). Of course, those who don't look to heaven for their savior, the Lord Jesus Christ, obviously don't have their citizenship in heaven. That's an important point which Paul was trying to make.

Christianity doesn't teach **deism**, the idea that God is completely separate and distant from the universe, which is now absolutely independent of God. It also doesn't teach **pantheism**, which says that God is so deeply embedded in this world that He is not distinguishable from it. God is certainly everywhere. The Psalmist announces: "Whither shall I go from thy Spirit? Or whither shall I flee from thy presence? If I ascend up into heaven, thou art there. If I make my bed in hell, behold, thou art there" (Psalm 139:7-8). Nothing is going on anywhere which God hasn't heard about. But He isn't part of His creation.

God is never to be identified with His creation. There is no "universal form of being," no "ultra something" in which both God and man participate. **There is no "scale of being" between God and His creation.** Men dwell in the presence of God, but they are not "one with God" in terms of their being. He is utterly different. The Psalmist says it best: "Lord, thou hast been our dwelling place in all generations. Before the mountains were brought forth, or even that thou hadst formed the earth and the world, even from everlasting to everlasting, thou art God" (Psalm 90:1-2). Man is, but God always was. When man wasn't, God was.

It can never be said of man: "For of him, and through him, and to him, are all things: to whom be glory forever. Amen" (Romans 11:36). But Paul said it of God. God never said this about man; He said it about Himself: "Yea, before the day was I am he; and there is none that can deliver out of my hand: I will work, and who shall let [prevent] it?" (Isaiah 43:13). Men cannot stick out their arms and stop God's plan. Even kings can't do it, for kings make their decisions in terms of God's plan. "The king's heart is in the hand of the Lord, as the rivers of water: he turneth it whithersoever he will" (Proverbs 21:1).

Men don't like to hear about this sort of God. They prefer to think of God as some sort of cosmic expert who can be called upon to bail us out every time we get in trouble. He can give us specialized information, as a professional counsellor might, but He certainly isn't the final authority. After all, men say to themselves, "We're all in this together: God, mankind, and the environment." God becomes, at best, "Dr. God," while all the rest of us are merely "Mr."

The Book of Hebrews, in the New Testament, paints a very different picture of God. "And, Thou, Lord, in the beginning hast laid the foundation of the earth; and the heavens are the works of thine hands. They shall perish, but thou remainest; and they all shall wax old as doth a garment. And as a vesture shalt thou fold them up, and they shall be changed: but thou art the same, and thy years shall not fail" (Hebrews 1:10-12). God is in absolute control, forever.

Why is it so important to keep stressing this Creator-creature distinction? Because it is the very essence of man's rebellion against God to deny it. When the evil tempter tempted Eve, he offered her a special hope: **to be as God**. She had been commanded not to eat the fruit of the tree of the knowledge of good and evil. Satan (Revelation 12:9) said: "For God doth know that in the day ye eat thereof, then your eyes shall be opened, and ye shall be as gods, knowing good and evil" (Genesis 3:5). So she ate, and her husband ate. They defied God. They tested God, to see whether His word would come true, or Satan's. They elevated themselves into judges, for they thought they would test God's word against Satan's. How would they do this? By assuming that they could determine good and evil in defiance of God's word to them. They acted as though they were sovereign creators even before they actually ate the fruit.

Again and again, throughout the history of man, people have compromised or actually rebelled against this doctrine of God the Creator. They have tried to elevate mankind into co-creators with God. They have said that men were once one with God, and that they shall be one with God in the future. They have said that men are endowed with a "spark of divinity." They have said that mankind, through a long evolutionary process, will become equal with God. They have said that since man and God share the same common "being" or substance, it is possible for men to bridge the gap and become divine. The Bible rejects all of these assertions.

In the ancient tyrannies of the Mesopotamian world, kings were said to be divine. The Egyptians believed that their Pharaoh was a divine being, the link between heaven and earth, the sustainer of Egypt's prosperity. This belief led directly to the idea of a **divine State**, a political order which could not be challenged by "mere men." The State, since it was the highest link between man and God, was therefore all-powerful, in the theologies of the ancient world.

Of course, you can accomplish much the same thing by denying that there is any God above the political order. Since the State is the most visibly powerful human institution, atheism removes a concept of some higher court of appeal beyond the State. The State becomes "divine" by default—the highest court of appeal, the highest moral authority. Not every atheist is a statist. But where atheism predominates, the State steadily encroaches on men's freedom, for they are left with no higher authority to appeal to, or to provide them with the moral justification for resistance to tyranny. Where the fear of God is absent, **the fear of the State** is a convenient, and universal, substitute.

Holiness

People who live in Protestant countries probably have heard the word "holiness" in several contexts. They have heard of "holy roller" churches. Or maybe they've sung the traditional hymn, "Holy, Holy, Holy." Another possibility: holiness sects. These are tightly knit groups of Christian believers who pursue a rigorous way of spiritual life.

The Bible has a doctrine of holiness. It begins with **God's holiness**. "And the Lord spake unto Moses, saying, Speak unto all the congregation of the children of Israel, and say unto them, Ye shall be holy: for I the Lord your God am holy" (Leviticus 19:1-2). "I am the Almighty God; walk before me, and be thou perfect" (Genesis 17:1). The New Testament doctrine is the same: "Be ye therefore perfect, even as your Father which is in heaven is perfect" (Matthew 5:48). Again, quoting the Old Testament: "Sanctify yourselves therefore, and be ye holy: for I am the Lord your God" (Leviticus 20:7). We start with God. We acknowledge the holiness of the God who created us. Then we apply the same standard of holiness, or perfection, to ourselves. Unquestionably, we find that **we don't measure up to the standard.**

But what exactly is holiness? God has it, we are supposed to have it, but what is it? The biblical meaning of holiness is "to be set apart," or different from the world. It is a kind of "set apart-ness," if I may invent a new term. It means "to distinguish oneself from others." God is set apart by His righteousness, His perfection. (He is also set apart because of His position as a separate kind of being, the Creator, but holiness refers to **ethics**, not the "stuff" we are made of.) We can see it better in God's words to the nation of Israel: "And ye shall be holy unto me: for I the Lord am holy, and have severed you from other people, that ye should be mine" (Leviticus 20:26). God wants us to conform ourselves to His moral standards. He **separates us** from those in the world who are immoral, who defiantly set up standards different from those established by God for mankind. We are His property, as we learned when we considered the Creator-creature distinction. He sets us apart ethically, requiring of us that we live different sorts of lives. He literally set apart the Hebrews in the ancient world, separating them geographically when He gave them the land of Canaan (the "Promised Land"). But in our day, He separates us spiritually by pulling our minds and hearts out of the corruption of the world around us, and by separating us socially (such as in our choice of marriage partners) and institutionally (membership in a fellowship, the church; education in Christian schools).

The Bible devotes considerable space to holiness. If you open a Bible concordance, which lists all the verses in which a particular word appears, and look up the word "holy," you will find hundreds of references. *Strong's Exhaustive Concordance of the Bible* has over five columns of extremely fine print listing the verses that appear in the King James Version of the Bible, the most popular of the English translations.

God's moral standards of holiness, the key to life, are set forth in His law. He is a **jealous** God, we are told. In the Book of Exodus, we find God's ten commandments. He tells His people not to bow down to other gods, "for I the Lord am a jealous God" (Exodus 20:5). So determined is God to defend His standards of righteousness, that He threatens us with punishment if we disobey. The prophet Amos, who was a simple sheep herder before God called him to challenge the people of his day, announced to them: "Hear this word that the Lord hath spoken against you, O children of Israel, against the whole family which I brought up from the land of Egypt, saying, You only have I known of all the families of the earth: therefore I will punish you for all your iniquities" (Amos 3:2).

But if God requires perfection, and men disobey Him, then how can any of us escape punishment? How can we meet such a standard of perfection? One defiant act, and we have lost perfection. In fact, as we will see in the chapter on man, we are born in sin. The great sin was the sin of our father, Adam. He acted for all of us when he defied God. We are all tainted with his transgression. So how can we attain perfection?

The answer is crucially important. We need a **substitute**. We need someone who **is** perfect to stand in front of God and say, in effect, "God, I have met your standard of perfection. I deserve your blessing. However, these people here, my friends, have sinned grievously. They deserve your holy judgment. But do this for my sake, as a perfect being. Punish me instead of them. Look at my perfection instead of looking at their imperfection. I will bear their punishment." This is exactly what the Bible required from the day of Adam's rebellion: a sacrifice. Specifically, **a blood sacrifice**, which would symbolize the greatest sacrifice of all time, the death and punishment of a perfect being, who was also a perfect man. The prophet Isaiah spoke concerning the coming Messiah: "Surely he hath borne our griefs, and carried our sorrows: yet we did esteem him stricken, smitten of God, and afflicted. But he was wounded for our transgressions, he was bruised for our iniquities: the chastisement of our peace was upon him; and with his stripes we are healed" (Isaiah 53:4-5). The Apostle Paul wrote: "For when we were yet without strength, in due time Christ died for the ungodly. For scarcely for a righteous man will one die: yet peradventure [perhaps] for a good man some would even dare to die. But God commendeth [proves] his love toward us, in that, while we were yet sinners, Christ died for us" (Romans 5:6-8).

This doesn't mean that the Bible teaches that we can become perfect in this life. The Apostle John wrote: "If we say that we have fellowship with him [God], and walk in darkness, we lie, and do not have the truth. But if we walk in the light, as he is in the light, we have fellowship one with another, and the blood of Jesus Christ his Son cleanseth us from all sin. If we say that we have no sin, we deceive ourselves, and the truth is not in us. If we confess our sins, he is faithful and just to forgive us our sins, and to cleanse us from all unrighteousness. If we say that we have not sinned, we make him a liar, and his word is not in us" (I John 1:6-10). **The right of confession of sins** before Christ through prayer, and also through restitution if we have sinned against another, is **the most important right Christ's people possess.**

What is sin? **Sin is the violation of God's revealed law.** "Whosoever committeth sin transgresseth also the law: for sin is the transgression of the law" (I John 3:4). Some people have misinterpreted John's words in the third chapter of his letter, concluding that John taught that absolute perfection is possible after a man is brought by grace into Christ's salvation. But what John taught was that the **definition** of a saved man is sinlessness, that he is sinless before God because God looks at Christ, not at the sins of the regenerate man. The regenerate man is characterized by his striving against sin, by his determination to root sin out of his life, but John taught the benefits of confession of sin, which proves that he knew that regenerate men, though viewed as men draped in Christ's righteousness, still transgress the law. The regenerate man cannot live a life characterized by sin. He cannot immerse himself in sinning as a way of life.

Without a substitute, a man faces inevitable judgment. The man who thinks he can stand before God in his own holiness, without Christ's righteousness covering him, has committed permanent suicide. He faces what the New Testament calls "the second death" (Revelation 20:14), eternal judgment. That's why God required animal sacrifices in the Old Testament. They represented the absolute sacrifice of Christ on the cross, although that sacrifice was almost 1,500 years in the future when Moses gave Israel the law. Even Abel, Adam's son, offered a blood sacrifice to God (Genesis 4:4). God's holiness is no trifling thing, nothing to be scoffed at. Men who do not take God's holiness seriously are making a terrible mistake. Such an attitude takes too seriously the righteousness of man in the face of a holy God. The prophet Isaiah warned: "But we are all as an unclean thing, and all our righteousnesses are as filthy rags [literally: menstrous rags]; and we all do fade as a leaf; and our iniquities, like the wind, have taken us away" (Isaiah 64:6). Graphic language, indeed; yet men continue to believe that "they are no worse than the next guy," as if the next guy weren't perishing, too.

The Trinity

What kind of God is this God of the Bible? A **personal** God. He has communion as a person has communion. But He does not need man for His communion. He exists throughout eternity; man's appearance was temporal. God was not lacking anything when man was not around. He was not lonely, as some pagan myths of the creation tell us. He was not lonely, for He possesses communion. We are not dealing with one uniform, isolated being; we are dealing with **Persons** who constitute a **Person**.

When God announced the creation of mankind, He said: "Let us make man in our image, after our likeness: and let them have dominion..."(Genesis 1:26a). When the rebels at Babel began to construct their tower, a monument to their one-world government, God said: "Go to, let us go down, and there confound their language, that they may not understand one another's speech" (Genesis 11:7). "Let **us**," God said; and **They** did. But They did it as one Person—one Person, yet more than one Person, in full communion.

The first chapter of Genesis tells us: "And the earth was without form, and void; and darkness was upon the face of the deep. And the Spirit of God moved upon the face of the waters" (Genesis 1:2). We also read concerning Adam and Eve: "And they heard the voice of the Lord God walking in the garden in the cool of the day ..."(Genesis 3:8a). Did a Spirit walk? The language indicates that this plural God exists in several Persons.

The Old Testament doesn't say specifically how many Persons constitute the Godhead. The New Testament does: Father, Son, and Holy Spirit. The Holy Spirit remains in the background in His relations with men. Christ told His disciples: "These things have I spoken unto you, being yet present with you. But the Comforter, which is the Holy Ghost, whom the Father will send in my name, he shall teach you all things, and bring all things to your remembrance, whatsoever I have said unto you" (John 14:26). Again, Christ said: "It is expedient for you that I go away: for if I go not away, the Comforter will not come unto you; but if I depart, I will send him unto you" (John 16:7). In other words, God the Father will send the Holy Spirit, yet Christ will also send Him. The Holy Spirit is an agent who has a special role to play in New Testament times. He comforts God's people during the time in which Christ is absent.

Christ also said: "When he, the Spirit of truth, is come, he will guide you into all truth: for he shall not speak of himself; but whatsoever he shall hear, that shall he speak: and he will show you things to come" (John 16:3). The Holy Spirit intercedes with God on our behalf: "Likewise the Spirit also helpeth our infirmities: for we know not what we should pray for as we ought: but the Spirit itself maketh intercession for us with groanings which cannot be uttered" (Romans 8:26). He stays in the background, but He does important work.

Who is the most important of the three Persons? What has to be said from the outset is that they are all equally important, for they are all of the same essence. They are, in the words of one Christian philosopher, mutually self-exhaustive. That means that each of them knows all things; that each of them is totally open to the others; that they share the same goals, exercise the same power, honor each other equally. They are equals, but they are not identical, for they are distinguishable. Christians usually say that they believe in one God in three Persons, but language is insufficient here. What we do know is that there is one God: "Hear, O Israel: The Lord our God is one Lord" (Deuteronomy 6:4). Yet at the same time, when the interrogators questioned Jesus regarding His claim of divinity, He asserted His full divinity. "Again the high priest asked him, and said unto him, Art thou the Christ, the Son of the Blessed? And Jesus said, I am: and ye shall see the Son of man sitting on the right hand of power, and coming in the clouds of heaven. Then the high priest rent his clothes, and saith, What need we of further witnesses? Ye have heard the blasphemy: what think ye? And they all condemned him to be guilty of death" (Mark 14:61-64). The Jewish Sanhedrin, the high court of the Jews in Christ's day, knew exactly what He claimed for Himself, and He was willing to affirm this much. Beyond this, He remained silent.

Time and again, those who reject Christianity argue that Jesus was only a man, not fully divine. Or they say that He was **almost** divine, or **became** divine, but that He was not, from the beginning, fully co-equal with the Father. This is the age-old error of **subordinationism**. It tries to put Christ below the Father in terms of His being, power, glory, or honor.

But didn't Christ acknowledge His own inferiority to God the Father? Didn't He say again and again that He was doing His Father's business? When He prayed in the garden, the night that He was captured by the authorities, He prayed with these words: "Abba, Father, all things are possible with thee; take away this cup from me: nevertheless not what I will, but what thou wilt" (Mark 14:36). But He also said "Heaven and earth shall pass away: but my words shall not pass away. But of that day and that hour knoweth no man, no, not the angels which are in heaven, neither the Son, but the Father" (Mark 13:31-32). He asserted the eternality of His own words, yet He claimed ignorance of the day of judgment. What can we make of all this?

Theologians struggle with these seeming paradoxes, and the best they have come up with is this: the Trinity is made up of equal persons, but as regards Their activities in relation to the creation, They have different functions. They are **equal in essence eternally**, but **subordinate in function historically**. God sent His Son to redeem men. Jesus said, "I am the way, the truth, and the life: no man cometh unto the Father but by me" (John 14:6). But He also said: "No man can come unto me, except the Father which hath sent me draw him [literally: **drag** him]: and I will raise him up at the last day" (John 6:44). There is a mutuality of purpose, but a difference in historical execution of their respective tasks.

Theologians like to make up fancy terms, so they distinguish between the **ontological** Trinity (equality of being) and the **economical** Trinity (subordination in function). All they're really saying is that they find traces of subordination in Jesus' ministry before His Father, and subordination of the Holy Ghost's ministry before both the Father and the Son, especially since He testifies not of Himself. With respect to **God's relation to His creation**, in time and on earth, there are **differences in function**. In relation to each other, the three Persons of the Trinity are mutually self-exhaustive, knowing, respecting, and loving each other completely.

By understanding these theological distinctions in advance, the new Christian gains an intellectual defense against those who would make Christ almost a God or a late-blooming God, or a God who really wasn't 100% human. He also protects himself against any variation of evolutionism, which argues that man is becoming a God, and that Christ was our first great example of man's upward march to full divinity. **Jesus started out being God.** Paul wrote: "Let this mind be in you, which was also in Christ Jesus, who, being in the form of God, thought it not robbery to be equal with God, but made himself of no reputation, and took upon him the form of a servant, and was made in the likeness of men. And being found in fashion as a man, he humbled himself, and became obedient unto death, even the death of the cross" (Philippians 2:5-8). God the Father didn't humble Himself; the Holy Spirit didn't humble Himself; but God the Son did. Each had a different task, but man cannot legitimately make himself into a divine being because of the historical humbling of the Son of God, who walked on earth as Jesus Christ, the Messiah, fully human and fully divine, one Person, with two natures, in perfect union, but without intermixture. (If Christ had possessed two distinct personalities, then we would wind up with a doctrine of one God, **four** Persons—the divinizing of the nature of man, a creature. This would deny the Creator-creature distinction, and it would also deny the reality of the ontological Trinity.)

Conclusions

If God is God, then man isn't God. If God created all things, then man is in no way the lord over creation. If God sustains the creation through the might of His power, then we must believe in the **providence of God**, not the providence of man. If we cannot legitimately believe in the providence of man, then we most certainly cannot legitimately believe in the providence of the State. The State is not the agency of human salvation. The State is not the source of our liberties. The State is not the source of our wealth, power, and hopes.

It was this implication of the doctrine of God that got the Hebrews into so much trouble with Nebuchadnezzar, king of Babylon, who believed himself to be a divine king in a divine State

(Daniel 3). He repented of this belief at the end of his life (Daniel 4). It was this same implication which enraged Pharaoh, another self-proclaimed divine ruler, when Moses asked that he allow the Hebrew slaves to go out of Egypt for a week in order to worship God (Exodus 5). If God is the Creator, then He must also be the Savior, which permanently denies this role to the State. The statists have never forgiven God because of this fact.

Something else must be understood. God is simultaneously **one** and **many**. God is **He** and God is **They**. God acts as a Person, yet He is three Persons. We have in the very being of God both individualism and collectivism (corporate being). We have in God's very being the theological foundation of the reconciliation of an ancient philosophical problem, namely, the "one and the many problem." Is man essentially individualistic or collectivistic? Is the State supreme or the individual? The Bible tells us the proper approach to this problem: **man, like God, is both individualistic and collectivistic.** We dare not emphasize one aspect and exclude the other.

Chapter 2

MAN

When we're trying to get to the bottom of things, it's usually best to get to the origins of things. What was the origin of man? The Bible provides us with the answer: "And God said, Let us make man in our image, after our likeness: and let them have dominion over the fish of the sea, and over the fowl of the air, and over the cattle, and over all the earth, and over every creeping thing that creepeth upon the earth. So God created man in his own image, in the image of God created He him; male and female created He them. And God blessed them, and said unto them, Be fruitful, and multiply, and replenish the earth, and subdue it: and have dominion over the fish of the sea, and over the fowl of the air, and over every living thing that moveth upon the earth" (Genesis 1:26-28). In the next chapter, God gives us more information about the specifics of man's creation: "And the Lord God formed man of the dust of the ground, and breathed into his nostrils the breath of life; and man became a living soul" (Genesis 2:7).

Man is **God-made**. He is not man-made. He owes his life, his goals, and his environment to God. God is the source of everything man has. God **owns** man just as surely as He owns all the other resources of the creation. God is absolutely sovereign over man and the creation.

But man isn't dust. He came from the dust, but he's more than dust. He is a special creation of God. God breathed a soul into man; no other creature received this special consideration. Other creatures have intelligence, but no other creature has a soul. No other creature is made in God's image.

This indicates a three-tiered system, at the very least. First, there is God, the Creator. Then there is man, the creature with a soul. Then there is the general creation. Man is part of the creation, yet he is in some special way distinct from the creation. Man is unique.

23

The Image of God

The Bible says that God made man in His image. Or, more precisely, God made man in Their image. Man is a person, endowed with a soul, and in communication with God. Man reflects the very character of God. He is not equal with God, for he is a creature. Nevertheless, he reflects God's nature in a way that no other creature does.

In the verse that first speaks of the creation of man, Genesis 1:26, we are told two things about man. First, he is made in the image of God. Second, he is to have **dominion** over the living beings of the earth. The link between the image of God and man's lawful dominion cannot be ignored. We are not told that the essence of the image of God is seen in man's moral nature. We are not told that the image of God is seen in man's ability to think. Neither are we told that the fundamental fact of the image of God in man is his ability to speak. All of these aspects of man's nature are related to God's nature, but of the essence of the image of God in man is dominion. "Dominion" follows God's "likeness" in man (Genesis 1:26a).

What God did initially was to create a man-free universe. This took five days. This man-less universe was incomplete. It was good; God said it was good after each stage of creation. But it was incomplete. **God created man as a means of completing nature**. Nature was not a coherent whole, even though it possessed God-given regularities, such as the reproduction of each species after its own kind (Genesis 1:24). **Nature was not lawless, yet it was incomplete**. It was governed by God, yet it was incomplete. Something was missing, despite nature's regularities. Man was the missing piece, for "there was not a man to till the ground" (Genesis 2:5b)

Ours is a **personal universe**. God, a personal being, created the universe. It has its very being in terms of God and God's comprehensive plan for the ages. Not a single fact in the universe exists apart from God, God's plan, and God's evaluation of each fact. No fact is isolated, self-existent. Every fact is fully interpreted by God, because God created every fact, gives meaning to every fact, and controls every fact. God is absolutely sovereign.

God created a kind of assistant, or a second lieutenant, to exercise dominion over His earth. This doesn't mean that man is independent of God, or in any way reduces the sovereignty of God. All of man's lawful sovereignty is **derived** sovereignty. God gave it to him when He gave man's assignment to him. God didn't lose some of His sovereignty when He created man. He still controls all that comes to pass. Nothing takes place that God tries to prevent, but somehow fails to prevent. Man's sovereignty is explicitly **delegated** sovereignty. Whatever sovereign power he enjoys, he enjoys as a result of the image of God in his very being. He doesn't have a so-called "spark of divinity" in him. Nowhere in the Bible can you find that doctrine taught. But he does have the image of God, which is a dominion-oriented image. **God is creatively constructive**, while **man is receptively reconstructive.**

Man is a personal being. He needs communion. Because he is a limited being, he also needs help. God therefore created an assistant, Eve. With Eve, he was to begin to bring the garden under dominion. In fact, he was assigned the task of naming (classifying) the animals before he was given Eve (Genesis 2:20). **He had a job to do before he was given a wife.** Man is defined in terms of the image of God, but this image involves man's normal inclination to dominate the creation. He did his job; then he got his wife.

Eve was his "helpmeet," to use a common term (Genesis 2:20). Actually, the King James Version never uses "helpmeet." That's a word which developed from the King James' phrase, "an help meet for him." What the phrase really meant was "a helper **fit** for him," or better yet, "**designed** for him." Eve was designed to complement Adam and make his work more efficient. Adam was limited from the start, an incomplete creation, just as the earth was an incomplete creation. Adam needed Eve. He needed her to work better, enjoy life better, procreate children, and most important of all, better reflect God's image.

Man is like God. He isn't identical to God, but he is like God. God now has a creature made in His image who can act as **God's agent on earth**, making the earth fruitful. He can work in the garden, dressing it (Genesis 2:15). But more than this: he can dress the whole world. He wasn't to stay in the garden all his life. The **garden of Eden** was simply a **preliminary training ground** for man. It set the **pattern**. It was to serve as a **school for dominion**. The rivers flowed out of the garden, and what better way for the sons of Adam to find their way into the world to subdue it (Genesis 2:10, 13-14)?

Man must dominate. This was never intended to be a license for misusing his powers. He was to dress the garden, not ravage it. He was to treat God's creatures well, for he was representing God on earth. He was to care for God's creation, as a steward cares for his master's property. Nevertheless, man must dominate. It is basic to his very being. He was designed to exercise dominion, as the image-bearer of God, in time and on earth.

Man started out as something like a second lieutenant. (Eve might be considered a non-commissioned officer, except in those days there was no rule against officers fraternizing with non-coms.) He had the opportunity to become a captain, a major, even a one-star general. He was to be tested in his assignments by God. But one thing was impossible for man: **he could never become the Commander-in-Chief.** He could never become the sole authority. He could never become God.

That's just what he wanted to become.

The Fall

The evil tempter came to Eve, the subordinate, and told her to violate God's law. He told her that she wouldn't really die on the day she ate of the tree (Genesis 3:4). No, he told her, she would have her eyes opened. She would become as God, knowing good and evil (Genesis 3:5). To become as God: what a marvelous opportunity! No muss, no fuss; **instant divinity**. No commissioned officer status for her, nor for her husband. She wanted to be Commander-in-Chief. What a promotion! No years of work in the garden, and then in the world at large.

Satan, the number-one rebel in the universe, knew how rebellions are made. He went to the obvious source of discontent: Eve. Here she was, the number-two person in a two-person outfit. In fact, she was really number five, if we count the three persons of the Godhead. She was at the bottom. So who do you think would be the most likely candidate for starting a rebellion? Satan thought so, too.

She started giving orders. She violated God's explicit instruction, which presumably had been passed on to her by her husband. God had told Adam not to eat of the tree before Eve was created (Genesis 2:17). Satan came to her and quoted God's words—selectively, of course, as Satan always does—in order to remind her of the restriction on the couple. Then he told her it wasn't really that dangerous, and besides, the pay-off was terrific: **to be as God**. She ate, and she gave to her husband to eat.

The chain of command was broken. Satan, the chief rebel, got the woman to begin the rebellion. Shortly thereafter, her husband took her advice, rejected God's explicit instructions, and he ate. Satan had brought disruptions to Eden.

The traditional view of this event in Christian circles (which is also my view) is that Satan was striking out at God by winning the allegiance of man, who bore God's image. In other words, **Satan sought a victory over God by striking at God through man.** He was using man as a means of disrupting God's universe. He was going to thwart God's plans by getting man to violate God's law. This is a theological speculation, but it makes a lot of sense, given the picture in Genesis 2.

What we find is that **God declares that man will be used to thwart Satan's plan for the universe.** God tells the woman: "And I will put enmity between thee and the woman, and between thy seed and her seed; it shall bruise thy head, and thou shalt bruise his heel" (Genesis 3:15). This is exactly what happened at the cross: Satan bruised the heel of the son of man, Jesus, but in satisfying the holy justice of God by His death, Christ bruised the head of the serpent. Christ made a way for His people to escape the wrath designed for Satan and his host (Matthew 25:41).

Satan had hoped to use man as a pawn in a kind of cosmic chess game. God then took that pawn and devised a strategy to turn the tables on Satan, using that same pawn to defeat him. The open sign of the turning point in the game was the crucifixion and resurrection of Jesus. The game obviously isn't over, but man, Satan's hoped-for pawn, is now a divided race. Like the angels, who are also divided, **God's human forces are guaranteed the victory.** Steadily, God's forces—in the heavens and on earth—are pushing back the kingdom of Satan. Satan's last outpost is hell, but the church of Jesus Christ is advancing toward that last outpost, "and the gates of hell shall not prevail against it" (Matthew 16:18). It takes time, effort, and the grace of God, but victory is assured. The gates of hell shall not prevail against God's holy (set apart) church. He didn't say that the gates of hell wouldn't hold against the onslaught of the angels. He didn't say that the gates of hell wouldn't withstand the onslaught of the three Persons of the Trinity. He said that the gates of hell cannot withstand the final onslaught of the **church**. Satan's hoped-for means of thwarting God will be used to thwart Satan.

Nevertheless, the ethical rebellion of man has had enormous consequences for the history of man and the history of God's contest against Satan. Man rebelled ethically. He set himself up as a judge between God and Satan. Would man really die? "Well," man said, "let's run an experiment. We will eat, and then we'll see what happens. Satan might be correct about all this, after all. Satan's word might very well be equal with God's." So man, the self-proclaimed sovereign judge, decided to test God's verbal promise against the ability of God to fulfill the terms of His promise.

This analysis underestimates the extent of man's rebellion. When man decided to test God's word, he actually had **already** passed judgment against God's word. After all, man ate the forbidden fruit. Given the horrendous consequences promised by God, the risks were high. In fact, they were so incredibly high that only someone who had already decided that **God's word couldn't possibly be true** would be willing to take that sort of risk. Man was calling God a liar, just as Satan had called Him. Man was implicitly calling Satan the truth-bringer, the light-bearer, while God was simply a lying despot who was placing man under an intolerable and completely unwarranted restriction. "Watch this, God!" Adam and Eve said to themselves. Or at least, they might as well have said it. That's certainly what their actions meant.

Satan promised that they would become as God, knowing good and evil. But the Hebrew word is stronger than that. It means "determining" or "establishing," not simply passively knowing good and evil. By the act of defiance, they were already asserting their status as co-equals with God. No, worse than that. They were establishing themselves, they believed, as the **supreme judges** between these two beings, God and Satan. They would test God's word and Satan's. They had already decided that Satan's word was true.

Satan could offer them something for nothing—status as gods, determiners of good and evil, apart from the long years of godly, **subordinate** service as garden-dressers and world-dressers— without endangering his own hoped-for position as the sovereign being of the universe. Why not? By their assertion of the right to judge between God and Satan, they had already acknowledged Satan's sovereignty as the being who brings truth. Satan could always demand full subordination, given his great power in comparison to man's power, **if** God would no longer protect man. That's what the Book of Job tells us that Satan thinks, or thought before Calvary's cross. He had to ask God for the power to harm this righteous man (Job 1:6-12). Without God's protection, man was nothing to worry about, Satan concluded. So why not let man think man was the sovereign judge between Satan and God? Man would be disillusioned soon enough. Man would be powerless soon enough. Man would be dead soon enough.

Did man die that day? Spiritually, he did. In principle, he did. But God did not slay his body that day. Why not? **God showed mercy to man because Christ's sacrifice was already scheduled.** God showed mercy to man for the sake of Christ.

This may seem difficult to believe, but the Bible unquestionably teaches it. For the sake of Christ and Christ's church, the assembly of saints, God preserved the lives of our first parents. The New Testament tells us, concerning God's healing work, that He has "saved us, and called us with an holy calling, not according to our works, but according to his own purpose and grace, which was given us in Christ Jesus before the world began" (II Timothy 1:9). Paul repeated this message in several of his letters. "Blessed be the God and Father of our Lord Jesus Christ, who hath blessed us with all spiritual blessings in heavenly places in Christ. According as he hath chosen us in him before the foundation of the world, that we should be holy and without blame before him in love, having predestinated us unto the adoption of children by Jesus Christ to himself, according to the good pleasure of his will, to the praise and glory of his grace, wherein he hath made us accepted in the beloved" (Ephesians 1:3-6). **Before the foundation of the world:** Satan's doom, and the blessings of God on His people, were guaranteed before Adam rebelled.

Man's Fall was real. It took place in time and on earth. The first man and the first woman were involved. Satan, the angelic rebel, was involved. This was no morality play written by some obscure Hebrew priest about 3,500 years ago. This was no mythical tale whispered in secret ceremonies during the initiation rites in the deserts of Palestine. God's word says that **this rebellion really took place, in time and on earth,** and that the reason we're in the plight that we so obviously **are** in, is because our parents made a disastrous decision.

Now the immediate response of the sons and daughters of
Adam and Eve runs along these lines: "Well, don't hold me
responsible. I would have had more sense than they did. I wouldn't
have touched that fruit. Why, I wouldn't even have looked at it. It's
not my fault. I wasn't there." But of course that's the typical
response of arrogant rebels. Here were Adam and Eve, created
perfect, with no history of sin behind them. They communed with
God. There was no sin separating them from a holy God. And
these two people, created good, rebelled. And now we find their
offspring, rebellious to the core, separated from God by a mountain of sins, blind to the doom that awaits all ethical rebels, trying
to tell themselves (not to mention God) that it would have been a
lot different if someone as terrific as **they** are had been assigned to
the garden of Eden.

The Bible tells us: "Wherefore, as by one man sin entered into
the world, and death by sin; and so death passed upon all men, for
that all have sinned" (Romans 5:12). Again, "For all have sinned,
and come short of the glory of God" (Romans 3:23). And most important of all for man: "For the wages of sin is death; but the gift
of God is eternal life through Jesus Christ our Lord" (Romans
6:23).

Man's Fall was **ethical**. It involved an **active rebellion** on man's
part against the law of God. God had told him not to eat of the
tree, but man wanted instant illumination, instant divinity. He rejected the processes of time, the effects of godly, obedient labor.
He rejected the thought that he would have to remain a subordinate. He would have to acknowledge his position as a creature
under God; he would have to spend his life thinking God's thoughts
after Him, as a creature, rather than stand as a tyrant over creation,
whipping creation into line as a self-made God. He would have to
mature over time, and always as God's subordinate. Awful!

God wouldn't permit this sort of nonsense to go on unrestrained.
First, man **is** a subordinate. He has to be; he is a **creature**. He is
under the sovereignty of God. Man has to serve God or Satan, as
the chief rebel. Now, Satan isn't choosy. He doesn't require that
we worship him explicitly. All he wants is that we worship him implicitly. He didn't tell Adam and Eve that they should eat of the
tree in order to spend eternity worshipping him. He only told them
that they should do what God had forbidden, so that they could
become god-like beings. **By rejecting the worship of God, man**

inevitably accepts the worship of Satan, even when man thinks he is worshipping himself, or idols, or the messianic State.

Christ said: "No man can serve two masters: for either he will hate the one, and love the other; or else he will hold to the one, and despise the other. Ye cannot serve God and mammon" (Matthew 6:24). Man cannot serve as a mediator between God and Satan. He cannot test God's word. He cannot serve them both, even when he thinks he is serving neither.

Man must serve. He was created as God's representative on earth. He cannot escape his calling (vocation, task, etc.) before God. He cannot escape his very being. He was designed to worship God. He was designed to be an obedient subordinate. Now, it's possible for him to become a **disobedient** subordinate, **but he remains a subordinate.** Dominion man is always subordinate man.

Man has tried many ways to escape this position. In Eden, he tried to do it by asserting his self-appointed sovereignty over God. He would test the reliability of God's word. What really happened? He wound up a subordinate to Satan, ethically speaking. Metaphysically speaking (I hate to use a word like "metaphysical," but I don't know what else to use), he remained subordinate to God. By this, I mean that in terms of the real world—a world in which God is absolutely sovereign—he was then, is now, and forever will be **subordinate to God**. But as an acting man he rebelled ethically. He was no less a man. He was no less under the sovereign control of God. He was no less God's second lieutenant, in charge of the earth. He was no less **dominion man**. He was, however, a **twisted** dominion man, a rebel.

Man must be subordinate. Man must also rule. How can he do both? Under his original calling, he was to be subordinate to God, but a ruler over creation. Now he has asserted his declaration of independence from God, so he finds himself under the power of some aspect of the creation. He tries to be a ruler in his own right, and he becomes subordinate to Satan. Now, as I've said, Satan isn't choosy. Man can become ethically subordinate to any aspect of the creation. It doesn't really matter that much to Satan. Man can pin his hopes to anything, so long as it isn't the God of the Bible. Man can obey anything or anyone, so long as it isn't the law of God.

Paul wrote these words concerning men's ability to believe in anything, no matter how crazy, in order to avoid believing in God. "For the wrath of God is revealed from heaven against all ungodliness and unrighteousness of men, who hold [literally: hold **back,** or restrain] the truth in unrighteousness, because that which may be known of God is manifest in them; for God hath shewed it unto them. For the invisible things of him from the creation of the world are clearly seen, being understood by the things that are made, even his eternal power and Godhead; so that they are without excuse. Because that, when they knew God, they glorified him not as God, neither were thankful; but became vain in their imaginations, and their foolish heart was darkened. Professing themselves to be wise, they became fools, and changed the glory of the uncorruptible God into an image made like to corruptible man, and to birds, and four-footed beasts, and creeping things. Wherefore God also gave them up to uncleanness through the lusts of their own hearts, to dishonour their own bodies between themselves, who changed the truth of God into a lie, and worshipped and served the creature more than the Creator, who is blessed forever. Amen" (Romans 1:18-25).

Quite a picture, isn't it? Here are human beings, who imagine themselves to be wise, but who become the worshippers of creepy-crawlies. They hold back the truth in unrighteousness. They are given the revelation of God in His creation, yet they restrain this knowledge, condemning themselves. They know what they're doing. They are actively restraining the truth of God. They aren't a bunch of supposedly innocent savages who just never had the opportunity to hear the message of salvation through faith in Jesus Christ's atoning death on Calvary. They are savages, all right, but active, systematic, truth-restraining savages. There is nothing innocent about them. They worship bugs instead of God. They worship snakes instead of God. And the really self-deceived ones tell themselves that they worship nothing at all, and then fall prostrate before the messianic State.

Man's Fall was ethical. It was active rebellion. Eve, admittedly, was deceived, Paul tells us, but Adam wasn't (I Timothy 2:14). It was not that Adam fell because of some flaw in his being, or a flaw in the creation. It was not that kind of rebellion. It was active sin, the overcoming of righteousness, the rejection of the truth.

This is important for the doctrine of salvation. God doesn't restore some lost aspect of man's being. Man is a rebel today, but he is still a man. He still is the image of God. He actively restrains the truth of this image, but he is nevertheless a subordinate to something, and he also dominates something else. He may worship a demon and beat his wife. He may worship money and cheat his neighbor. He may worship the State and suppress the free market. Since he is still a man, still made in the image of God, still a subordinate, and still dominion man, **he is still completely responsible before God**. That's why, through the grace of God, some men respond to the message of salvation. They are still men. They still have the testimony of their very being to condemn them. **If men were not men, they could not repent.** Angels don't repent. Men do. When God regenerates a man, He doesn't "put back" something that man lost in the Fall—some aspect of his being that made man a "true" man in Eden, but whose absence makes man something less than a man today. God "**untwists**" the man, **restoring him ethically** before God.

Man was a man before he rebelled. Man is a man today, though a twisted rebel. Man will be a man in the new heavens and the new earth, when sin is abolished. And man will still be a man in hell, with one exception: he will no longer be dominion man. Any will to dominion will be eternally frustrated. That is part of the curse of the second death. Satan suffers the same fate: possessing power before his rebellion, after his rebellion, but not in hell. Still subordinate, like his associates, he loses power. That is his final curse. Refusing to acknowledge their metaphysical subordination to God—their subordination in the very essence of their being as creatures—Satan and his host, including rebellious men, will wind up completely dominated by God, but without a trace of their original power, their delegated authority as responsible creatures. They sought absolute power; they will wind up with none.

The Curse

God's response to the sin of Adam and Eve is revealing. First, He began His questioning of the pair. He began with Adam, the head of the household. Satan had begun his revolution with Eve; God returned to Adam. He asked Adam if he had eaten of the forbidden fruit. "And the man said, The woman whom thou gavest to be with me, she gave me of the tree, and I did eat" (Genesis 3:12). That woman whom **Thou** gavest to me: Adam was attempting to place the blame elsewhere. It was the woman's fault, but ultimately it was God's fault. "You gave her to me, God; you created a flawed environment for me. I'm just an innocent victim of my environment, after all. I'm not really all that responsible."

God then asked the woman if this was true. Had she given her husband the fruit? "And the woman said, The serpent beguiled me, and I did eat" (Genesis 3:13b). "The devil made me do it! It's this terrible environment, God. Temptations everywhere. What's a poor girl to do?"

God asked the serpent nothing. He just condemned it. From then on, it would be the most cursed of beasts, and the son of man would bruise its head, even as it would bruise the heel of the woman's seed (Genesis 3:14-15). That curse extended, God then returned to the woman. She will have pain in childbearing, indicating a change in her anatomy. The serpent would hereafter crawl on the earth, indicating a change in its anatomy, and the woman would be in pain when giving birth.

Then came Adam's curse: "And unto Adam he said, Because thou hast hearkened unto the voice of thy wife, and hast eaten of the tree, of which I commanded thee, saying, Thou shalt not eat of it: cursed is the ground for thy sake: in sorrow shalt thou eat of it all the days of thy life. Thorns and thistles shall it bring forth to thee; and thou shalt eat the herb of the field. In the sweat of thy face shalt thou eat bread, till thou return unto the ground; for out of it wast thou taken: for dust thou art, and unto dust shalt thou return" (Genesis 3:17-19). God had cursed the anatomies of the first two rebels; now he cursed not only Adam's body, but his labor. His calling before God would henceforth be painful. He had been turned back into dust. He would forever be reminded of his creaturehood. Shape dust into any form, and it eventually crumbles and blows away. So would it be with man.

But more than Adam's body was cursed. The ground was cursed. It would henceforth resist man. It would produce thorns and thistles. This, in effect, was a change in nature's anatomy. Nature would now rebel against man, even as man had rebelled against God, and woman had rebelled against both man and God. Adam had been placed as a kind of second lieutenant over nature. He had rebelled against his Commander-in-Chief. Now he would learn what all insubordinate commanders learn: the process is hard to stop. When second lieutenants disobey senior officers, non-commissioned officers tend to disobey second lieutenants. And so on, right down the chain of command. Rebellion was loose among the troops. Now man would learn how troublesome insubordinate subordinates can be. Satan, the number-one-rebel, had launched a universal rebellion by means of man.

Unquestionably, nature was cursed. Nature, man's subordinate, participated in the defeat of her commanding officer. Adam's punishment dragged nature into the brig, too. Nature's fate was sealed by the fate of her commander. His defeat was nature's defeat. **What happens to commanding officers is crucially important to their subordinates.** Whether a man serves under the command of Jesus Christ or Satan makes all the difference in the world, and even more important, all the difference **beyond** this world. Men will serve under a conquerer or the conquered, but they must serve someone. **There are no neutral observers in this cosmic struggle.** Everyone is drafted into one army or the other. Men are born into Satan's army, since it's a hereditary office; **Adam volunteered himself and all his posterity for service in Satan's forces.** Only God can draft men into His forces. There have only been two true volunteers: the first Adam, and the second Adam, Jesus Christ. Satan tempted them both: Adam in the luxurious garden, and Jesus in the barren wilderness, after He had fasted forty days (Matthew 4). Adam fell in the midst of luxury; Christ resisted in the midst of a hostile environment. Adam had everything but the forbidden fruit—a perfect environment, according to God. He abandoned God's word and volunteered for the wrong army. Christ had practically nothing, a harsh environment, and He resisted Satan's offer to defect. **Commitment to God's word, not man's environment, determines man's success or failure.**

Adam rebelled against God. Nature rebelled against Adam. Satan is in rebellion against God, man, and nature. With nature rebellious, has God's plan been thwarted? Will man be defeated in his assignment of subduing the earth, under the sovereign control of God? Did Satan defeat God? Is Satan, in time and on earth, the successful commander of the best troops? Or is his strategy doomed, in time and on earth? We know it's doomed in eternity, but is it doomed before eternity? Is Satan that good a commander? Will Christ's troops suffer endless humiliation, endless defeats, in time and on earth? Will Christ's draftees be apologetic until the very last day concerning their Commander's skills in battle, the strategy devised by their Commander, the insufficient training of God's troops, the woefully second-rate equipment, and the inability of God's angels to offer protection to men from Satan's angels? Did God in fact defeat His own plan when He cursed the ground, thereby undercutting His former subordinate, Adam?

Concerning God's strategy, and its likelihood of success, in time and on earth, we will defer a discussion for now. That topic will be considered at the end of this book, in the chapter on the Kingdom of God. But what about Adam's task? Did God remove the dominion assignment from Adam? Not at all; He just made it **harder** for Adam to complete his assignment. Adam would now find out how miserable it is to get finished with a project when all your employees are goofing off, or making trouble, or actively dragging their feet. God would have trouble with Adam and his heirs from now on, so Adam and his heirs would have trouble with nature. But the dominion assignment is still in force. Only now there is a new incentive: **eating**. No more free lunches for mankind. No more luxurious garden for basic training. It was the end of Adam's basic training. He had wanted instant illumination, instant power, instant divinity. He hadn't been content with the pleasant, but time-consuming, basic training in the garden. Fair enough, God said in effect: get out there right now and start subduing the earth. You wanted "on-the-job training"? You wanted to speed things up? You've got it!

But God is gracious. He made coats for them out of animal skins. He killed the animals for the sake of man (Genesis 3:21). He didn't send them out to be killed or embarrassed by their own nakedness. He sent them out with physical capital, plus whatever mental capital they had.

They had amazing mental capital. **Adam was incredibly smart**. He had named (classified) all the animals of the garden in a few hours, for he had completed his assignment before Eve was given to him, on the sixth day. His mind must have been like a computer. We know from ancient records and buildings how amazingly advanced the immediate post-Flood technology was—far more advanced than anything in the modern world until about two centuries ago. (Books showing this fact include Peter Tomkins' *Secrets of the Great Pyramid* [1971] and Charles Hapgood's *Maps of the Ancient Sea Kings* [1966].) Human evolution is a myth; human **devolution**, at least in the area of man's life span and man's grasp of technology, is closer to the mark. From the days of

Noah's Flood until about the sixteenth century, it was downhill, technologically, except for occasional breakthroughs and very slow advancement during the Middle Ages (say, 700 A.D. until 1500 A.D.).

Was this curse of the ground a total curse? If so, Adam would have been defeated in his assignment. But the curse also constitutes a **blessing**, given man's rebellious nature. If man had continued to live in an uncursed garden and an uncursed world, with total wealth at his immediate disposal, what would he have done with his spare time? The slaying of Abel by Cain tells us. Man, the murderer, the rebel, the dominion officer on earth, would have tolerated no back-talk, no insubordination, from other men. If Adam was willing to alienate himself from God, would his now twisted image have made him into a trustworthy voluntary associate with other men? If Adam, made in the image of God and without sin, was willing to alienate himself from his Father in heaven, what would his heirs have been willing to do to each other if they had lived in luxury with endless time on their hands? It would have been a world filled with murder, rape, pillage, and arson. It would have been a world of constant warfare.

God restrained man precisely because He wanted man to continue working out the implications of man's dominion assignment. It may be hard work to pull weeds; it's a lot more pleasant than getting murdered. Dead men don't exercise dominion. What man would have done, as he does now to a lesser degree, is strike out against the most obvious manifestation of God, namely, other men, who are made in the image of God. Allowing mankind total abundance is comparable to allowing murderers access to nuclear weapons, and zero-cost nuclear weapons at that.

Men now have an **economic incentive to co-operate** with each other. They have to work together to get rid of those thorns and thistles. They work in groups, or trade with each other, in order to increase their per capita income. They may not love each other, they may not even like each other, but it makes economic sense to cooperate with each other. There is a built-in incentive program in this cursed world—an incentive program to substitute co-operative labor for uncooperative violence. **A world of scarcity is necessary for a race of murderers.**

One of the implicit beliefs of all socialists is that nature is innately abundant, but evil capitalist institutions reduce the wealth of the masses. This is nonsense. Nature was originally abundant, but now nature is cursed. **Scarcity is normal**; it is prosperity which is abnormal. This doesn't mean that scarcity is **normative**. It should not be our goal, either as individuals or societies. **Abundance is normative**, says the Bible. Abundance is our legitimate goal. Whole chapters are devoted to the relationship between following God's law and gaining external, visible blessings (Deuteronomy 8 and 28). But for rebellious man—ethically rebellious man—scarcity is normal. Long-term poverty for a nation, generation after generation, is a sign of God's curse—His active, continuing judgment on that society (Deuteronomy 28:15-68). He keeps them poor because He doesn't trust them with wealth. The responsibility of stewardship is too great for them; they will use their external wealth for destructive purposes. God can entrust wealth to a society of Abels; He doesn't entrust such wealth to a society of Cains, except as a preliminary step to national judgment (Deuteronomy 8:10-20).

Cursed nature is not normative, any more than fallen man is. We cannot look at nature and discover absolute standards of thought, absolute standards of law, or absolute standards of judgment. Even if cursed nature were normative, perverse men would misinterpret nature. If Adam rebelled against the verbal revelation of God Himself, before he fell into sin, what should we expect from the sons of Adam, now that nature is cursed and no longer the same kind of revelation of God that it was in the garden? It still testifies of God, as we read in Romans 1:18; **man holds back the truth in active unrighteousness**. But cursed nature is not the same open revelation of God that it once was, and we dare not use nature as an ethical, political, or any other kind of guidepost for building human institutions. We have to abandon "natural law" as a source of reliable information. Nature is cursed, and we are ethical rebels, spoiling for a fight or a misinterpretation. That's why we need the revelation of God in His word, the Bible, and through His Word, Jesus Christ.

Salvation

The doctrine of salvation is the most important doctrine in the Bible, from the point of view of man's self-interest. It isn't as important as the doctrine of God, because man isn't as important as God. But from man's perspective, the doctrine of salvation is the critical doctrine. Without this doctrine, the doctrine of God would serve only to condemn man, for man is an ethical rebel.

It's a complex doctrine. It has been the error of many Christians to oversimplify this doctrine. For the sake of sorting out some of the details of this doctrine, I have used three ordering principles: God's court of law, man's ethical condition, and man's earthly assignment. These can be classified as the **judicial**, the **moral**, and the **dominical**. They refer, respectively, to these three subdoctrines of salvation: justification, sanctification (regeneration), and adoption. Because there is so much confusion concerning the idea of the fatherhood of God, I prefer to begin with adoption. Then we can take up the other two doctrines, sanctification and justification. The whole process is related to God's sovereign choice: **election**.

Adoption

"In the beginning was the Word, and the Word was with God, and the Word was God. The same was in the beginning with God. All things were made by him; and without him was not any thing made that was made. In him was life; and the life was the light of men. And the light shineth in darkness; and the darkness comprehended it not" (John 1:1-5). Who was this Word, this light? Jesus Christ. "He was in the world, and the world was made by him, and the world knew him not. He came unto his own, and his own received him not. But as many as received him, to them gave he power to become the sons of God, even to them that believe on his name" (John 1:10-12).

Have you ever heard someone talk about the "universal fatherhood of God and the universal brotherhood of man"? Well, it's absolutely true. There is a universal fatherhood of God, and there is a universal brotherhood of man. And we can see how it works in practice by reading the story of Cain and Abel, two brothers. Abel offered God a blood sacrifice. He was a herdsman. Cain thought his offering would be just as good: an offering from the field. He was a farmer. God accepted Abel's sacrifice and rejected Cain's. Cain slew Abel in his wrath (Genesis 4). People who use the phrase "the universal brotherhood of man" to prove an underlying unity based on mutual respect and love are misusing the Bible's testimony. **The universal brotherhood of man is a brotherhood of death and destruction.** Men see the image of God in their brothers, and they despise its testimony of their continuing subordination to their universal Father, God.

But does the Bible really teach the universal fatherhood of God? Of course. Paul, when he preached to the Greeks of Athens, used the doctrine of the universal fatherhood of God to bring them to repentance from their sins against their Father. Paul reminded them: "And he hath made of one blood all nations of men for to dwell on all the face of the earth, and hath determined the times before appointed, though he be not far from every one of us. For in him we live, and move, and have our being; as certain also of your own poets have said, For we are also his offspring" (Acts 17:26-27).

God created man. He is the Father of man. But what misusers of the Bible fail to tell their listeners is this: God the Father has **disinherited** His children. He has rejected them, as He rejected Cain. He has cut them off from their inheritance. He threw Adam out of the garden, so that Adam could not eat of the tree of eternal life that grew in the garden (Genesis 3:22). Men want their inheritance back, but only on their own murderous terms. Because there is a universal fatherhood of God—a God who has disinherited His children from true life—men should turn back to God in repentance. But they won't do it.

God has therefore inaugurated a new program of sonship and fatherhood. That system is called **adoption**. To as many of those who believe on the divinity of Jesus Christ, and trust in His atoning work of blood-shedding at Calvary for their ticket to eternal life, to them gives He the power to become the sons of God. Paul wrote: "For if ye live after the flesh, ye shall die: but if ye through the Spirit do mortify the deeds of the body, ye shall live. For as many as are led by the Spirit of God, they are the sons of God. For ye have not received the spirit of bondage again to fear; but ye have received the Spirit of adoption, whereby we may cry, Abba, Father" (Romans 8:13-15). Paul told the Athenians that they were the sons of a universal God. He told the Roman Christians that they were the sons of God. Was Paul confused? Had he forgotten what he had told the Athenians? On the contrary, he remembered quite well. Paul taught the truth: there are **two forms of sonship**. Natural sons are condemned from birth because of Adam's rebellion; adopted sons—**adopted before the foundation of the world** (Ephesians 1:4-5)—are the sons whose inheritance has been restored. **Adopted sons are the sons of the complete restoration.**

The Book of Job tells us of a righteous man who had great

wealth. Satan came before God and said that Job's righteousness would crumble if God allowed Satan to remove his wealth, his health, and his visible signs of God's favor. After agonizing, Job finally was told by God that God is sovereign over all creation (Job, chapters 38-41). God can do anything He wants with anything that is His, which included Job. Having made His point, He then restored wealth, health, and a large family to him (Job 42). The end result was better than before: Job had a proper understanding of the absolute sovereignty of God, and he also had greater external wealth. That's what adoption is all about: **restoration that is better than the original.**

God adopts; men respond to the announcement of their adoption by acknowledging faith in Jesus Christ. "The word is nigh thee, even in thy mouth, and in thine heart: that is, the word of faith, which we preach, that if thou shalt confess with thy mouth the Lord Jesus, and shalt believe in thine heart that God hath raised him from the dead, thou shalt be saved. For with the heart man believeth unto righteousness; and with the mouth confession is made unto salvation" (Romans 10:8-10). **God acts; men respond.**

Paul's letter to the Ephesians outlines what we **were,** who we **are** (through God's grace), and what we are **supposed to do.** "And you hath he quickened, who were dead in trespasses and sins; wherein in time past ye walked according to the course of this world, according to the prince of the power of the air [Satan], the spirit that now worketh in the children of disobedience: among whom also we all had our conversation in times past in the lusts of our flesh, fulfilling the desires of the flesh and of the mind; and were by nature children of wrath, even as others. But God, who is rich in mercy, for his great love wherewith he loved us, even when we were dead in sins, hath quickened us [given us life] together with Christ, (by grace ye are saved;) and hath raised us up together, and made us sit together in heavenly places in Christ Jesus: that in ages to come he might shew the exceeding riches of his grace in his kindness toward us through Christ Jesus. For by grace are ye saved through faith; and that not of yourselves: it is the gift of God: Not of works, lest any man should boast. For we are his workmanship, created in Christ Jesus unto good works, which God hath before ordained that we should walk in them" (Ephesians 2:1-10). **From** death **to** life, **through** faith, **by** grace, **unto** good works that were ordained by God for us to do: here is the path of restoration.

What a marvelous doctrine the doctrine of adoption is! It raises some very important questions, however. How can God look at a sinful man and declare him a true son of God? What about the man's sin? Here we come to the problem of the **order of salvation.** What comes first (logically, though sometimes simultaneously)?

Election

What comes first, predictably, is **God's decision to choose a man.** No better statement of this exists than Paul's declaration: "And we know that all things work together for good to them that love God, to them who are called according to his purpose. For whom he did foreknow, he also did predestinate to be conformed to the image of his Son, that he might be the firstborn among many brethren. Moreover whom he did predestinate, them he also called: and whom he called, them he also justified: and whom he justified, them he also glorified. What shall we say to these things? If God be for us, who can be against us?" (Romans 8:28-31). **God chose us before the foundation of the world.** We must not minimize Paul's words: "According as he hath chosen us in him before the foundation of the world, that we should be holy and without blame before him in love, having predestinated us unto the adoption of children by Jesus Christ to himself, according to the good pleasure of his will" (Ephesians 1:4-5). It was **God's sovereign choice before time began** to adopt some for His own, conforming them to the image of His Son. The twisted image of God in man has been straightened out by God, in principle, and as we mature as adopted sons, that image will be progressively untwisted by God's sanctifying grace through time.

God **calls** us to Himself. He makes a general call to all men, but a saving call is a special call. The general call is the one mentioned by Jesus: "For many are called, but few are chosen" (Matthew 22:14). That call is like the call of a father to a wayward child—one which the child hears, refuses to accept, and runs away from. But the "call of explicit choosing," or the "effectual call," or the "inescapable call," is **the call of God to His about-to-be adopted sons.** They cannot resist this call. He chose them before time began. "But God hath chosen the foolish things of the world to confound the wise; and God hath chosen the weak things of the world to confound the mighty" (I Corinthians 1:26). Why? "That no flesh should glory in his presence" (I Corinthians 1:29). It is the work of God, not of man's flesh. To prove it, He chooses the "losers" of the world, who become the ultimate victors with Him.

Adopted sonship is as independent of a man's planning as biological sonship is. It is God who adopts some men as His ethical sons. They do not adopt God. They respond to their newly acquired adopted sonship, but only because it has in fact been acquired already. Like the newborn infant who screams when slapped on the bottom, newly adopted sons voice their response. They do not shout in pain; they shout for joy.

Sanctification (regeneration)

Having called men, He then **regenerates** them in the midst of time. "A new heart also will I give you, and a new spirit will I put within you: and I will take away the stony heart out of your flesh, and I will give you an heart of flesh. And I will put my spirit within you, and cause you to walk in my statutes, and ye shall keep my judgements, and do them" (Ezekiel 36:26-27). God's adopted sons will conform themselves to the image of His Son, Jesus, and like Jesus, they will do the works of the law, for the law of God will be in their hearts.

Regeneration means being **born again,** or as the Greek phrase can also be translated, **born from above.** "Jesus answered, Verily, verily [truly, truly], I say unto thee, Except a man be born again, he cannot see the kingdom of God" (John 3:3). **Man must be born of the Spirit of God.** "That which is born of the flesh is flesh; and that which is born of the Spirit is spirit. Marvel not that I said unto thee, Ye must be born again. The wind bloweth where it listeth, and thou hearest the sound thereof, but canst not tell whence it cometh, and whither it goeth: so is every one that is born of the Spirit" (John 3:6-8). The Spirit of God actually regenerates a man, untwisting the fallen image of God in man, making that man **a new creation.** "Therefore if any man be in Christ, he is a new creature [creation]: old things are passed away; behold, all things are become new" (II Corinthians 5:17).

God **chooses** a man as an adopted son. God **calls** this man. God **regenerates** this man, making it possible for him to respond to the call. He must be regenerated **before** he can respond to the call, otherwise, he would never listen to the call. "But the natural man receiveth not the things of the Spirit of God: for they are foolishness unto him: neither can he know them, because they are spiritually discerned" (I Corinthians 2:14). Again, "For the preaching of the cross is to them that perish foolishness; but unto us which are saved it is the power of God" (I Corinthians 1:18). We are back to that familiar principle: **God acts; men respond.** At this point, you may be saying to yourself: "This sounds too complicated to me. After all, it's really faith that counts. Why get involved in a lot of theological speculation? What does it matter, whether God regenerates a man first, or whether the man responds in faith and then God regenerates him? Isn't it all the same in the end?"

No, it isn't all the same. We have to understand the nature of man. **Man is totally depraved**—not a bit, not a whole lot, but **totally**. Adam's one sin buried us. "For whosoever shall keep the whole law, and yet offend in one point, he is guilty of all" (James 2:10). Comprehensive, isn't it? Total, isn't it?

Adam, created perfect, could do only one thing to gain God's curse. Anything else in the whole world was open to him. He headed straight for the forbidden fruit. Now his heirs are totally depraved. They have transgressed the whole of the law. There is nothing on earth they can do to gain the favor of God, except one thing: have faith in Jesus Christ. If Adam, a perfect man, could have retained God's favor by doing anything in the world, except one thing, and wound up doing that one thing, how can fallen men expect to be able to discover and then **do** the one thing that can bring God's favor, out of an infinite number of things they can do that won't bring God's favor? It's ridiculous. They can't do it. They won't do it. Only if God regenerates them first can they possibly do it, and then, being regenerated, they **will** do it.

When the Bible says that **the natural man receiveth not the things of the Spirit,** it really means it. People who say they believe the Bible, people who even quote this verse, often don't believe it. They rewrite it to say: "The natural man receiveth not the things of the Spirit, except, of course, the most important thing the Spirit ever says, the thing that is absolute foolishness to the world. **Some** natural men **do** receive this." Well, this rewritten version is absolutely false. God acts; men respond. God elects; men respond. God regenerates; men respond. **Regenerate** men receive the things of the Spirit. Natural men don't. Ever. Not even a little bit. That's what the Bible says, and that's what Bible-believing people had better believe.

What is the **response** of a newly regenerated man? **He professes faith in Jesus Christ.** Understand: he **is** regenerated; **therefore** he believes in Christ. It is not the other way around. He does **not** manufacture faith out of his own autonomy. He does **not** offer his faith to God in payment for salvation. He does **not** earn his way into heaven. A man doesn't choose to be born, physically or spiritually. John speaks of the adopted sons, "Which were born, not of blood, nor of the will of the flesh, nor of the will of man, but of God" (John 1:13). It couldn't be any clearer. The will of man, including the will of the adopted son, is not involved as an independent, originating factor. It is **all** God's grace, from start (choosing which men to adopt before time began) to finish (bringing them into the new heavens and new earth).

Men usually resent this doctrine. Like Adam, they want at least a little original sovereignty. They want "a piece of the action" in their own salvation. But they can't have it. "But the natural man receiveth not the things of the Spirit of God" (I Corinthians 2:14a). **This means exactly what it says,** that the natural man (natural son) really cannot respond to the call to repentance until **after** he has been regenerated. He responds after he is adopted, no longer a natural man (son).

Once a man is regenerated, he can respond to God's grace. **Faith and repentance,** which are essentially **a single response by man,** immediately follow. By grace are we saved, through faith (Ephesians 2:8). Men know that Christ has saved them, they assent to the fact, and they trust on His continuing grace to sustain them. They repent—turn away from—their sins. "Thus is it written, and thus it behooved Christ to suffer, and to rise from the dead the third day: and that repentance and remission of sins should be preached in his name unto all the nations" (Luke 24:46-47). This is what we are to believe; this is what our assignment is: **to preach the message in all nations.** This is what the apostles preached from the beginning. "And when the Gentiles heard this, they were glad, and glorified the word of the Lord: and as many as were ordained to eternal life believed" (Acts 13:48).

This act of regeneration on the part of God is sometimes called ·**definitive sanctification** by theologians. It is the **moral transformation** of man, the **new heart and new attitude** which God imparts to man. They have Christ's perfect humanity (though not His divinity) imparted to them, in principle, at the moment of regeneration. This implies a **final** sanctification, that on the day of judgment, we will be conformed to the image of God's Son (Romans 8:29). "Blessed be the God and Father of our Lord Jesus Christ, which according to his abundant mercy hath begotten us again unto a lively hope by the resurrection of Jesus Christ from the dead, to an inheritance incorruptible, and undefiled, and that fadeth not away, reserved in heaven for you, who are kept by the power of God through faith unto salvation ready to be revealed in the last time" (I Peter 1:3-5). This **definitive** sanctification belongs to every Christian at the moment of conversion. Christ's righteousness is imparted to us. It's ours, in principle, **now**.

However, we aren't perfect, in time and on earth. So we have to work out our salvation with fear and trembling. Paul used the analogy of the **athlete** who always struggles toward the finish line, no matter how tired he is. "I press toward the mark for the prize of the high calling of God in Christ Jesus" (Philippians 3:14). "Know ye not that they which run in a race run all, but one receiveth the prize? So run, that ye may obtain" (I Corinthians 9:24). "Let us lay aside every weight and the sin which doth so easily beset us, and let us run with patience the race that is set before us" (Hebrews 12:1). "I have fought a good fight, I have finished my course, I have kept the faith: henceforth there is laid up for me a crown of righteousness, which the Lord, the righteous judge, shall give me at that day: and not to me only, but unto all them also that love his appearing" (II Timothy 4:7-8). Setting aside those sins that weigh us down in our race: this is **progressive** sanctification. It is our life on earth. It is the subduing of our own sins, by means of God's revealed law, by the grace of God. It is the working out of our salvation, that is, working out the implications of our faith. It is a **moral** struggle.

Both aspects of sanctification must be believed. We receive Christ's righteousness at the moment of the new birth. We add nothing to his righteousness. We can **rest** in His good works. But at the same time, this righteousness is not fully developed in our own lives, in time and on earth. So the definitive, absolute sanctification must produce progressive sanctification. **We don't earn salvation, but we work out its implications.** History has meaning. Our lives have meaning. What we do makes a difference, in time and on earth, and also at the day of judgment, when we will receive our rewards (I Corinthians 3). Then we will receive our **final** sanctification.

Justification

Men are chosen. They are adopted, meaning they are born again (from above). They respond in faith and repent. God also **justifies** them. **Justification is a judicial act.** God, the sovereign judge, looks at Christ's righteousness, finds it perfect, and then imputes this righteousness to Christ's people. He **declares** them "not guilty." We have seen Romans 8:30 before, but here it is again: "Moreover whom he did predestinate, them he also called: and whom he called, them he also justified: and whom he justified, them he also glorified." We are safe from any successful accusation by Satan. "It is God who justifies: who is he that condemns?" (Romans 8:33). God declares us righteous because of Christ: "Being justified freely by his grace through the redemption that is in Jesus Christ" (Romans 3:24). It is not man's work which justifies man: "Therefore by the deeds of the law there shall no flesh be justified in his sight: for by the law is the knowledge of sin" (Romans 3:20).

This is strictly a **judicial** act of God, the Supreme judge. He **declares** us innocent, not because of any innate or original righteousness in us, but because of the righteousness of Jesus Christ. God looks at Christ's conformity to His law, as a perfect man (not as the second Person of the Trinity), and declares us righteous. He formally releases us, as rightfully condemned criminals, from the otherwise inevitable wrath to come. This declaration is **definitive** (immediate), and it will be **final** on the day of judgment.

We are continually in **God's court of law**. As we work out our salvation with fear and trembling, God continually brings judgment on our activities. This continual rendering of judgment is the basis of institutions of government—families, civil governments, church courts—in time and on earth. God views our actions, and declares our righteous acts to be acceptable before Him. Our unrighteous actions are covered by the blood of Christ. There are standards of law and order, and God is the source of these standards.

His continual declaration of our innocence is His response to Christ's imputed perfection. God is not saying that our works are somehow the source of our innocence. We are not innocent, except as recipients of Christ's imputed (declared) righteousness. We are not, however, timeless beings. We make decisions, think about our situations, and carry out actions. All of these acts are judged by God. God **continually evaluates** our actions, and **He declares us progressively righteous,** as we mature as spiritually regenerate creatures. His declaration of our righteousness matches our progressive sanctification. But again, it is **Christ's righteousness in us** which enables God to declare our acts righteous. Our acts of righteousness are God's gift to us. "For we are his workmanship, created in Christ Jesus unto good works, which God hath before ordained that we should walk in them" (Ephesians 2:10).

If we sin, God judges us. He brings punishment upon us. "Blessed is the man whom thou chastenest, O Lord, and teachest him out of thy law" (Psalm 94:12). "Chasten thy son while there is hope, and let not thy soul spare for his crying" (Proverbs 19:18). This is God's attitude toward His adopted sons. "For whom the Lord loveth he chasteneth, and scourgeth every son whom he receiveth" (Hebrews 12:6). There is this **continual rendering of judgment,** but it is not judgment unto condemnation. It is God's process of **progressive justification,** His means of bringing His judgments of our actions, in time and on earth, progressively into conformity to His definitive justification, which was announced and imputed to us at the moment of our conversion. Meaning is restored to history, as **God declares His people righteous over time,** as they advance in their spiritual maturity, both **individually** and **collectively.**

Summary

Let's review this important but complex doctrine of salvation. There are three spheres in which man's sin and God's salvation are worked out: the **judicial** or legal sphere, the **moral** sphere, and the **dominical** sphere. Adam was created legally guiltless, morally upright, and dominically in charge of the earth. When he rebelled against God, Adam was declared legally guilty; he became morally perverse, and he was exiled from Eden and lost dominion over the earth. The plan of salvation, however, made it possible for Adam to acquire **legal justification** before God's court of law, **moral renovation** through the work of the Spirit of God, and **dominical**

adoption as son and ambassador of God.

The **law of God** can be seen to have application in these three areas as well. **Juridically** or legally, the law condemns sinners, declaring them guilty. **It puts men under the curse and wrath of God.** Jesus Christ, God's perfect Substitute for sinners, though perfectly sinless Himself, took the legal guilt and wrath of the law upon Himself. Being a sinless man, He could take the place of those He came to save; being God, He could bear the infinite wrath of God against sin. The Bible calls on men to lay hold of this sacrifice by faith, acknowledging our guilt before God's law, and declaring our trust in the substitutionary sacrifice of Christ as our only means of salvation. Those who exercise this faith-commitment are **justified** before the court of heaven; that is, they are **declared** righteous on the basis of Christ's righteousness **imputed** to them.

This brings us to the **second** use of the law. **Morally,** the law is God's **standard of righteousness**. It shows us right from wrong. Sinful man hates God and thus rejects the law as the binding standard for his life. Although Jesus Christ never broke the law of God, on the cross God put the sins of His people on Christ, as the Scripture says, "For he hath made him to be sin for us, who knew no sin; that we might be made the righteousness of God in him" (II Corinthians 5:21). Death is God's penalty for sin, and a fitting penalty it is, for **death destroys sin.** Christ's death was the destruction of the sins placed on him, and it made possible the new life of His people. Those placed into union with Christ by God through faith experience death to sin and newness of life. They are morally renovated, and now rejoice in God's law. This moral aspect of salvation is called sanctification. **Sanctified man progressively subdues his own evil tendencies.**

The **third** use of the law is its **dominical** use. The law shows God's way of life for all of life, and man, as ruler of the earth, is **to rule by means of God's law**. Sinful man has forfeited legitimate dominion, however. The Bible associates dominion with sonship, since the son is the vice-president of the father in the family. Adam was the son of God, according to Luke 3:38. Cast out of Eden, Adam was expelled from God's family, losing his title to legitimate sonship, and losing his legitimate dominion. Jesus Christ assumed that place for His people. He owned nothing, exercised no occupational dominion after His baptism into the role of Savior (though

He had been a carpenter before this), and had no place to lay His head. On the cross He experienced **the ultimate form of forfeiture of dominion—hell**. Because of this, the people of God are restored to dominion and sonship by being **adopted** back into God's family. Christians are no more to imitate Christ's poverty than they are to try to die for the sins of the world. Christians may be called to a life of poverty, but essentially every Christian is a restored dominion man (or woman). **Dominion man progressively subdues the earth.**

Justification, sanctification, and adoption—these are the three aspects of salvation, corresponding to the **judicial, moral**, and **dominical** spheres of life. It is important to observe that there is an order to this salvation. God does not grant long-term dominion to immoral men, nor does he impart new life and righteousness to any who have not been declared legally just in His sight.

This logical order is not a temporal order, however. While we must **distinguish** the three aspects of salvation, we cannot **separate** them. God never imputes justification without also imparting sanctification and adoption. Every Christian who is justified in God's sight will also live a new life in essential conformity to God's law, and will inevitably exercise dominion in whatever sphere (however limited) God places him. We may further note that each of these three aspects of salvation has a **definitive**, a **progressive**, and a **final** aspect.

First, there is **justification**. When God sovereignly grants salvation to a person, and sends the Holy Spirit to create faith (loyalty) in that person's heart, God **declares** that person to be justified at that moment. This is **definitive justification**. Throughout the Christian life, redeemed man will have his acts of righteousness declared by God to be acceptable to Him. That man will also progressively learn what it means to be cleared of guilt and to live as a free man. This is **progressive justification.** Then, on the day of judgment, there is God's final rendering of judgment, the **final justification** of God's people. What must be understood is that in all three cases, it is **God's declarative act**, not man's, that is the source of redeemed man's justification. The decision to declare one person righteous, and another person eternally guilty, is solely God's decision. Fallen man initiates nothing in his own justification. **Nothing**.

Similarly, when saved, the sinner is **regenerated** and given new life. His attitude of hatred is replaced with an attitude of love for God, and a desire to obey Him and His law. This is **definitive sanctification**. No Christian, however, is perfect in this life, for he is still influenced by the world around him and by the remaining tendency to sin within himself. Thus, he must gradually grow in holiness. This is **progressive sanctification**. When he dies, however, he is finally separated from all sinful influences, and is made perfect in holiness. This is **final sanctification**. Each aspect of sanctification (regeneration) is a gift from God.

The same is true of **dominion**. God adopts us at the moment of our salvation. He then gives us our own personal "garden of Eden" to dress and to keep. As we grow in grace, in time and on earth, our dominion is expanded. At the resurrection, our dominion is consummated. Dominion is definitive, progressive, and final. It is a gift from God.

The Christian life in all aspects is lived by **faith**. Faith is not a mystical experience nor is it something that we exercise only once at the point of conversion, nor is it mere intellectual belief. Sometimes people assume that we are justified by faith and sanctified by work. This is fundamentally wrong. **Faith is an attitude which accompanies all activity**. All men have faith, loyalty to some set of ideas. The Christian has faith in, and loyalty to, the Creator of the universe. This **faith loyalty attitude** gives rise to good works, moral and dominical. The Christian looks to God for the power to live a righteous life, and for the power to exercise dominion. Looking to God is an exercise of faith, trust, loyalty. Thus, all Christian activity is grounded in faith. The preeminent expression of faith is **prayer**. In prayer, the Christian expresses his acceptance of God's word and covenant by saying "amen" to God's word. In prayer, the Christian expresses his total dependence on God by asking Him for the grace to live as God wants him to. Practically speaking, then, faith is seen in prayer.

Restoration

We know from the Bible that man's rebellion brought a curse to the ground. This curse was designed to restrain men's evil acts toward each other, yet it was also to burden man, making his dominion assignment more difficult to complete. We are all sinners, so we are all under the curse's burdens. At the same time, God wants His sons to continue the assignment—his **adopted** sons.

His natural sons, who rebelled in Adam and continue to rebel, are doomed. They will spend eternity in the lake of fire, **impotent** in a way unimaginable to us. They will no longer have any responsibility before God to work on their dominion assignment, for they will no longer have even a trace of power. No power—no responsibility. This is their judgment. They sought autonomous (independent) power; they will have no power at all, independent of God or under God's sovereignty in history. So God is not worried about the inability of rebellious sons to fail in their dominion assignment. They will fail, and adopted sons will **replace** them as the true humanity, which is defined as the responsible family of God— responsible for subduing the earth to the glory of God. This **process of replacement** begins on earth.

If the ground is now cursed because of man's rebellion, should we not expect to see the removal of the curse in the future, when the adopted sons come into their inheritance of sinless eternal life? When the natural sons have all their power removed, they will then be no threat to other men. This is what the Bible teaches: "For the earnest expectation of the creature [literally: the creation] waiteth for the manifestation of the sons of God. For the creature [creation] was made subject to vanity, not willingly, but by reason of him who hath subjected the same in hope, because the creature [creation] itself also shall be delivered from the bondage of corruption into the glorious liberty of the children of God. For we know that the whole creation groaneth and travaileth in pain together until now. And not only they, but ourselves also, which have the first fruits of the Spirit, even we ourselves groan within ourselves, waiting for the adoption, to wit, the redemption of our body" (Romans 8:19-23). A day of **final release** is coming—release from the curse.

We also know that each man's personal victory over sin is a lifelong task. Paul told the Philippian church members to "work out your own salvation with fear and trembling" (Philippians 2:12b). Work out the **salvation which is yours** conveys the meaning better; not that they were saving themselves by their own efforts, but that **they were working out the implications of their faith, in time and on earth.** So are all men all of the time. They are working out the implications of their particular faiths, their primary commitment, for good or evil. Shouldn't we therefore expect a **progressive release** for nature, before the final day of release?

As godly men work out the implications of their faith, shouldn't the world immediately around them steadily improve? If one man is honest, helps those in his immediate surroundings, and makes life more pleasant, shouldn't we expect to see him do better materially? Not every man in every instance, of course; but when a **group** of men sharing faith in the Christ of the Bible work out their faith in fear and trembling, won't **most** of them grow more powerful, more influential, if only because other people recognize them as being more reliable?

We know that man has a dominion assignment. We know that God intends His adopted sons to continue to work. We know that this labor is a life-long process. Should we expect God to increase His blessings on the work of the natural sons, while reducing His external blessings in the lives of His adopted sons? Should we really expect the rebels to go from victory unto victory, in time and on earth, while the adopted sons, who have been selected by God to fulfill the terms of the dominion assignment, are cursed with more poverty, more burdens, less capital, and endlessly increasing frustration, in time and on earth? We will consider the Bible's answers to these questions in the chapter on God's kingdom, but think about them for the time being. But keep this question in mind: If God has assigned His adopted sons the primary responsibility for fulfilling the terms of His dominion assignment, cannot Satan claim victory over God, in time and on earth, if God's adopted sons become progressively less able to complete their assignment? If this is the case, hasn't Satan been successful in His attempt to thwart God in history? Hasn't he effectively replaced God on earth as the master of those who are fulfilling the terms of the dominion assignment, the natural sons? In short, **will not Satan be able to boast, throughout eternity, that he personally had thwarted God, at least for a few thousand years**? Hasn't his claim to operating sovereignty been justified, since it was his people, not God's adopted sons, who fulfilled the terms of man's dominion assignment, in time and on earth? Hasn't he, in effect, locked up God's sovereignty inside the gates of heaven? Shouldn't the Bible have read something like this: "The gates of **heaven** shall prevail"? Isn't it the kingdom of God which is under siege, rather than the gates of hell (Matthew 16:18)? Does the Bible really teach such things?

Conclusions

Man is made in the image of God. His rebellion against God did not remove God's image from man's being, but it twisted it. Man chose to test God's word, hoping to become sovereign over God. Instead, man only switched allegiances: he now serves Satan. He can serve only one master at a time, and there are only two possible masters. The universal fatherhood of God has become God's judgment on man, for God has disinherited His natural sons. Yet because He chose some men to become adopted sons—a choice made before time began (Ephesians 1:4)—some men are restored to original sonship, meaning **ethical sonship**. The others await a fate worse than physical death: the second death, in which all power is taken from them. The dominion assignment will then be fully and visibly reconfirmed with the adopted sons. Before the day of judgment, however, all sons labor in terms of the dominion assignment, and the earth has been cursed to make their work more difficult, less rewarding, and less productive without co-operation on the part of their fellow man. Restoration of the ground is guaranteed, for restoration of full ethical sonship, through regenerating adoption, is also guaranteed.

Chapter 3

LAW

When God created the animals, He put them under law. He determined that they would reproduce after their own kind (Genesis 1:24-25). When God created man, He put man under law. He told Adam that he should not eat of the tree of the knowledge of good and evil (Genesis 2:17). Adam was physically able to eat its fruit, but he was under moral, legal restraint not to.

The law of God is a testimony to His unchanging character. "I am the Lord, I change not," God told His people (Malachi 3:6). He is reliable. His character is fixed. Everything else in creation changes, but not God. His permanence is the very standard of permanence.

Christ, speaking of that final day of judgment, announced: "Heaven and earth shall pass away, but my words shall not pass away" (Matthew 24:35). No clearer statement of His own divinity could be imagined. He was equating His words with the permanence attributed to God. **Only God speaks a permanent word.**

In the sermon on the mount, Christ informed His listeners: "Think not that I am come to destroy the law, or the prophets: I am not come to destroy, but to fulfill. For verily [truly] I say unto you, Till heaven and earth pass, one jot or one tittle shall in no wise [way] pass from the law, till all be fulfilled" (Matthew 5:17-18). The word "destroy" could refer to a tearing down, or dismantling something. Jesus did not come to dismantle the law of God. But that's a peculiar way to speak of the law. What He meant was that He had not come to **abrogate** or **annul** the law. He did not come to **invalidate** the law. God's law structure of the cursed creation will not be changed for as long as the old creation (our world) remains. The opposite concept of "abrogate" or "annul" is **confirm, establish, ratify.** Christ said, therefore, that He did not come to abrogate the law but to ratify it—to confirm it, to put His

55

"seal of approval" on it. He confirmed its validity by teaching its precepts, living His life in terms of its requirements, and overcoming temptation (in the wilderness) by citing its provisions to Satan (Matthew 4).

The law is as permanent as God. But wasn't Jesus promising the final abolition of the law, once the earth ends? True, not one jot or tittle, the smallest letters in the Hebrew alphabet, will pass away until then, but after that, will the new heavens and new earth (Revelation 21) be free of the law? That would be a misinterpretation of Christ's words, since He already stated that His words will never pass away. What He meant was that those laws applying to the **fallen** world will be in force until the world is restored. Then the **applications** of the law may change, since the external circumstances will change. For example, the laws of marriage will no longer be in force, for there is no marriage in heaven (Matthew 22:30). We are today no longer faced with the problem of whether or not to eat from the tree of the knowledge of good and evil; that tree is not part of our testing any longer. But the **general principles** of marriage will always hold: faithfulness, communion, service, etc. The general principle of the tree is still in force: don't disobey God's revealed commandments. Nowhere in the Bible can we find any hint of a final abolition of the rule of God through law and its principles.

Law's Purposes

God is a holy being, set apart from His creation. He is set apart by His very being; He is fundamentally different from the creation. He is also set apart by His moral perfection. He is the standard of righteousness. He is the source of all moral standards. He is not under law, but is the source of law. We don't examine the acts of God and try to compare them with some self-existing, sovereign set of standards; God is the source of the standards.

Law is the basis of control for man: control of man's own moral behavior, control of rebellious acts by other men, and control of the creation itself. Without the regularities of nature, all would be incoherent. But man is given dominion as God's assistant on earth, and man's knowledge of nature's regular patterns is his primary means of directing nature and subduing it. **Law is power**. Yet all power, if it is to be exercised legitimately, must be under moral law. There are lots of terrible things we have the power to do, but they should not be done. So man gains dominion by means of law, yet he is also restrained by law. God's law has **moral** and **dominical** functions.

God has revealed His standards in the Bible, especially in the first five books of the Old Testament, called the Pentateuch. They are **moral** standards. They also provide **dominical** standards. They tell man how to deal with **other men** and **nature**. The revealed law of God gives men **guidelines for action**. They are valid guidelines because God made both man and the creation, and **He designed these laws to be in conformity with man and nature**. Or we might say that the whole creation, including man, is governed by both moral and physical principles, and these principles are expressions of the holiness and power of God. Man can grasp these moral and dominical principles because he is a creature made in God's image.

Psalm 119, the longest chapter in the Bible, deals with the relationship between God and man, and its focus is the law of God. Anyone who is really serious about discovering God's legal relationship to man should read this passage carefully. "Wherewithall shall a young man cleanse his way? By taking heed thereto according to thy word. With my whole heart have I sought thee: O let me not wander from thy commandments. Thy word have I hid in mine heart, that I might not sin against thee. Blessed art thou, O Lord: teach me thy statutes" (Psalm 119:9-12). Man's life is literally saturated with law; he lives in a universe of law, cannot escape from law, and exercises dominion in terms of law. **Law is man's tool of dominion**: over himself, his fellow men, and the creation.

Law is also a means of **judging** one's conformity to God's standards. God's law has a **judicial** function. Without these standards, a man could not test his relationship with God. Paul wrote: "I had not known sin, but by the law: for I had not known lust, except the law had said, Thou shalt not covet" (Romans 8:7). The law tells us what we are: **rebels**.

Law therefore is a **schoolmaster** which leads us to Christ. "Wherefore the law was our schoolmaster to bring us unto Christ, that we might be justified by faith" (Galatians 3:24). Our knowledge of our own rebellious nature as disinherited sons is intended to lead us to Christ, to believe in Him, and to receive confirmation of our position as adopted sons.

Law is also a means of **judging the spiritual condition of others**.

Christ warned: "Beware of false prophets, which come to you in sheep's clothing, but inwardly they are ravening wolves. Ye shall know them by their fruits. Do men gather grapes of thorns, or figs of thistles? Even so every good tree bringeth forth good fruit; but a bad tree bringeth forth evil fruit. A good tree cannot bring forth evil fruit, neither can a corrupt tree bring forth good fruit. Every tree that bringeth not forth good fruit is hewn down, and cast into the fire" (Matthew 7:15-20). But how could we recognize good fruit or evil fruit if we didn't have **permanent standards from God** which serve as our standards of evaluation?

Law is a means of **establishing the holiness—the "set apartness"—of God's people**. It is a segregating device. God tells us, "Be ye holy, even as I am holy," which means, "Be ye set apart from rebels, for I am set apart from rebels." We are told: "And have no fellowship with the unfruitful works of darkness, but rather reprove them" (Ephesians 5:11). Again, "Be ye not unequally yoked together with unbelievers: for what fellowship hath righteousness with unrighteousness? And what communion hath light with darkness?" (I Corinthians 6:14). The law helps us to fulfill these requirements; we have **standards of righteous fruit**. The law is also a means of **calling the nations to repentance**, for they will understand how they are separated from the law of God and His holiness: "Behold, I have taught you statutes and judgments, even as the Lord my God commanded me, that ye should do so in the land whither ye go to possess it. Keep therefore and do them, for this is your wisdom and your understanding in the sight of the nations, which shall hear all these statutes, and say, Surely this great nation is a wise and understanding people. For what nation is there so great, who hath God so nigh unto them, as the Lord our God is in all things that we call upon him for? And what nation is there so great, that hath statutes and judgments so righteous as all this law, which I set before you this day?" (Deuteronomy 4:5-8). This is the Old Testament background to Christ's statement: "Ye are the light of the world. A city that is set on an hill cannot be hid. Neither do men light a candle, and put it under a bushel, but on a candlestick; and it giveth light unto all that are in the house. Let your light shine before men, that they may see your good works, and glorify your Father which is in heaven" (Matthew 5:14-16).

It works both ways, however. **Evil on the part of God's people is**

used by the enemies of God to blaspheme God. Nathan the prophet came to King David, the ruler of Israel, to challenge him for his great evil in committing adultery with Bathsheba, and in ordering her husband into the front lines of battle to be killed. Nathan told David, "this deed hast given great occasion to the enemies of the Lord to blaspheme..." (II Samuel 12:14). The enemies of God recognize the holiness of God, God's law, and God's people. They are alert to ridicule the sins of His people, so that they might ridicule His law and His very existence. They say things like this: "Why go to church to sit around with a bunch of hypocrites? I can meet all the hypocrites I need outside of church." By implication, they're saying, "In fact, those inside the churches are the most hypocritical of all. At least those outside the churches don't put on airs." Which is a way of saying, "Actually, I'm a lot **better** than those inside the churches, and my way of life, when you come right down to it, is **superior** to the way of life lived by Christians."

Those outside of God's fellowship recognize the holiness of God. It confronts them all day, every day. The invisible things of the world testify to the existence of God, but they restrain this knowledge in unrighteousness (Romans 1:18-20). Since they recognize the holiness of God in the creation, they also need to recognize His "set apartness" in His law. This is why it is imperative that God's people adhere to God's law. **It is a schoolmaster for those outside the fellowship.** Without God's law, they will not recognize the horror of their plight.

How can Christians preach an effective gospel to sinners without also preaching the law of God? Do we preach about a holy God? **How** do they know He is holy? Do we preach that His people must be holy? **How** can they know what holy lives are without the law? Do we tell men they need to turn from their sins and repent? **How** can they recognize what a sin is without the law of God? Do we tell them that God hates sin? **What** is there to hate without the law? Do we wonder why men fail to recognize the affront to God that sin entails? **Why** should they, if we don't preach the binding nature of God's revealed law?

Paul devoted considerable space in his letter to the Christians at Rome to this very subject. He told them about his own experiences before he repented and believed on Christ's atoning work on the cross for his salvation. "For I was alive without the law once; but when the commandment came, sin revived, and I died. And the commandment, which was ordained to life, I found to be unto death. For sin, taking occasion by the commandment, deceived me, and by it slew me. Wherefore the law is holy, and the commandment holy, and just, and good'' (Romans 7:9-12).

Paul taught that Christians are no longer under the **curse** of the law. **Law no longer slays us.** That's the reason he could declare that he was once dead when he recognized the deadly nature of sin. Sin no longer strangles the Christian. It no longer drags him to the eternal grave. But it did once, Paul said, and that's why law is such a good thing. It woke him up to just exactly what he was, a sinner, and where he was going: hell.

If Christians ignore the law of God, and regard it as irrelevant, just because we are no longer under God's curse, how will unbelievers recognize us being different? How will they respond to men who do not acknowledge the law as externally binding? We know how they'll respond: ''Those Christians are just a bunch of **hypocrites**. They tell me that I'm doomed because I haven't obeyed God's law 100%, yet they pay absolutely no attention to the law once they're supposedly converted to Christ. They use their religion to make me feel guilty, and then they lie, cheat, and steal worse than anyone, because they say that they're free from the law now. **Hypocrites!**''

Well, isn't that just about what we are, if we use the doctrine of grace as a license to sin? As Paul said, ''Do we then make void the law through faith? God forbid: yea, we establish the law'' (Romans 3:31). And again, ''What shall we say then? Shall we continue in sin, that grace may abound? God forbid. How shall we, that are dead to sin, live any longer therein?'' (Romans 6:1-2). What Paul argued against, over and over, is the mistake of relying on **our own independent attempts to fulfill the requirements of God's perfect, and comprehensive, law structure.** If a man puts himself under the terms of the law, and then thinks he can earn his way to heaven by doing the law, he's an eternally dead man. ''For as many as are of the works of the law are under the curse; for it is written, Cursed is every one that continueth not in all things which are written in the book of the law to do them'' (Galatians 3:10). That's what Christ has saved us from: ''Christ hath redeemed us from the curse of the law, being made a curse for us: for it is written, Cursed is every one that hangeth on a tree'' (Galatians 3:13). Jesus Christ actually fulfilled the terms of the law, and then, as our fully righteous substitute, was sacrificed on God's altar, so that we will not wind up on that fiery altar. Christ, by fulfilling the law, has removed the **curse** of the law from His people; but as He said in the sermon on the mount, He came not to annul the law but to **confirm** it. If Jesus Christ died to confirm the validity of the law, Christians should never say anything that might lead lost men to conclude that there is any escape from our requirement to obey the law. No one escapes that requirement. What men **can** escape is their requirement to **pay for** their transgression. Christ never said we don't owe God a debt for our transgression; He did say that He had paid the debt for our transgression. What are lawless Christians trying to do, increase their portion of the debt Christ lovingly paid? Are they continuing to live in sin that grace may abound? God forbid, said Paul.

Our King's Treaty

God tells us that sinners deserve His wrath. He is a holy God, who despises both sin and the sinner. He casts **sinners** into hell, forever, not just sin. **Sinners** pay, not sin. God said that He despised Esau, Jacob's brother, even before the two had been born, even before they had committed sin. Paul wrote: "(For the children, being not yet born, neither having done any good or evil, that the purpose of God according to election might stand, not of works, but of him who calleth;) It was said unto her [Rebecca], The elder shall serve the younger. As it is written, Jacob have I loved, but Esau have I hated" (Romans 9:11-13).

Most people don't like this kind of preaching. Paul was never a very popular fellow. But he was a very smart fellow. He knew what most listeners would conclude. He answers them before their question gets asked: "What shall we say then? Is there unrighteousness with God? God forbid. For he saith to Moses, I will have mercy on whom I will have mercy, and I will have compassion on whom I will have compassion" (Romans 9:14-15). The average man thinks to himself: "Poor old Esau. What a tough break. After all, what had he done in his mother's womb to deserve God's wrath? That God: what an arbitrary character! Loving Jacob and hating Esau. It's not fair." But Paul has answered this objection: "It's fair because God did it. Is there unrighteousness with God?" You see, what the sinner is **really** thinking, is this: "Man is really a decent species. Each man is born with a clean slate. He makes it or breaks it on his own. He performs or he doesn't. He earns his way to heaven, or maybe to hell, but it's his work that counts. God is being unfair to decent, clean-slate man when He doesn't give a guy a fair shake.''

What does the Bible say about man? That he sinned in Eden, and from that point on, he is perverse. He has twisted the image of God which is his character. As David said, ''Behold, I was shapen in iniquity; and in sin did my mother conceive me'' (Psalms 51:5). It is not sex as such which is sinful; it is the **entire character** of sinful mankind. Man is not born with a clean slate. **He is born a disinherited son of God the righteous Father**. He needs adoption. And God decides who is to be adopted and who is not. The astounding thing about the account Paul gives of Jacob and Esau is not that Esau was hated by God. The astounding, miraculous thing is that **God loved Jacob.** God doesn't owe us a ''break''; God owes us punishment, and He graciously gives some of us a break, not because we deserve it, but because He wants to do it, out of loving mercy. This is the biblical doctrine of **election**.

God is gracious even to the hated natural sons. He offers them a **peace treaty**. That treaty is His law. When a king places his people under his protection, he sets forth their obligations to him in return. **A civil government always has law.** Its citizens must obey the law in order to gain the benefits of protection. **We never find peace treaties without mutual obligations**. The terms may be harsh. The nation which loses a war may be faced with terms that involve unconditional surrender. But the treaty ends the war. Sign the treaty, and the war ends.

God put Adam under a treaty. Live in the garden for a while, enjoy your wife, and then go out and subdue the earth. ''All I ask, Adam, is that you avoid the fruit of a single tree.'' So there were terms to God's treaty. And there was punishment for disobedience; in this case, Adam's immediate spiritual death, his eventual physical death, the curse of the ground, and the same for Eve, plus pain in childbearing. The treaty offered protection and benefits. It had terms of obedience. It had punishments for disobedience. That is typical of every treaty. It is God's way of dealing with men. It is also every ruler's way of dealing with his subjects.

God offers all men His treaty. They know it, too. They see God in the invisible things of the world, and they restrain this knowledge (Romans 1:18-20). They even have the **work** of the law written in their own hearts, and they don't even meet this standard. "For when the Gentiles, which have not the law, do by nature the things contained in the law, these, having not the law, are a law unto themselves: which shew the work of the law written in their hearts, their conscience also bearing witness, and their thoughts the mean while accusing or else excusing one another" (Romans 2:14-15). The law of God isn't in their hearts, but the work of the law is. That is sufficient to condemn every man, but still man refuses to look up to God and acknowledge the comprehensive law-order that God has spelled out in His treaty of peace. Men prefer to continue their war against God—a war which cannot be won. He offers all men peace, but He knows that not one will accept the terms of the treaty apart from His grace. Why won't men capitulate to a treaty of complete righteousness? The prophet Jeremiah told us long ago: "The heart is deceitful above all things, and desperately wicked: who can know it?" (Jeremiah 17:9). And a few lines later, he uttered this mighty prayer on the enemies of God: "Let them be confounded that persecute me, but let not me be confounded: let them be dismayed, but let not me be dismayed: bring upon them the day of evil, and destroy them with double destruction" (Jeremiah 17:18). That's how our king wants us to pray against His enemies: **let them be destroyed**. If they repent, of course, they are no longer His enemies, which is why it is also legitimate to pray for their conversion, meaning their formal signing of God's peace treaty. May God's enemies **be destroyed** or **sign the peace treaty**.

God is nevertheless **merciful**, even to His enemies. He requires men to offer a peace treaty before attacking another nation. "When thou comest nigh unto a city to fight against it, then proclaim peace unto it. And it shall be, if it make thee answer of peace, and open unto thee, then it shall be, that all the people that is found therein shall be tributaries unto thee, and they shall serve thee. And if it will make no peace with thee, but will make war against thee, then thou shalt besiege it; and when the Lord thy God hath delivered it into thine hands, thou shalt smite every male thereof with the edge of the sword" (Deuteronomy 20:10-13). No sneak attacks are allowed, even by God's people who marched in the Old Testament era under the protection of God. He Himself offers all rebels a peace treaty; we must do the same.

Most Christians understand that they are **ambassadors** of Jesus

Christ. Paul wrote his letter to the church at Ephesus from a prison cell in Rome. How did he describe his task there? "And for me, that utterance may be given unto me, that I may open my mouth boldly, to make known the mystery of the gospel, for which I am an ambassador in bonds: that therein I may speak boldly, as I ought to speak" (Ephesians 6:19-20). But what is an ambassador? It's someone who goes to another nation or another people as a representative of a foreign monarch. He comes before the people of one nation as an official agent of another. **An ambassador visits one kingdom as an official agent of another kingdom.** He speaks in the name of his home kingdom's government.

The Christian evangelist is unquestionably an ambassador. More than this, he is an ambassador who is on a specific mission: to call God's enemies to **surrender** to the great King. He comes into Satan's kingdom and **demands** the capitulation of Satan's forces. He tells them of the futility of continuing the fight. He tells them of the sovereignty of God. He tells them of the awful, eternal future which awaits all those who are found in the uniforms of the enemy on the final day. He calls them to reject their current ruler and to defect, just as Rahab the harlot defected to Israel and Israel's God when she was visited by the Hebrew spies (Joshua 2). He tells them of the majesty of his King, who protects His people and gives them hope. He tells them of the justice of his King, of the wonderful laws under which he lives. He tries to make them jealous of the law of God, just as God promised Israel that foreign nations would be jealous of Israel's laws if Israel remained faithful to those laws (Deuteronomy 4:5-8). He tells them that their chosen ruler, Satan, is a usurper, that he does not deserve their allegiance. He tells them that his King is a universal King, not just some local monarch. He tells them that his King holds them completely responsible for obeying His law, to the last jot and tittle, whether they admit it or not. He tells them that they had better surrender now, and learn about his King's peace treaty and all its requirements, for if they refuse to submit themselves to its terms before the final battle, then they will be utterly destroyed. **The ambassador is not to pretend that there are no terms in the peace treaty.** He is a fool, or a liar, if he tells the foreign usurpers that by capitulating now, they will never have to obey the treaty's laws, but if they refuse to surrender, they will be held fully responsible for obeying them. The whole idea of requiring their surrender is to extend the reign of the monarch throughout the whole world. **The whole idea is to bind men by the terms of the treaty now, before the final battle, so that they be not bound up later and thrown into the fire.** As Christ warned, concerning the final judgment on the tares (but not the true wheat): "Let both grow together until the harvest: and in the time of the harvest I will say to the reapers, Gather ye together first the tares, and bind them in bundles to burn them: but gather the wheat into my barn"(Matthew 13:30).

God's ambassadors extend His kingdom by making plain the terms of the treaty. The law of God is man's tool of dominion. Why? Because God's law is man's way to become humble in front of God. He who is **meek before God** will inherit the earth (Matthew 5:5). If a man humbles himself before God, he need have no fear of the world. Remember, man must be **subordinate**, and man must exercise **dominion**. This is basic to man's very nature, and it is basic to the law structure of the creation, which was designed as a garden for man, meaning humble, obedient man. **He must be subordinate to God and exercise dominion in terms of God's law-order.** He must not be humble before Satan and spend eternity in hell, along with Satan, where neither Satan, his angels, nor man can exercise any dominion whatsoever. **The terms of God's peace treaty are the terms spelled out in His law.** They are the means of dominion. His adopted sons are to adhere to God's law in order to bring the earth under the rule of God's law. His adopted sons are to adhere to God's law in order to become honest ambassadors of God in Satan's temporary, and steadily eroding, kingdom. His adopted sons are to adhere to God's law in order to deflect the predictable charge of hypocrisy from the natural, rejected sons. The adopted sons are to adhere to God's law for the same reason that David should have: to avoid giving the enemies of God an opportunity to blaspheme (II Samuel 12:14). In short, **God's peace treaty is also a declaration of war on Satan's kingdom.** It serves as a weapon of war; His people possess it, and can steadily subdue the earth in terms of it. His enemies don't acknowledge its validity, and they are left without God's tool of dominion.

Law's Blessings

The Book of Deuteronomy contains a great deal of material on the law. Perhaps the two most relevant passages are chapters 8 and 28. Both of them have the same outline. First, God has given His people a particular set of laws. These laws must be respected. Second, if they obey His laws, God will see to it that they receive external, visible blessings as a people. Third, if they rebel, they will have these blessings removed, and a period of hardships will come upon them.

Deuteronomy 28 devotes the bulk of its message to listing the horrors that will come upon them, from verse 15 to the end of the chapter, verse 68. Deuteronomy 8 has a somewhat different approach. It tells the Hebrews that they will go into the land and prosper if they follow His law. This will bring external prosperity. The external prosperity will then become a temptation to them. They may begin to think that their power has brought their prosperity, rather than their humbleness before God and their adherence to His law-order. Finally, if they do capitulate to their temptation, and they elevate themselves before God and the world, they will be judged, even as the cities of Canaan were judged when God brought them into the land.

We might call this outline the "paradox of Deuteronomy 8." First a **gift**: the land of Canaan. Next, **the law**: the means of dominion. Next, **prosperity**: nature's response to godly rule. Next, **temptation**: forgetting God and attributing prosperity to man. Next, **arrogance**: attributing their prosperity to their own power. Next, **judgment**: God's denial of sovereignty to self-professed autonomous (independent) man. From a gift to the law; from the law to prosperity; from prosperity to arrogance; from arrogance to the removal of both prosperity and the gift. The gift, of course, was the land of Canaan. "And it shall be, if thou do at all forget the Lord thy God, and walk after other gods, and serve them, and worship them, I testify against you this day that ye will surely perish. As the nations which the Lord destroyeth before your face, so shall ye perish; because ye would not be obedient unto the voice of the Lord your God" (Deuteronomy 8:19-20).

The power of God's law in producing external prosperity is **not** dependent upon the spiritual condition of the adherents. The terms of the treaty can, for a time, be adhered to by rebels. So long as they adhere to the externals, they receive external blessings. Of course, no one can adhere 100% to the law, and therefore God has the right to smash anyone at any time. However, because of God's commitment to the terms of His treaty, He grants to rebels the possession of law-produced prosperity for the time in which they adhere to His law. For example, Egypt prospered under the rule of Joseph, even though the Egyptians were ethical rebels. Babylon prospered under the rule of Daniel, until the king of Babylon, Nebuchadnezzar, died, leaving his rebellious son on the throne (Daniel 5). The kingdom of the Medes and Persians prospered while Daniel was again raised to a position of preeminence under King Darius (Daniel 6). These kingdoms were pagan, but **for a time** they submitted to the rule of a servant of God, and they prospered.

The problem, of course, is arrogance. The blessings bring temptation; and the temptation is submitted to by ethical rebels. **It takes the active intervention of God to restrain the hearts of evil men.** Eventually, a Pharaoh arose who knew not Joseph. A Belshazzar replaced a Nebuchadnezzar. **Rebels cannot forever submit to God's law-order.** In the very last days of this world, we learn in Revelation 20, Satan's army rebels, and the wrath of God falls on them. (You might ask yourself, "rebels against what?" If Satan's rule expands through time, what is it that is so good and prosperous that provokes his rebellion? His own kingdom? Is it good and prosperous? Is not the essence of his kingdom the impotence and arrogance of the Pharaoh of the Exodus, who perished in the Red Sea, or King Belshazzar, who saw the handwriting on the wall and died a defeated monarch before morning? Is not the very essence of Satan's rebellion a striking out in impotent fury against the visible goodness of God and God's law: in heaven, in the garden of Eden, on the last day? We will consider this problem in the chapter on God's kingdom, but keep this question in mind: What will Satan be rebelling **against** that is visibly good on that final day?).

What we learn from the Bible is that God's law-order, when adhered to by any people, including ethically rebellious cultures, produces blessings. At the same time, we also learn that no unregenerate culture can sustain forever its outward adherence to God's law-order. If the Hebrews couldn't, then rebellious nations can't. The blessings create a temptation: to be arrogant. Or better put: **to be as God.** To be the source of law, the source of prosperity, knowing (determining) good and evil: here is the familiar temptation for mankind. It was the temptation which destroyed Adam in the garden. How can it be resisted by rebellious men, this side of paradise, this side of perfection? It can't. This is why God's law-order has a built-in protection against "unauthorized use" by ethical rebels. Rebels cannot forever pretend to be humble servants before a sovereign Creator. It grates against their very nature. They cannot stand it. They want the prosperity that is the fruit of obedience to God's law, but the terms of the treaty remind them of its first principle: total submission to a totally sovereign God. They rebel openly. They set up other gods to worship. They do what Moses warned the Hebrews against. "Beware that thou forget not the Lord thy God, in not keeping his commandments, and his judgments, and his statutes, which I command thee this day" (Deuteronomy 8:11). And what else? "And thou say in thine heart, My power and the might of mine hand hath gotten me this wealth. But thou shalt remember the Lord thy God: for it is he that giveth thee power to get wealth, that he may establish his covenant which he sware unto thy fathers, as it is this day" (Deuteronomy 8:17-18).

It takes the **special grace** of God's redeeming Spirit to drag men to the foot of the cross. They need to be adopted in order to enable them to remain faithful to the outward, written, comprehensive requirements of God's law-order. This doesn't mean that we should neglect the preaching of the law. If men submit themselves to the law of God, and they stop murdering each other, stop stealing from each other, stop seducing each other's daughters and wives, stop worshipping the false god of humanism, and stop committing evil in the sight of God and men, we all benefit. We all become the beneficiaries of a godly law-order. Who wouldn't rather live next door to men who honor the externals of biblical law, rather than men who constantly violate its rules? Even if our neighbors reject the testimony of the Bible that Jesus Christ is God, that He died on the cross to make atonement for sin, and that without faith in Christ, through the grace of God, every man will perish eternally, it is nevertheless preferable to live next door to those who adhere to the external terms of the treaty.

No society ever faces the choice between living in terms of law and living under no law whatsoever. It is never a question of "law vs. no law"; it is always a question of **which** law. Man must serve a master. That master imposes a treaty on his servants. The master may be the humanistic State. It may be a church. It may be a personal demon. It may be some imaginary invention, such as "the forces of history." Or it may be the God of the Bible. **But man**

**must serve a master, and every master brings a peace treaty for
man to sign.** Any ambassador of a king who supposedly has no
peace treaty for man to sign, no covenant between king and servants, no terms of obedience, no promise of benefits for submis-
sions, and no promise of judgement for an arrogant unwillingness
to submit, represents a lying king, or else the ambassador is lying
about what his king really demands from his servants. Beware of
any king, or any ambassador of a king, who claims that the peace
treaty is without terms of obedience. That would mean **unconditional surrender on the part of the king to man,** and the advent of
a new king, the tyrant Man. And Man, the self-proclaimed
monarch, imposes terrible terms of surrender on his fellow men,
not to mention the environment.

There is no neutral king. There is no neutral law. There are no
neutral blessings. And there are surely no neutral men. Ours is a
universe of law, but this law is the systematic regularity imposed by
God. God has not repealed His law, and He has not called us to
submit to Him apart from **a treaty with very specific terms.** The
quest for an alternative law structure—"natural" law, "neutral"
law, or no law at all—is an innately demonic quest. It is man's attempt to revoke unilaterally the terms of the treaty imposed by
God. To assert that we have found such a non-revelational law-
order is a declaration of independence from God. It is a revolt that
must fail.

Progressive Conquest

A conquered territory is not completely conquered overnight. It
is filled with pockets of rebellion. Like a garden full of weeds, it
takes time to bring it under dominion. It takes effort, capital, and
a continual resolve to extend the dominion of one's monarch. It
takes perseverance on the part of the monarch's ambassadors and
officers to bring a conquered kingdom under the king's rule. It is
only the patience of the king which permits this kind of conquest;
otherwise, he would burn down the city, burn up the farms, and
replace all the present inhabitants with his own subjects.

God did precisely this in Canaan. More precisely, he ordered the
Hebrews to root out the inhabitants, either by killing them all or
chasing them out of the land. Yet even here, God knew it would
take time. "I will not drive them out from before thee in one year;
lest the land become desolate, and the beast of the field multiply

against thee. By little and little I will drive them out from before thee, until thou be increased, and inherit the land" (Exodus 23:29-30). He told His people to conquer the land totally, to make a "clean sweep." That they failed to obey him only testified to their unfaithfulness (Judges 1:2).

God was establishing a **temporary** kingdom in Palestine. It was to have been a training ground for dominion, as the garden was also intended to be. But the Hebrews failed in Canaan, just as Adam had failed, so God took the kingdom away from them and made it universal, spreading it by means of His ambassadors, who take the gospel of Jesus Christ throughout the earth. Satan's kingdom was all the world before Christ's death and resurrection, with the exception of tiny Israel. Now his kingdom has been invaded by Christ's ambassadors, who bring an offer of peace to Satan's own subjects. The kingdom is no longer "bottled up" in Palestine. That's what Jesus meant when, early in His ministry, He said: "And no man putteth new wine into old bottles: else the new wine doth burst the bottles, and the wine is spilled, and the bottles will be marred: but new wine must be put into new bottles" (Mark 2:22). The new wine of Christ's gospel broke the old bottles of Israel, and this wine poured forth across the face of the earth. Satan's kingdom has been invaded. **Beaten definitively at the cross, Satan now is in retreat, fighting a rear-guard action against the invaders.** He is powerful. He is more dangerous than a wounded water buffalo. But he is nonetheless fighting a losing battle. He wins some defensive battles, but God's strategy achieved a permanent victory at the cross.

(Let me insert this parenthetical observation. Grape juice does not burst wine skins. It is the fermenting process which expands the liquid. **The bubbling over of the now-fermenting product is what bursts the old wine skins.** When the Bible speaks of wine, it means **wine**. To argue that it really means grape juice is to destroy the analogy which Christ used to describe His church's actions in history, and His gospel's power in history. Oh, how Satan must wish that Christ's church and Christ's gospel were really grape juice, sitting safe and sound in the old wine skins of Palestine! Why do you suppose Christ said that the wine of His communion table was His blood? **Because His blood is to cover the sins of sinners throughout Satan's kingdom, all over the world.** Yet there are millions upon millions of Christians today who insist on celebrating the Lord's Supper with grape juice. Grape juice breaks the analogy because grape juice won't break wine skins. Grape juice at the communion table symbolizes the **historical impotence** of Christ's blood, Christ's gospel, Christ's church, and Christ's expanding kingdom. Grape juice stays "bottled up," confined to the historical skins of Palestine.)

The law of God is our means of progressively subduing Satan's kingdom. It begins in our own lives, since Christ's first outpost is the heart of man. This is the **moral** sphere, the work of **sanctification.** Like an athlete in perpetual training, or a soldier in perpetual training, the Christian is perpetually subduing his own sinful flesh, by the grace of God, by the power of God's Spirit, and in terms of the law. Paul wrote: "For I delight in the law of God after [according to] the inward man. But I see another law in my members, warring against the law of my mind, and bringing me into captivity to the law of sin, which is in my members" (Romans 7:22-23). Paul didn't reject God's law; he delighted in it! It was this law which revealed another law in his flesh, the law of sin. It was Christ's triumph at Calvary—a triumph based on Christ's prior fulfilling of the terms of God's comprehensive law—that gave Paul hope. He was justified by faith, he said, not by law (Galatians 3:24).

What did he mean, "justified by faith"? It meant that God the Father will look at Christ's perfection and not Paul's sin on the day of judgment. But this does not deny the role of God's law in the individual's life. The second chapter of the letter of James tells us not to abandon law. "Even so faith, if it hath not works, is dead, being alone. Yea, a man may say, Thou hast faith, and I have works: shew me thy faith without thy works, and I will shew thee my faith by my works" (James 2:17-18). Adherence to God's standards of external, visible righteousness is how we judge the reality, the validity, of our grace-given faith in Christ's atoning work. **No adherence to God's law—no faith,** said James. No fruits of the Spirit, said Christ, then no redemption; for by fruits do we know true faith (Matthew 7:16).

This brings us to the doctrine of **sanctification**. The doctrine of sanctification has three parts: **definitive** sanctification, **progressive** sanctification, and **final** sanctification. We know that all of Christ's good works, all His adherence to the law, is put on our account at the point of our conversion. Still, we must work out the implications in our lives of this salvation. As Paul said, "let us lay aside every weight, and the sin which doth so easily beset us, and let us run with patience the race that is set before us" (Hebrews 12:1). (We think it was Paul who wrote Hebrews; no one can be sure today.) How do we recognize a sin? By the law of God. How do we lay aside these sins? By imposing the rule of God's law in our life. Without the law of God, we cannot possibly recognize and subdue sins.

We have covered this material in the chapter on man. However, sanctification has another application, one which is not discussed very often. The doctrine also applies to **collectives**: state, church, family, etc. God raises up whole nations that are composed of people who have declared their submission to God and His peace treaty. Israel is one example, and the pagan city of Nineveh, for a while, is another (Jonah 3:5-10). God deals with them **collectively**.

In the case of Sodom, God agreed with Abraham to spare the city for the sake of the family of Abraham's nephew, Lot, if Abraham could show that there were as few as ten righteous people in the city (Genesis 18:32). There weren't ten righteous people in the city, so only Lot and his two daughters escaped the wrath that fell on Sodom. But the point is, **God was willing to deal with a city for the sake of a tiny handful of righteous people**. Furthermore, because of God's judgment on a collective, Sodom, Lot had to flee to avoid being destroyed. Because of God's judgment on Israel and Judah, the prophets also went into captivity (Ezekiel 1:3; the Book of Daniel). The Hebrews were judged—chastised, if you prefer—because they and their ancestors had been under God's national covenant. Judah went into captivity for 70 years. Why 70 years? Because for 70 times 7 years, they had not obeyed the law of the sabbatical year, when the land was to be rested (no planting, no harvesting) for one year in seven, a law given by Moses in Exodus 23:10-11. So the land was given its rest while the Hebrews were slaves in Babylon (Jeremiah 50:34).

God is a Trinity. He is one acting agent, yet three Persons, in unity but without intermixture. God is both **one** and **many**. Three individuals, yet one being. There is **unity** and **particularity** in God. The creation reflects this aspect of God. Species are made of individuals, yet they are governed by regularities established by God: they reproduce after their own kind (Genesis 1:24-25). They are individual creatures, yet they are governed by laws that affect them as a species. So it is with human society. God deals with us as individuals, but He also deals with us as collectives. Both the one (the collective) and the many (individuals) are respected. God dealt with individual Hebrews, but also with the tribes. He dealt with the tribes, but also with the nation.

Did God choose the nation of Israel because of its might or faithfulness? He said He didn't choose them for anything they possessed. He set them apart from other nations, calling them holy. He does this with individual people. He chose them because He loved them, as a national entity; He does that with collective people. "For thou art an holy people unto the Lord thy God: the Lord thy God hath chosen thee to be a special people unto himself, above all people that are upon the face of the earth. The Lord did not set his love upon you, nor choose you, because ye were more in number than any people; for ye were the fewest of all people. But because the Lord loved you, and because he would keep the oath which he had sworn unto your fathers, hath the Lord brought you out with a mighty hand, and redeemed you out of the house of bondmen, from the hand of Pharaoh king of Egypt" (Deuteronomy 7:6-8). Isn't this just exactly what He does with individual people? He redeems them out of the house of bondmen, where Adam our father sold us. Men are in slavery to sin as individuals; Israel was in slavery to Pharaoh. God delivers both **individuals** and **nations** out of bondage.

How are individuals to work out their salvation? By suppressing sins in their own life. How are nations to work out their salvation? The same way. This is why God told the nation of Israel to cleave to His law, to keep His commandments. This is why He tells Christians to do the same thing as individuals. **This is progressive sanctification individually and collectively**: in families, churches, nations. There can be chastising of both individuals and nations. There can be total judgment on individuals and nations, as Sodom and Gomorrah should remind us.

Biblical law is our tool of dominion. It enables us to subdue sin in **inner** places (the moral sphere) and **outer** places (the dominical sphere). It is our standard of righteous performance in our daily lives as individuals and as collectives. Blessings and cursings come to us as individuals and collectives. In short, the treaty of the great king is established between God and His ambassadors as individuals, but also between God and His church, and also between

God and the nations. After all, the Bible doesn't promote a one-world State. That was what God destroyed at Babel. The nations (or peoples) persist beyond the day of judgment (Revelation 21:24,26; 22:2). God deals covenantally with individuals and with collectives. His **treaty of peace**, which is at the same time a code of law, establishes His **terms of surrender** for men and nations.

Should we really expect **victory**, in time and on earth? The Bible says that we ought to. We have been given the weapon that cannot be defended against over the long run, namely, **the word of God**. This weapon is imposed steadily, not in violent revolutions, but by the preaching of the gospel. Nothing could be more powerful. **The enemies of God are destroyed by it, step by step**. "But the word of the LORD was unto them precept upon precept, precept upon precept; line upon line, line upon line; here a little, and there a little; that they might go, and fall backward, and be broken, and snared, and taken" (Isaiah 28:13). This is the means of **progressive dominion**. God requires unconditional surrender, but He does not demand immediate, instant unconditional surrender, for that would require the abolition of history at the final judgment. That will come eventually, but He has established other requirements for history.

Restitution

This is the underlying principle of biblical justice. The individual who sins against another must **compensate the victim**. This is why God requires that a sacrifice be offered to Him by man, for man has sinned against a holy God. This sacrifice must be unblemished and perfect. God demanded full payment of this sacrifice from His own Son, Jesus Christ. The letter to the Hebrews is the New Testament book which deals most thoroughly with this human sacrifice. The writer declared, "we are sanctified through the offering of the body of Jesus Christ once for all" (Hebrews 10:10). It is **Christ's perfect sacrifice** which established the **foundation of our dominion:** "But this man, after he had offered one sacrifice for sins for ever, sat down on the right hand of God; from henceforth expecting till his enemies be made his footstool. For by one offering he hath perfected for ever them that are sanctified" (Hebrews 10:12-14). This is the doctrine of **definitive sanctification**: the one-time-only sacrifice of God's Son, which is then imparted to those chosen by God from before the foundation of the world. The righteousness of Christ is the basis of the acceptability of that sacrifice, which is our sacrifice as redeemed (bought-back) men.

The doctrine of **redemption** implied a **payment**. Why a payment? Because we owe God such a payment to **compensate Him** for our transgression. This is the ultimate restitution payment. The magnitude of the sin of Adam was so great, that God's Son, the second Adam (I Corinthians 15:45), had to lay down his life as the only sufficient payment. Redemption means "to buy back," or "to redeem," as a debtor "redeems a pawn" in a pawn shop, that is, buys back his collateral for the loan extended to him by the pawn broker. And this payment must be comparable to the original debt. It must be of the same magnitude. Furthermore, restitution requires an additional penalty payment.

Exodus, chapter 21, begins the detailed account of the requirements of God's law. It follows Exodus 20, in which the Ten Commandments appear. Exodus 21 is devoted to crimes and punishments. The general principle of compensation is established: "Eye for eye, tooth for tooth, hand for hand, foot for foot, burning for burning, wound for wound, stripe for stripe" (Exodus 21:24-25).

Isn't this overly harsh? Isn't this **vengeance**, pure and simple? Yes. So what? It is God's way of reducing future crimes of violence. It is also God's way of **reducing the power of the State**. The State may not legitimately establish the death penalty for theft, or torture for assault. The State is limited by the extent of the crime's impact on the victim. Did people actually have their eyes poked out when they had poked out an innocent victim's eye? What good did that do the victim? The victim had the option of asking for such punishment, but would he not have preferred economic compensation? The judges had the option of imposing comparable damages, if the victim agreed and the guilty party agreed (Exodus 21:30). The poor man who could not pay had the option of selling himself into slavery for up to six years in order to pay the fine. This payment was not made to the State; it was made to the **victim** (Exodus 21:19). The guilty party had every reason to avoid having his own body damaged, and the victim had many reasons to gain financial restitution, now that he was in some way hampered by his injury. It was in the interest of the victim to accept another's **substitute payment**. This, after all, is what God permits: a substitute payment. Instead of killing mankind, He accepts a substitute. Instead of maiming the guilty party, the victim accepts payment for damages. This helps both victim and criminal to recognize man's need for a substitute. But **someone** always has to pay. No exceptions.

The point of the law, however, is to drive home the magnitude of the payment. **Man cannot legitimately pay the victim a tooth's worth of value for an eye's worth of damage.** There must be comparable restitution. **The law reminds man of the magnitude of his debt to God for his sin against God.** He is reminded that he needs access to a substitute payment, for the magnitude of his sin is too great for him to repay. Man cannot hope to buy off the wrath of God by means of his own efforts. He cannot substitute a hangnail's penalty payment for a capital crime.

Restitution for all sin must be **made to God**. This is the first principle of biblical law. It must be **made to the earthly victim**. This is the second principle of biblical law. It must be **comparable to the crime**. This is the third principle. For crimes so horrible that no restitution payment is sufficient to compensate the victim (such as murder) or compensate God (adultery, witchcraft, idol worship, etc.), the civil government is empowered by God to execute the criminal. Exodus 22:18-20 lists some of these capital crimes; others include rape (Deuteronomy 22:23-24), adultery (Leviticus 20:10). and striking or cursing ones father or mother (Exodus 21:15,17). The family's integrity was to be protected. Paul was so convinced of the validity of **the civil government's right to execute criminals**, that when he was charged with blasphemy and brought before a Roman judge, he said: "For if I be an offender, or have committed any thing worthy of death, I refuse not to die..." (Acts 25:11a).

It is unfortunate, but many Christians who have not studied the law of God, or who believe that God has abolished His law, argue that the civil government must never execute a man, because a dead man cannot confess Christ. All criminals supposedly must be allowed to live, so that they may confess Christ at some indeterminate future date. Question: Why are criminals today allowed to avoid execution in order to give them a lifetime to be converted, but criminals in the Old Testament kingdom of Israel were required by God to die for certain crimes? Was God being unfair to criminals in Old Testament times? Second question: Isn't the threat of death for committing a capital crime **a very effective**

incentive for a man to consider his sins against God? If he thinks he has forever to repent—or an indeterminate period, which is psychologically "forever" in the mind of a present-oriented man—will he not put off repentance until it is too late? But most important of all, salvation is by grace, and if God tells us that a rebel should be executed, and He chooses not to regenerate him, isn't that God's business? We find too many Christians who still think that man "has a piece of the action" in salvation, and that if we in any way interfere with his life by condemning him to death, we have in some way violated his supposed innate right to be converted. We say, in effect, that God's revelation to man isn't good enough, including (and especially) God's revelation of Himself in His holy law. We think we are doing God a favor by refusing to execute people who have committed crimes that God says are worthy of execution. And we do this in the name of evangelism. Incredible! We attempt to mask the magnitude of capital crimes, so that evil men will not have to face up to the true magnitude of their crimes, and then we tell them to repent because they have sinned against a holy God. We tell them that God is a God of wrath who executes perfectly horrible justice—horrible to those who don't rest in Christ's atoning death—and then we seek to cover up the visible, institutional signs of God's wrath, even though God established these visible, institutional signs in His law.

Modern evangelicals who deny the right of the civil government to enforce biblical law are **embarrassed by God's righteousness. They** don't want to acknowledge the holy nature of the God revealed to us by the Bible. Yet they want **unbelievers** to acknowledge the existence of just such a God, even though modern evangelicals are embarrassed by His law. They say they want to "give the unbelievers a chance to repent," yet they have simultaneously attempted to blur ungodly men's perception of the Person and nature of God. Why should unbelievers repent (turn around) from their sins, when the God of the modern evangelicals is less willing to enforce His standards of righteousness through external punishment than the God of the Old Testament was? Why has God, in this age of Christian evangelism, decided to provide modern man with a **less** visible sign of His holiness? Why has God hidden His character, in the age of international evangelism, when He revealed His character through His law to the Israelites, when they were bottled up in Palestine? Why has He instructed His followers to de-emphasize (and even eliminate) the institutional sign of His impending judgment, namely, capital punishment, in the era of Jesus Christ, which is closer to the day of judgment than the era of Israel was? The answer to all these questions is the same: God **hasn't**. But many of his followers have acted in terms of these false assumptions.

By What Standard?

In the Old Testament, the law of God as enforced by the priests, kings, and tribal rulers was to serve as a beacon to the foreign nations, but evangelism on a personal level was not emphasized. The prophets did preach to foreigners, as the Book of Jonah indicates, but the establishment of godly rule through Israel's institutions was God's first step. It was the wisdom of Israel, as demonstrated by Israel's laws, which was to bring the nations to repentance (Deuteronomy 4:5-8).

In the New Testament times, evangelism on a face-to-face basis has been emphasized, because the kingdom of God is no longer associated with any single geographical region or any single nation. When the New Testament documents were written, there was no longer any civil order which could be associated with God and God's law. But this fact of the first century, A.D. should not be used as an excuse for avoiding the tasks of dominion in the realm of civil government. The law of God is still morally binding. It is therefore still **judicially** binding. If a law is not worth enforcing judicially, when it relates to **external crimes** against God or man, then it is not morally binding, either. If a man is **morally prohibited** from murdering his neighbor, seducing his neighbor's wife or daughter, or stealing from his neighbor, then he should be **judicially prohibited** as well.

We are back to the neutrality question, the great myth of neutrality. The **work** of the law is in the heart of the pagans, but not the law itself (Romans 2:14-15). Vague imitations of God's law are imposed by pagan civil governments, but not God's law. There is no universally recognized "natural law." There is no logically irrefutable "natural law." There is God's revealed law, and there are all other law-orders. By denying the legitimacy of God's law in the realm of civil government, men are affirming the validity of **some other law-order**, meaning some variation of the society of Satan. There are no universally recognized humanistic definitions of theft, murder, or assault. There are certainly no universally agreed-upon punishments for these crimes. How, then, can anyone calling himself a Christian be satisfied with anything less than the reign of Old Testament law in the civil government? Would he choose to live under Pharaoh? Would he choose to live under Belshazzar? Why, then, do so many Christians say that there's no such thing as biblical law for today's civil governments? Why do they choose to live under the control of something other than God's civil law? Why do they continue to choose Egypt and Babylon as their homes? How long will they continue to argue that **any** law-order can be accepted by Christians, no matter where or when they live, **except** one law-order, namely, the law-order ordained by God for His people and delivered by Moses and the prophets? How long will they continue to defend the legitimacy of Egypt and Babylon, and continue to deny the legitimacy of Jerusalem? **How long will they allow themselves to be deceived by Satan's myth of neutral laws, neutral judges, and neutral civil governments**? When will they recognize the truth of Jesus' warning? "He that is not with me is against me; and he that gathereth not with me scattereth abroad" (Matthew 12:30). They have not come to grips with Jesus' announcement: "Think not that I am come to send peace on earth: I came not to send peace, but a sword. For I am come to set a man at variance against his father, and the daughter against her mother, and the daughter in law against her mother in law. And a man's foes shall be they of his own household" (Matthew 10:34-36). Christ divides His people from members of their own households, yet there are literally millions of Christians today who say that it's impossible for Christ to divide men from their civil governments and the anti-Christian laws of those governments. Incredible, isn't it? Christ divides the most important of human institutions, the family, yet leaves intact the relationship between His people and any civil government on earth, now or in the future. Do you think this is likely? Really? And if it sounds silly, then on what basis should the Christian judge the performance of the civil government ruling him? Obviously, by **the laws of God that pertain to civil governments**. And where do we find such judicial standards? (This is going to come as a shock to millions of modern evangelical Christians!) The Bible. Specifically, in the Old Testament. Where else could we possibly find these standards? And if we continue to argue that there are no such standards, that the Old Testament isn't binding on us any more, and that we are prohibited from exercising godly rule in terms of the Old Testament, then **we have placed ourselves, in principle, under the dominion of Satan and his pagan kingdoms**. We are right back in Egypt or Babylon, from which God delivered His people long ago.

Conclusion

The law of God is a **revelation of God's character**. To deny the binding nature of law is to blur man's perception of this revelation of God's character. The message of the gospel of Jesus Christ is this: **restitution has been made**. A sacrifice has been offered. Men who cling to the righteousness of Christ cannot be condemned for the rebellion of Adam. We are delivered from the **curse** of the law, not the obligations of the law. The law is a tool of dominion for us: dominion over our own lives (the **moral** sphere), dominion over the lawless external acts of rebels (the **judicial** sphere), and dominion over the creation (the **dominical** sphere). If we reject that marvelous tool in the name of lawless "freedom," in the name of grace, then we are surrendering the world in principle to Satan. The Bible tells us that Satan's kingdom is steadily being displaced, that it cannot stand, that the gates of hell cannot survive. We must not abandon the tool of dominion, God's law, for to do that is to abandon the fight, to abandon the task assigned to His people, **the dominion assignment**.

One generation can always abandon its assignment. Israel did immediately after the deliverance from Egypt. God punished the whole generation, except for two men, Joshua and Caleb. These two men alone recommended to Israel's leaders that they should invade the land of Canaan, that God had delivered the Canaanites into their hands. The other spies sent out by Moses came back to report on the giants in Canaan, and the sure defeat that lay ahead. The incident is recorded in the Book of Numbers, chapter 14. Only Joshua and Caleb were allowed by God to enter Canaan; all the others died in the wilderness.

Though one generation can abandon the dominion assignment, not all of them can. Eventually, a generation of Christians becomes convinced that their God is sovereign, that God's law is valid, and that God's people are victors, in time and on earth. When these opinions spread across a nation, or a group within a nation, the blessings begin anew. The people cease wandering in the self-imposed wilderness. They turn back to God, His law, and His dominion assignment. They begin anew the extension of God's kingdom, in time and on earth.

SUMMARY OF PART I

Are you ready for that examination of "What is a Christian society?" I said in the introduction that three questions are the most important ones when you start to examine a society: 1) What is its view of God? 2) What is its view of man? 3) What is its view of law?

The Christian view of **God** is the crucial issue. God is a Trinity, three Persons, yet one Being, in fellowship, yet acting as one Person. This God is therefore **one** and **many**, at the same time, and beyond time. God is both unity and particularity. This God is the Creator of the universe. All the universe was created out of nothing in response to His word. No part of this universe shares any of God's being. Christianity affirms the **Creator-creature distinction**: God is fundamentally different from the universe. The universe is held together by God through His providential administration. The universe cannot be impersonal, for it rests wholly on God, a personal being. Christianity therefore affirms **cosmic personalism**. There are no independent forces directing the creation forces that are above God or apart from God. Everything that happens has meaning, for the plan of God governs all history. The universe has a foundation in the plan of God. God knows everything exhaustively. He controls everything completely. There is no zone of neutrality in the universe, no zone of autonomy (independence), no cosmic "King's X" from God and His providential administration. All sin is personal, for it is always rebellion against a personal Being by a creature. There is not a single shred of chance in the universe, no sort of cosmic "might have been," no area of existence unknown to God. God is absolutely sovereign over the universe because He created it and presently sustains it. The first chapter of Genesis and chapters 38 through 41 of the Book of Job tell us about the creative acts of God and His complete authority over all creation. So does the ninth chapter of Paul's letter to the Romans.

The Christian has a unique view of **man**. Man was created in the image of God. He was created to bring God's law over the creation. Man was created as God's personal representative on earth. Man's task is to subdue the earth, and this dominion assignment (or dominion covenant) was repeated to Noah, after the worldwide flood (Genesis 9:1-7). Man cannot escape this assignment except in hell, and subsequently in the lake of fire. **The closer a man or a society conforms itself to the revealed standards of biblical law, the more that man or that society will come to fulfilling the terms of God's assignment to man.** This assignment is both personal and collective, and both men as individuals and as collectives are held responsible for fulfilling this assignment.

Man, however, is a rebel. He fell ethically when he defied God's law and ate of the tree of the knowledge of good and evil. He wanted instant illumination, instant knowledge, instant authority to determine good and evil. God threw him out of the garden of Eden, along with his wife, who had been given to him as a helper. They were cursed physically, as was the earth itself. This curse was to make the fulfillment of the dominion assignment much more difficult, and yet it also made fulfillment possible, for the curse of economic scarcity now forces hostile men to cooperate with each other for the sake of greater productivity and greater personal income. The division of labor principle increases everyone's output when men cooperate voluntarily, rather than using force to conquer and destroy each other. Man is still in the image of God, but this image is twisted ethically, so that man refuses to acknowledge God's authority over him, and he chooses instead to worship creatures rather than the creator. Man is therefore bound for eternal destruction, unless God intervenes and brings individual men to faith in Jesus Christ, God's sacrificial lamb, God's high priest, and God's Son, the King and sustainer of creation.

Men cannot escape the dominion assignment, but they work out their salvations or damnations as subordinates to God. Some men believe they aren't subordinate to God, and so they become slaves of Satan, the fallen angel. Since the cross, each kingdom struggles for victory, but Christ's kingdom is assured of victory, whereas Satan's is guaranteed final defeat.

As the terms of the dominion assignment are progressively

fulfilled by God's subordinates, the Christians, the creation will be progressively restored. The curse on the ground will be progressively lifted, just as the curse on man will be progressively lifted. But there will never be perfection on earth as long as there is sin, and there will be sin until the final judgment.

Man therefore cannot save himself. God saves man by His grace, through man's faith in Christ, the only atonement satisfactory to God. Man is not saved through his own law-keeping. Man is not saved through the abolition of law. Man is not saved by revolution. Man is saved by God, by means of Christ's law-keeping, imputed and imparted to man by grace, through personal faith in Jesus Christ. God has chosen those He will save before the foundation of the world (Romans 9; Ephesians 1).

Finally, there is **law**. Law includes the God-imposed and God-sustained regularities of the universe. It also includes the moral law, under which man operates, and in terms of which man is judged. This also includes the laws of man's institutions, for which men in groups are held responsible. Blessings and cursings are imposed in terms of God's law. Law is a tool of dominion. It serves to restrain the evil in men (conscience) as well as the visible evils among men (judicial enforcement). Law's areas of human operation can be summarized: moral, judicial, dominical. Man is simultaneously under God's moral law, under judicial law, and over the creation by means of dominical law. Man is responsible to God for the proper exercise of the law. He is simultaneously subordinate and domineering. He is supposed to be subordinate to God and above the creation, but because of man's rebellion, **he subordinates himself to the creation** and **rebels against God**. Rebellious man reverses the order of creation, being domineering where he should be subordinate and vice versa.

The law has not been abolished, abrogated, or annulled by Jesus Christ. Some of the Old Testament's ceremonial laws are fulfilled in Christ, for they were shadows, while He is the foreshadowed reality. The principles of law are unchanging, for they reflect the character of God, who is unchanging. The applications of a law may change, as the historical circumstances change. But if a law hasn't been specifically altered in application by God's revelation, it is still in effect.

God's sacrifice of His Son on the cross serves as man's substitute. Christ fulfilled the law and is therefore spotless, a sacrifice without a blemish. This is what God requires to satisfy His own holiness. Nothing less will suffice. So Christians have been **delivered from the curse of the law,** but they are **still under the terms of the law,** God's peace treaty with mankind. The law is to bring men and nations to repentance. The law is therefore a schoolmaster for men, both as individuals and in their capacity as representatives of corporate groups.

Christian man therefore has a written set of standards that are applicable to the creation, for the same God who created man and nature delivered His revelation to man, who is made in God's image. Man is responsible for dominion because man was created to exercise dominion. Man and nature "fit," with man in a position of superiority because of the image of God which defines him. The law serves as the intermediary between man and nature. This law "fits" man's mind and nature's processes. God created them all to be a harmony. Only man's rebellion distorted this harmony, and the progressive sanctification of man by God's grace and the man-subduing law is steadily restoring this harmony.

With this outline in mind, we are now ready for the next step: understanding the three primary institutions given to man by God. These are: the family, the church, and the civil government. We will also consider the economy. All of these are forms of government. In fact, the most important form of government is **self-government.** But these institutions were designed by God to meet man's needs. God controls all of them. We should not attempt arbitrarily to relate God to the church, man to the family, and law to the state. God is related to all three institutions. Man is involved in all three. Law governs all three. These institutions are the structural basis of the kingdom of God, in time and on earth. And the economy is related to all three, for scarcity affects all three.

PART II

INSTITUTIONS

INTRODUCTION TO PART II

If Christianity presents us with a unique view of society's crucial foundations—God, man, and law—then we should expect to see important differences between Christianity's view of social institutions and rival religions' view of these same institutions. We should expect to see these institutions constructed on different philosophical foundations. We should also expect to see vast differences in the efficiency of these institutions, depending on whether they are found in a Christian society or a pagan society.

One of the most important features of Christian social theory, or at least Protestant social theory, is **the absence of any totally sovereign human institution**. No institution is granted final authority, for no human institution is free from the destructive effects of sin. **Only Jesus Christ can claim total sovereignty in time and on earth. Jesus Christ alone is the link between man and God**. His revealed word, the Bible, is the final authority for man, not the pronouncements of committees, bureaucrats, or religious leaders.

The source of social order is God. Specifically, it is the Holy Spirit, who was sent to comfort the church (John 16:7). The Holy Spirit came to guide men into all truth: "Howbeit when he, the Spirit of truth, is come, he will guide you into all truth: for he shall not speak of himself; but whatsoever he shall hear, that shall he speak: and he will show you things to come" (John 16:13). And we know that "where the Spirit of the Lord is, there is liberty" (II Corinthians 3:17b). It is God's sovereign power over the creation that holds all things together, and we know that the established relationship between God's law and external blessings guarantees the preservation of social order for those societies that strive to conform themselves to the revealed law-order of God.

Biblical social theory therefore affirms the order-producing effects of a **decentralized** system of competing, yet ideally cooperating, institutions. No single institution needs to provide this social order. Indeed, no single institution can, since the concentration of power involved in such an attempt is self-defeating and in total opposition to biblical social order. Freedom and order are achieved only when men throughout a society are striving to reconstruct all their social institutions along the lines outlined in the Bible.

Whenever we see a social theory that proclaims the validity of a **pyramid structure of institutions**, with some institutions at the bottom, and a single institution at the top, we are facing **the society of Satan**. The pyramid structure, both in social theory and architecture, was basic to pagan antiquity. It is also the reigning social theory of modern socialism and Communism. It places men at the base of the pyramid, and it places the State at the top.

The Bible proclaims the existence of **multiple sovereignties**, multiple institutions that bear lawful authority. Human institutions possess legitimate sovereignty, but all such sovereignty is limited and derivative. God alone possesses absolute sovereignty. Any attempt by any institution to command final authority is demonic. All institutions are under God and governed by God's law. No single institution commands permanent authority over all the others.

What the Bible proclaims as binding is this: **responsible men under God,** but never autonomous men under God. Neither the **one** (State, Church, Family) nor the **many** (individuals) can claim absolute sovereignty. Neither collectivism nor individualism is valid as an exclusive principle of social order. What the Bible proclaims is **covenantalism**: individuals and institutions under God, and under God's applicable laws.

With this framework in mind, we turn now to four social institutions: family, church, state, and economy.

Chapter 4

FAMILY

Man and woman were created as a functioning team. Their task was, and is, **to subdue the earth to the glory of God** (Genesis 1:26-28; 9:1-7). This is the task of dominion. It is basic to the very being of man to fulfill this assignment. Man's punishment for rebellion involves God's withholding of man's ability to fulfill this command, an eternal longing, a feeling of impotence, that will gnaw at every rebel's mind forever.

Adam was created first. He was assigned the preliminary task of naming (classifying) the animals before he was given his wife (Genesis 2:19-20). Man completed this assignment, and then God gave him a wife. This indicates that **a woman is given to man to help him fulfill his calling before God**. Paul put it this way: "For the man is not of the woman; but the woman of the man. Neither was the man created for the woman; but the woman for the man" (I Corinthians 11:8-9). At the same time, they are now a functioning unit under God: "Nevertheless neither is the man without the woman, neither the woman without the man, in the Lord. For as the woman is of the man, even so is the man also by the woman; but all things of God" (I Corinthians 11:11-12). Originally, the woman was made for the man, but all children emanate from both man and woman. All are under God.

There was, and is, a **hierarchy**. God is absolutely sovereign over both men and women, but He establishes His chain of command through the husband. Peter wrote: "Likewise, ye wives, be in subjection to your husbands" (I Peter 3:1a). Again, "Even as Sara obeyed Abraham, calling him lord: whose daughters ye are, as long as ye do well, and are not afraid with any amazement [terror]" (I Peter 3:6).

Husbands owe their wives righteous judgment and support. "Likewise, ye husbands, dwell with them according to knowledge,

91

giving honour unto the wife, as unto the weaker vessel, and as being heirs together of the grace of life; that your prayers be not hindered" (I Peter 3:7).

Paul's lengthy statement concerning the mutual duties of husbands and wives compares this relationship with Christ's love for His church and the church's responsibility to the one who loves her. "Wives, submit yourselves unto your own husbands, as unto the Lord. For the husband is the head of the wife, even as Christ is the head of the church: and he is the saviour of the body. Therefore as the church is subject unto Christ, so let the wives be to their own husbands in every thing. Husbands, love your wives, even as Christ also loved the church, and gave himself for it; that he might sanctify and cleanse it with the washing of water by the word. That he might present it to himself a glorious church, not having spot, or wrinkle, or any such thing; but that it should be holy and without blemish. So ought men to love their wives as their own bodies. He that loveth his wife loveth himself" (Ephesians 5:22-28). Given the perceived necessity of Paul and the other writers of commanding wives to submit to their husbands, and telling the husbands to love their wives, we should expect to find the opposite in life: disobedient wives and unloving husbands.

God gave strict orders to Adam to refrain from eating of the tree of the knowledge of good and evil. The tempter approached Eve first, in his successful attempt to foment a revolution. Adam, in turn, carried his revolution to God. He also ate. Satan knew what he was doing when he began his revolution by undermining the family hierarchy. He cut the chain of command at its weakest link, the woman. Peter spoke of the wife as "the weaker vessel" (I Peter 3:7). Paul said the woman was deceived by the serpent, but the man was not deceived (I Timothy 2:14). Adam was the stronger link.

The family hierarchy extends downward to the children. Paul repeats the familiar refrain: "Wives, submit yourselves unto your own husbands, as it is fit in the Lord. Husbands, love your wives, and be not bitter against them. Children, obey your parents in all things: for this is well pleasing unto the Lord. Fathers, provoke not your children to anger, lest they be discouraged" (Colossians 3:18-20). This chain of command is designed to reflect God's relationship to the creation—a hierarchy of functions, but without any superiority or inferiority of being—which means that the Christian view of marriage upholds both sexes without confusing the two. **Functional subordination does not imply ethical inferiority.** It simply means that mankind as a collective unit is composed of different sorts of people, and there can never be functional equality between men and women. Their tasks are different, and for mankind to fulfill the terms of God's dominion assignment, men must respect the differences God has built into the sexes. Men are functionally superior to their wives in a way analogous to Christ's functional superiority over the church. The church will never be functionally superior to Christ.

The family is God's specially designed unit. It is designed to extend God's visible sovereignty over the face of the earth. The family is the chief agency of dominion. Dominion is its task.

Children

Children are a blessing of God. "Lo, children are an heritage of the Lord: and the fruit of the womb is his reward. As arrows are in the hand of a mighty man; so are children of the youth. Happy is the man that hath his quiver full of them: they shall not be ashamed, but they shall speak with the enemies in the gate" (Psalm 127:3-5). The enemies in the gate are opponents who have come before the judges of the city, who in Old Testament times sat at the gate, to bring a charge against a man. Men with large families have confidence in themselves, and so are not afraid of such enemies. This appears to indicate that **the self-discipline involved in being the head of a large family carries over into other human relationships**. Large families produce heads of households who are better fit to lead in the community.

One of the requirements for holding the offices of elder or deacon in the church is for a man to be married (I Timothy 3:2,12). They are to rule over their households effectively (I Timothy 3:4-5,12). **The family is a training ground for leadership in the church.** One of the obvious failures of almost all denominations and local churches—a failure which goes back to the early church—is the unwillingness of church authorities to write into their denominational handbooks guidelines defining successful rule over a family. The modern churches place great emphasis on where a man went to college or seminary, on whether he can raise money, or on whether he can deliver a red-hot sermon. The Bible puts little or no emphasis on any of these factors. It puts emphasis on the leader's abilities as the head of his household.

Children are a tool of dominion. They are to be sacrificed for in their youth. They are to be instructed carefully and continually in the law of God. "And these words, which I command thee this day, shall be in thine heart; and thou shalt teach them diligently unto thy children, and shalt talk of them when thou sittest in thine house, and when thou walkest by the way, and when thou liest down, and when thou risest up" (Deuteronomy 6:6-7). The time spent in training children in God's law is time well spent, for it is a capital investment. It does produce the next generation of godly, dominion-minded families. The Bible says, "Train up a child in the way he should go: and when he is old, he will not depart from it" (Proverbs 22:6).

This leads us to an extremely significant conclusion: **education is the moral responsibility of parents**. They are the ones who must determine whether or not their children are being taught the truth. They are responsible before God for the rearing of their children. They are held responsible even for the content of their children's education. This is why it is a great responsibility to bring children into the world.

The modern State has asserted its responsibility to educate children. This is the means by which the modern State has arrogated to itself the position of the established god on earth. The government schools have become the established religion of every nation on earth. Humanism, which is the worship of man and his works, rests on this crucial institutional foundation: the tax-supported, State-regulated, hypothetically neutral, deeply religious humanist school system. There can be no neutrality, yet the government schools have almost completely stamped out Christianity and the law of God by means of the neutrality myth. The State forces Christians to finance schools that teach a rival religion, the religion of humanism. The State has also attempted to regulate Christian and independently financed schools. At every point, the State has substituted tenured bureaucrats who are virtually impossible for parents to remove from authority, while it has removed parents from the seats of power in setting curricula or any other standards. The modern State, which is a messianic, supposedly man-saving institution, has used the tax-supported, compulsory schools as the primary means of stealing children from God, by removing them from parental control.

Christians complain about taxation, but **they have tithed their children to the State**. They have abdicated their financial responsibilities—"Let the State finance my children's educations"—and in our day, they have abandoned almost all other aspects of their instructional responsibilities. They have turned the production of citizens over to tax-financed, State-directed schools. The priests of the religion of humanism have been able to enlist the support of many generations of Christian parents, who have decided that it is easier to transfer the responsibility for educating their children to bureaucrats hired by the State.

Naturally, parents have to delegate responsibility to someone. Few parents have the time or skills to educate their children at home. But the fundamental principle of education is the **tutor** or the apprentice director. Parents hire specialists to teach their children along lines established by parents. The private school is simply an extension of this principle, with several parents hiring a tutor, thereby sharing the costs. But the parents, not the tutors, are institutionally sovereign. **Since sovereignty must bear the costs, education should be parent-financed**. Anything else is a transfer of authority over education to an imitation family.

Children are to honor their parents (Exodus 20:12). It is the first promise which is attached to a commandment: ". . . that thy days may be long upon the land which the Lord thy God giveth thee" (Exodus 20:12b). So the parents owe their children educations, food, shelter, and care, but the children owe their parents honor. This means financial support. There are mutual obligations based on personal bonds. **No one in the transaction is to become an endless giver**, and **no one is to become a perpetual recipient**.

The modern messianic State has intervened here, too. The State promises to uphold men from womb to tomb. The State promises to become the new father. The impersonal, bureaucratic State has substituted its rule for the father's rule, and its children—perpetual children—are to remain obedient to it all the days of their lives.

The Bible tells us that children grow up and begin new families. "Therefore shall a man leave his father and mother, and shall cleave unto his wife: and they shall be one flesh" (Genesis 1:24). There should be no perpetual one-way obligations. Parents are to train their children to be obedient, but also independent. They are to foster maturity in their children. The State wants perpetual children, complete obedience. The State is a sad imitation of a family. It is a **pseudo-family** which threatens human freedom.

Welfare

The family is designated by God as the chief agency of human welfare. It is the agency that is most effective in solving the problems of poverty, sickness, and crisis. It is the only agency which knows its limitations and strengths, for the self-interest of every household head is to count the costs of every project undertaken by the family. No other human agency links mutual self-interest, mutual understanding, mutual obligations, and mutual support in the way that a family can. Members are close. They know each other's weaknesses and strengths. The family is also an extended institution, with bloodline contacts that can spread out widely. It can call upon related families for help in a crisis.

It is a **fundamental principle of charity** that charity be **personal whenever possible**. The Samaritan in Jesus' parable of the good Samaritan came across a helpless, injured man. He helped him. He could see how badly the man was hurt. He could see that he was not being tricked. He had the resources necessary for helping the man. He was close to a place where the man could be cared for. He hired the caretaker personally, which meant that he could hold that man responsible for the care of the injured man, since he was paying him to do the work (Luke 10:33-35). This is how Jesus defined the term "neighbor." It means someone who is in a position to help, and who does so, based on accurate information concerning the plight of the injured or helpless.

The person most likely to be able to help a poor man is a **slightly less poor** man. The slightly less poor man is closer to the poor man (geographically and socially), he can recognize true need better than a distant man, and he can more accurately assess the short-term solutions to the poor man's problems. This means that **charity from the rich should be filtered down through institutions that are close to the poor**. The church is one such institution. Other private charities may also qualify. But well-paid, bureaucratic agents of the State, with its compulsory programs financed by taxes, will not be able to help the poor except at the expense of everyone's independence. The rich will pay, the poor will receive a fraction of the payments, and the bureaucrats will multiply. The relationship is invariably permanent, until the welfare State, that pseudo-family, goes bankrupt and is overthrown internally or defeated by external nations.

The family cares for children. It finances their educations. It cares for sick relatives. It provides work for the partially employable members in its midst. It supervises with feeling, not with forms in triplicate. It provides insurance, but not a lifetime of compulsory Social Security tax payments that are finally wiped out by the mass inflation necessary at the end of such programs in order to finance them. It provides aid, but not to everyone, not to blocs of special-interest voters.

The eldest son is entitled to a double portion of the family's estate (Deuteronomy 21:17). This means that if a man has four children who are legally responsible for him, then he must divide the estate into five equal shares, with the eldest son receiving two-fifths. Why? Because it is the eldest son who has the primary responsibility for caring for aged parents. The child who is willing to bear this responsibility is treated as the eldest son, such as Isaac's position of favor before Abraham, not Ishmael, the firstborn, or Jacob's position before Isaac because of God's choosing of Jacob over Esau, the elder twin. There is a mutuality of service and blessings. Costs and benefits are more closely linked. Family disputes among the children are minimized.

The State, in modern times, has become the "eldest son." Estate taxes in some nations will take virtually the whole of very wealthy estates. Families are forced to sell off lands and family heirlooms in order to pay the estate taxes. **The State has asserted its position as the pseudo-family, and now it demands payment for its services.** Those who voted for the creation of the caretaker State two or more generations ago should have known what would happen. **The State becomes the heir of family capital.** The true families are progressively bankrupted, yet the State, as an inefficient, tyrannical, life-long pseudo-parent, is also steadily bankrupted, for the State is not creative; it is parasitic. It needs new wealth to confiscate, yet its steady destruction of family capital withers up the sources of new taxes.

The Bible provides evidence that God has entrusted the bulk of the welfare obligations to the family, secondarily to the church, and almost no responsibilities whatsoever to the civil government. The Old Testament required citizens to journey to specified cities once every three years for a communal celebration. "At the end of three years thou shalt bring forth all the tithe of thine increase the same year, and shalt lay it up within thy gates. And the Levite (because he hath no part nor inheritance with thee), and the stranger, and the fatherless, and the widow, which are within thy gates, shall come, and shall eat and be satisfied; that the Lord thy God may bless thee in all the work of thine hand which thou doest" (Deuteronomy 14:28-29). While the civil government required this celebration tithe (or so it would appear), the individual families had to make this sacrifice, which involved financing for Levites, strangers, and widows, only once every three years. A committed socialist would be hard-pressed to make a case for "Christian socialism" based on this meager evidence for statist power.

The church is required to take in widows who have reached the age of 60, but whose families refuse to support them (I Timothy 5:3-13). Nephews are considered responsible by the church authorities in such cases. It is a matter of excommunication for any family member to refuse such support to a deserving widow who meets the criteria specified in this passage. "But if any provide not for his own, and specially for those of his own house, he hath denied the faith, and is worse than an infidel" (I Timothy 5:8).

It should be obvious that **the family, and not the civil government, is the central agency in the battle against poverty**. The incentive to increase the assets of the family leads directly to increased production. The incentive to maintain the reputation of the family by providing charity for indigent members is also present in societies governed by biblical principles. Because the family is the agency of social welfare, the civil government can remain small, limiting itself to protecting property, providing for national defense, enforcing God's civil law, and defending the public peace. The family, as the chief agency of **self**-government, reduces the need for civil government.

Trustee

The family is the primary trustee of a society's capital. The family serves as a bridge between generations. The family name is an important aspect of biblical rule. To increase the capital of the family unit is a basic impulse in Christian societies.

A promise to Abraham concerning the inheritance of his descendants was central to God's covenant with Abram, whose name was changed to Abraham ("father of nations") by God. God promised to give his heirs the land of Canaan (Genesis 15:18). Abraham had been concerned about a lack of an heir for his capital, having only a steward to leave his wealth to (Genesis 15:2-3). He wanted a son to inherit his capital, and presumably to inherit the family name.

The family was understood to be an institution ideal for the **preservation of capital**. Abraham recognized this, as did the people of his day. By extending one's family, one extended the dominion of the family, the most important institution a man could belong to in Abraham's day. This hope was part of God's promise to Abraham when He called him out of Haran. "Now the Lord had said unto Abram, Get thee out of thy country, and from thy kindred, and from thy father's house, unto a land that I will show thee. And I will make of thee a great nation, and I will bless thee, and make thy name great; and thou shalt be a blessing. And I will bless them that bless thee, and curse him that curseth thee: and in thee shall all the families of the earth be blessed" (Genesis 12:1-3). A man with no children who had reached age 75 was promised heirs. A man with no heirs would have his name made great. This was a true incentive to pick up and leave one's home.

The future mattered to Abraham, even though he would never see the entry of his heirs into the land of Canaan. That promise from God could be trusted. It was as good as done, four centuries before they entered Canaan (Galatians 3:16-18). His family, though presently without blood heirs, would receive the land of Canaan as its inheritance from Abraham, by the grace of God.

This **future-orientation** is central to the life of a biblical family. The dominion assignment was given to Adam, reconfirmed with Noah, and is now part of the covenant between God and His church, meaning individuals who belong to His church. **We are to extend the rule of God's law across the face of the earth.** We are to subdue it and have dominion over it. One of the means of extending dominion is the family. No wonder one of the promises to Moses was that if the nation remained faithful to God's law, wives would not have miscarriages. Even the female domesticated animals would avoid miscarriages (Exodus 23:26). The promise of **a growing stock of human capital** is basic to God's covenant with His followers.

The family serves as a trustee of the most important capital asset, the **faith** delivered to the saints. This is why Deuteronomy 6 requires parents to teach their children the law of God. **By bringing**

children under the dominion of God's law, parents rear up families of dominion-minded children. The subordination to God's law inaugurates the dominion aspect of God's covenant. Dominion-minded families then extend God's rule even further, as they bear more children, who in turn are brought under the rule of God's law.

Christians have **time** on their side. It may not always seem to be so, but it is. Time is under God's sovereign control. He allots time to everyone, but He blesses those who conform themselves to His law. Long life and large families are both aspects of God's blessings to the faithful. They are blessed because they use their capital in kingdom-oriented ways. Christians can look to their earthly futures in confidence, even as Abram did (before God renamed him Abraham). They know that they have the tool of dominion, God's law. They know that God promises blessings to the faithful. They can rest in Christ's work on the cross. The future belongs to them and their heirs. Their names will extend into the future.

Given this perspective, is it surprising that Christians should amass capital? Is it surprising that the Protestant Reformation of the 1500's led to the growth of capitalism in the next century? There is a Protestant ethic, and its view of time is fundamental to its success. **Men who are confident concerning the future, in time and on earth, can plan for a very long run: centuries, if necessary**. Their vision extends beyond their own graves. They see victory in terms of linear development over time. They can invest a bit of money today, even at a very low rate of return, and if God blesses its growth long enough, the law of compound interest takes over, leading to a long-run expansion of capital. It is revealing that charities established by Puritan businessmen in London in the late 1500's and early 1600's were still operating in 1900. The original capital base had been reinvested over the years, leading to an expansion of charitable activities. The growth in productivity—the basic rate of return—was sufficient to operate the charities and still expand their influence.

Men will not sacrifice for the future of a bureaucratic State with the same enthusiasm with which they will sacrifice present consumption for the sake of their families' futures. The State is a pseudo-family, and men treat it as such. If the State confiscates family wealth at the time of death of the "founding father," then the sons, not to mention the father himself, will have an incentive to spend the family fortune today, if only to keep the tax collector from getting the bulk of the estate. **This drastically shortens men's time perspective**. The long run becomes no longer than the lifetime of the founder when the State confiscates the estate at his death. A bit of money invested today must make a high return if it is to grow to any considerable capital base in the lifetime of one man. Such a return is not that easy to achieve. Men turn to gambling to "make the big killing" when they recognize the improbability of building a capital base with today's few assets, given the tight boundaries of a single lifetime.

The Roman Catholics in the Middle Ages recruited their brightest young men for the ministry. They required celibacy to insure their full commitment to the institutional church. In contrast, medieval Jews recruited their brightest young men for the Rabbinate. The families sacrificed to provide such training. Then the young men were encouraged to marry bright (or rich) young women and produce large families of (hopefully) equally bright children. The results of the two social policies were very different. The Jews expanded their genetic pool of bright people, and trained them to be industrious. The Roman Catholics got one lifetime of labor out of their best men, leaving no family heirs behind to inherit the amassed capital. The Jews were to gain influence vastly out of proportion with their numbers. The difference lay, to a great extent, in the institutional trustee: church vs. family. The **family name** is symbolic of a lot more than just a name.

Communion

The family is a **fellowship of faith**. Concerning Christian fellowship in general, Paul remarked: "Be ye not unequally yoked together with unbelievers: for what fellowship hath righteousness with unrighteousness? And what communion hath light with darkness?" (II Corinthians 6:14). Marriage, as a true communion, involves separation from the enemies of God. A man needs a cooperative wife, who can uphold him, help him, and give him encouragement in their shared tasks. He has to be able to share his hopes and dreams with her, and she with him. If they don't share first principles, how can they share their hopes for the future? Their hopes would be shared only on the basis of the least-common-denominator principle. But a successful marriage is based on higher principles than these.

A couple's home is a refuge against the battles of the day. If the man is battling the world, spiritually and economically, he needs a place to gain new strength. He needs "rest and recreation" to help him win the battles of the world. His family life should provide a zone of mutual support against the pressures of the outside world. But what if the same spiritual battles are in store for husband and wife, since they share different outlooks? Life becomes a constant battle, or at the very least, battles interrupted by temporary truces. **Marriage should be more than a temporary cease-fire**. The warfare of the spirit cannot easily be fenced out at the front door. The Christian partner must subdue his mate's influence in the home, to the extent that his or her influence is at war with the unbelieving mate's anti-Christian first principles. Dominion is vastly more difficult for one who is exhausted from battles inside the home, as well as outside.

Marriage is compared with the relationship between Christ and His church. Godly marriage is therefore a true fellowship, the archetypal fellowship among human institutions. Men cannot normally operate successfully without wives, which is why God gave Adam a wife. If a man has no fellowship, he is normally less effective in his dominion labors. God provides a wife to provide a man with a fellow laborer, but also with a fellow dreamer, fellow learner, fellow restorer. Men work better when they are members of a tightly knit team. Marriage is just such a team.

Conclusion

God has established families. God's own being is a family: Father, Son, and Holy Ghost. It has worked well for God throughout eternity; it can work well for His servants on earth.

The family is a unit, yet it is made up of different individuals. It is both **one** and **many**. It provides a basic division of labor, and this leads to greater productivity. It provides a zone of safety against life's battles with a fallen, recalcitrant environment. It offers fellowship and communion to its participants. It provides men and women with a stake in the future, both through children and economic capital. It gears men to the future, and in so doing, makes possible habits of thrift that lead to vast capital growth. It gives men some idea of Christ's love for His church. It provides welfare and education for its members. It reduces the need for a huge State bureaucracy, so it acts as a weapon against the illegitimate expansion of State power. It will not survive into heaven (Matthew 22:30), but short of heaven, it offers mankind incomparable benefits.

This is not to say that in a fallen world, marriage doesn't sometimes create problems for its members. Paul even advised people in his day not to marry, if they could live comfortably as single (I Corinthians 7). Some scholars have argued that he probably was referring only to his era, since he was concerned about impending judgment from the authorities (which came under Nero's reign in the 60's): "But this I say, brethren, the time is short" (I Corinthians 7:29a). His recommendation: "I say therefore to the unmarried and widows, It is good for them to abide even as I" (I Corinthians 7:8). Paul was unmarried, probably a widower, although we can't be certain of his status as widower. Yet in his first letter to Timothy, he advised younger widows to remarry (I Timothy 5:14), which seems to indicate that his opinion in his letter to the Corinthian church was temporary. Paul admits that there are times when the concerns of marriage interfere with one's service to God: "He that is unmarried careth for the things that belong to the Lord, how he may please the Lord. But he that is married careth for the things that are of the world, how he may please his wife" (I Corinthians 7:32-33). It is important for men to choose wives who are fully committed to their husbands' work before the Lord. Without this, the marriage threatens to compromise the man's actions as a responsible agent of God.

When a man and a woman are working together to subdue the earth to the glory of God, self-consciously applying their labors, content to be servants of God, working to produce a family in conformity to God's law, marriage is a blessing. It is not the only blessing, Paul told the Corinthians, but it is still a good thing. For most people, he implied, the single state leads to sexual problems, so people need the marital bond (I Corinthians 7:2). **For most people, marriage is the most effective institutional means of dominion.** Without the family, the work of dominion could not continue effectively. Men could not multiply and fill the earth except outside the faith, if Christians were forbidden to marry—not without breaking God's law, anyway. The family is God's primary institution for dominion.

Chapter 5

CHURCH

The church is another institution which assists men in the discipline of **personal self-government**. The church is God's specialized institution for the preaching of the gospel, the maintenance of the required sacraments (baptism and the Lord's Supper), and the discipline of its members. These are the marks of a true church. Without these, there can be no institutional church.

Protestants traditionally distinguish between the **institutional church** and the **invisible church**. Some people within the churches are deceivers, possibly self-deceivers. Jesus, in His parable of the sower, revealed that of four plantings sown, only one grew to full maturity (Matthew 13:3-8). This, He explained, referred to the entanglements of the world and the trials Christians suffer. A minority of those professing faith in Christ actually persevere in life. So the institutional church, at any point in time, will have the devil's troops on the membership rolls. Peter even warned against false teachers: "But there were false prophets also among the people, even as there shall be false teachers among you, who privily shall bring in damnable heresies, even denying the Lord that bought them, and bring upon themselves swift destruction. And many shall follow their pernicious ways; by reason of whom the way of truth shall be evil spoken of" (II Peter 2:1-2).

The invisible church is the assembly of faithful people who will be found entering heaven at death, and will be found in the new heavens and new earth. These are those whom Christ chose before the foundation of the world (Ephesians 1:4). It is this church, which overlaps the institutional church, but is fewer in number than the institutional church, which God has promised to bring into His heavenly kingdom (John 14:2). (We might use the words "historical church" to describe all baptized, professing Christians, and "eschatological church" or "final-day church" to describe the

105

assembled saints on the day of judgment.)

The institutional church is of necessity **hierarchical**. It reflects the relationship among the Persons of the Trinity with respect to the creation. There are separate functions within a congregation. There are rulers, and there are followers, just as we find in the family. There are bishops (Greek word: *episkopos*), also called elders (Greek word: *presbuteros*), and the terms are used interchangeably. There are also deacons. The deacons are assistants to the elders. They "wait on tables," to use the graphic term describing the deacons' function which the twelve apostles adopted (Acts 6:2). Instead of burdening the early apostles with the problems of caring for widows, the people were supposed to approach the officers who held this newly created position in the church. The deacons could baptize new converts in certain situations, for the deacon Philip baptized the Ethiopian eunuch (Acts 8:38). They were assistants to the elders, yet they were able to perform some of the tasks normally reserved in modern churches to the ministers, meaning full-time preachers. The requirements for both offices are almost identical: married, well-reputed managers of their own households, sober. Elders are supposed to serve first as deacons: "And let these also be proved: then let them use the office of a deacon, being found blameless" (I Timothy 3:10). The elder's wife also has to be blameless (I Timothy 3:11).

There are many ways to divide up the functions of these officers: ruling elders, preaching (teaching) elders, bishops who supervise other elders, committee members who supervise church (denominational) affairs in between church-wide assemblies, evangelists, teachers. "And he gave some, apostles; and some, prophets; and some, evangelists; and some, pastors and teachers" (Ephesians 4:11). Paul did not draw any sharp distinctions among offices; he did point to differences of talents possessed by men in that single office. But modern churches tend to segregate separate skills into separate offices, with a far more rigid hierarchy, and far more detailed hierarchy, than Christ ever announced. What we have seen in the church's offices is **bureaucratization**. The early church imitated the structure of the collapsing civil government of the Roman Empire (which to some extent it was actually replacing). Modern churches have done much the same thing.

The Old Testament recognized the head of the household as the family's priest. The father led the family in services at the passover. "And it shall come to pass, when your children shall say unto you, What mean ye by this service? That ye shall say, It is the Lord's passover, who passed over the houses of the children of Israel in Egypt, when he smote the Egyptians, and delivered our houses. And the people bowed the head and worshipped" (Exodus 12:26-27). When the Hebrews left Egypt, God established a centralized priesthood (Leviticus 3), but this priesthood never replaced the family priest's activities; it only supplemented those activities. The bulk of the family's worship was in the home.

Just before God gave Israel His Ten Commandments, He announced: "And ye shall be unto me a kingdom of priests, and an holy nation. These are the words which thou shalt speak unto the children of Israel" (Exodus 19:6). This prophecy was fulfilled by Christ's coming, said Peter: "But ye are a chosen generation, a royal priesthood, an holy nation, a peculiar people; that ye should shew forth the praises of him who hath called you out of darkness into his marvellous light" (I Peter 2:9). **Every believer is a priest.** This does not make him a solitary figure with unquestioned authority. It does make him (or her) a lawful priest when he (or she) is the head of a household. Church authorities must be males, never women, but widows are lawful priests performing priestly duties in the home. Certainly wives are priests, for they wait on tables continually, making them assistants to elders in the home.

On the question of female officers in the church, there is no question among those who believe in the testimony of the Bible. Anyone who refuses to acknowledge this teaching doesn't believe in the Bible. It can serve as a means of testing a church's commitment to the Bible. Paul wrote: "Let the woman learn in silence with all subjection. But I suffer not a woman to teach, nor to usurp authority over the man, but to be in silence. For Adam was first formed, then Eve. And Adam was not deceived, but the woman being deceived was in the transgression" (I Timothy 2:12-14). Paul was adamant about this: "Let your women keep silence in the churches: for it is not permitted unto them to speak; but they are commanded to be under obedience, as also saith the law. And if they will learn any thing, let them ask their husbands at home: for it is a shame for women to speak in church" (I Corinthians 14:34-35). **Churches that ordain women to positions of authority, or which ordain them to ministers of the gospel, are in the open, flagrant rebellion against God.** That's what the Bible teaches. (Sunday schools are not generally considered to be actual church meetings, although they meet in the church buildings. Having women teach the adult Sunday school, however, borders on rebellion, for most people consider the Sunday school "almost church," and some seem to think it's "more than church," since they take their children to some local Sunday school, but they never accompany their children into a church meeting. This, however, was the reason the earliest Sunday schools were developed in modern urban areas: to reach sinners through the conversion of their children. Today, the Sunday school has tended to be a replacement for declining parental, especially paternal, instruction in the home. Women can legitimately instruct children in Sunday school, for they are not exercising authority over men.)

Community

A community in communion: this is the standard for the institutional church. It is the family of God, with all the problems of a family. It is the assembly of the faithful, meeting every week on what we unfortunately call Sunday (a relic of the Roman calendar). It is a true community, based on shared goals, shared beliefs, shared burdens, shared blessings.

Christ told His disciples: "This is my commandment, That ye love one another, as I have loved you" (John 15:12). Again, "These things I command you, that ye love one another" (John 15:17). John wrote: "Hereby perceive we the love of God, because he laid down his life for us: and we ought to lay down our lives for the brethren" (I John 3:16). In fact, "We know that we have passed from death unto life, because we love the brethren. He that loveth not his brother abideth in death" (I John 3:14). Peter wrote: "Seeing ye have purified your souls in obeying the truth through the Spirit unto unfeigned love of the brethren, see that ye love one another with a pure heart fervently" (I Peter 1:22). The church is to be an institution of cooperating, loving, people. This is **a mature love by stable people**, not wildly emotional children: "That we henceforth be no more children, tossed to and fro, and carried about with every wind of doctrine, by the sleight of men, and cunning craftiness, whereby they lie in wait to deceive, but speaking the truth in love, may grow up into him in all things, which is the head, even Christ, from whom the whole body fitly joined together and compacted by which every joint supplieth, according to the effectual working in the measure of every part, maketh increase of the body unto the edifying of itself in love" (Ephesians 4:14-16). That's a lengthy sentence, but it says a lot. The church is Christ's body, and He is the head. It is to edify itself, through sound doctrine. It is not to be tossed to and fro by every wind of new doctrine that comes along. Christ holds His body together by **sound doctrine** and **mutual love**. Both are absolutely vital to the survival of the institutional church. Sadly, in practice, churches seem to specialize in one or the other: sound doctrine and frozen people, or lots of love and no sense. It's too often a choice between mature stabilty without visible indications of love, or else bubbling joy coupled with shifting crackpot doctrines.

Love involves a strong personal commitment. We read that "the love of money is the root of all evil" (I Timothy 6:10a), which indicates a grasping or clinging on the part of the lover. It's an unwillingness to let go, a systematic dedication of one's life to something else. This is a good description of love, and it applies to human relationships, too. But this is a definition without content. We must ask ourselves, "Love in terms of what?" What are we to love in our fellow Christians? What are the standards of love? How are we to act toward them? The answer is found in Paul's letter to the church in Rome: "Love worketh no ill to his neighbor: therefore love is the fulfilling of the law" (Romans 13:10). Love is lawful. It takes note of God's standard of righteousness. It seeks to apply those standards in every human situation. Men do not lie about their fellow Christians, or turn them away empty-handed when a crisis strikes. Love is the visible manifestation of the law in action. It is an emotional clinging to like-minded followers of Christ, but a clinging in terms of revealed law. It is not simply unguided and distinctionless emotional commitment; **it is systematic commitment to the welfare of others in terms of God's law**. Love is not an excuse for lawlessness.

By equating the love of God and the law of God, we can better understand the cross. God's love to the world was manifested in the same event as His vengeance against law-breaking. God executes His judgment. He does so without respect of persons. "For the Lord your God is a God of gods, and Lord of lords, a great God, a mighty, and a terrible [God], which regardeth not persons, nor taketh reward. He doth execute the judgment of the fatherless and widow, and loveth the stranger, in giving him food and raiment.

Love ye therefore the stranger: for ye were strangers in the land of Egypt'' (Deuteronomy 10:17-19). Since strangers were foreigners to God's covenant, uncircumcised dwellers in the land, God's judgment in history was against them. Nevertheless, men were told to love them. What did this mean? It meant that the Hebrews were to deal honestly with them, giving them the full protection of the law of God. God, who is a universal sovereign, requires all men to heed His commands. **This is the biblical doctrine of love: to render honest judgment, and bring the rule of God's law over all men, including the stranger.** Love is the fulfilling of the law. This is why the cross is the supreme symbol of both God's love and God's absolute justice: Christ died on the cross to satisfy God's justice, and this sacrifice of God's Son reveals God's incomparable love for His adopted sons.

The Greek words for brotherly love and love of money are different. Love of money is self-oriented, the service of man's lusts. Brotherly love is oriented toward the welfare of others, even as Christ died for His friends. A man can love money, if money is to him simply a sign of his effectiveness in selling consumers what they want at prices more competitive than other sellers are willing to offer consumers. Money within the framework of a competitive free market needn't be an evil. If men regard money as a kind of indicator of consumer satisfaction, then money is legitimate, and the quest for money is legitimate. But money sought for its own sake, irrespective of the damage the quest does (selling pornography, for example, or cheating the poor), is the sign of rebellious man's god, himself. It is the orientation of a man's activities that is important in defining good love from bad love. Again, **the law of God provides us with standards that allow us to test the kind of love in our hearts.**

The healthy church is made up of many sorts of people. Paul described the church in terms of a body: head, hands, eyes, lesser parts, but all under the direction of Jesus Christ, the true head of the church (I Corinthians 12). The division of labor is basic to any functioning church. Different people have different skills. The church needs all sorts of people if it is to be a functioning body, or living unit. It is a collective, responsible before God for its collective actions. Blessings come to individuals because of their membership in collectives; so do judgments. God is both one and many; we are one and many as members. This is why God wants a comprehensive church, one which is able to bring a sense of meaningful community to isolated, lonely men. Men serve something higher than themselves. They serve something that will survive their brief lives. They serve a cause which is permanent and which is guaranteed victory. The accent is on **service**. Men serve God rather than Satan. The sign of their service to God is their service to other men, especially those in the community of faith. The criterion for **leadership in the church** is **service to the church**: "...but he that is greatest among you, let him be as the younger; and he that is chief, as he that doth serve" (Luke 22:26). Christ was the suffering servant. His suffering service was instrumental in establishing the foundations of His all-encompassing victory. He served God and men; we must serve God and men. He gained total power by His willingness and ability to serve perfectly; we gain derivative but comprehensive authority in the same way, though as creatures.

The church has welfare functions. It cares for the elderly and defenseless widows (I Timothy 5). It cares for those members facing a calamity, and not just those who are members of the local congregation (II Corinthians 9). But its charity is not to be lawless or indiscriminate. Paul wrote: "For even when we were with you, this we commanded you, that if any would not work, neither should he eat" (II Thessalonians 3:10). The church is the body of Christ, and Christ has provided the church with eyes, ears, and a standard of law, so that the leaders might not waste the tithes and offerings of the faithful. **Charity must not subsidize evil**, as the pseudo-charity of the messianic State has subsidized evil, failure, and the enemies of God throughout the 20th century. Charity must not subsidize sloth. It must not subsidize rebellion against the laws of God.

Covenant

God established His covenant with Adam, and again with Noah. It was a dominion covenant. It was man's authorization to subdue the earth, but under God's overall authority and under His law. God also covenanted with Abram, changing his name to Abraham, and instituting the sign of His covenant, circumcision. He covenanted with Jacob, Abraham's grandson, changing his name to Israel, promising to bless Jacob's efforts (Genesis 32:24-30). God covenanted with Moses and the children of Israel, promising to bless them if they conformed to His laws, but curse them if they disobeyed (Deuteronomy 8; 28). The covenant was a **treaty**, and it involved **mutual obligations and promises**. The ruler, God, offers the peace treaty to a selected man or men, and they in turn accept its terms of surrender. The treaty spells out mutual obligations: protection and blessings from the King, and obedience on the part of the servants. It also spells out the terms of judgment: cursings from the King in case of rebellion on the part of the servants.

This same covenant is extended to the church today. It covers the institutional church, and it also applies to nations that agree to conform their laws to God's standards. Paul wrote: "And as many as walk according to this rule, peace be on them, and mercy, and upon the Israel of God" (Galatians 6:16). He also wrote to the Gentiles at the church of Ephesus: "Wherefore remember, that ye being in time past Gentiles in the flesh, who are called Uncircumcision by that which is called the Circumcision in the flesh made by hands; that at that time ye were without Christ, being aliens from the commonwealth of Israel and strangers from the covenants of promise, having no hope, and without God in the world. But now in Christ Jesus ye who sometimes were far off are made nigh by the blood of Christ" (Ephesians 2:11-12). They were strangers no longer to the covenants of promise; neither are we. God has made a new covenant with us Gentiles, fulfilling the prophecy of Jeremiah 31:32-34: "For finding fault with them, he saith, Behold, the days come, saith the Lord, when I will make a new covenant with the house of Israel and with the house of Judah: not according to the covenant that I made with their fathers in the day when I took them by the hand to lead them out of the land of Egypt; because they continued not in my covenant, and I regarded them not, saith the Lord. For this is the covenant that I will make with the house of Israel after those days, saith the Lord; I will put my laws into their mind, and write them in their hearts: and I will be to them a God, and they shall be to me a people" (Hebrews 8:8-10).

One of the most effective ways that Satan has deluded converts to Christ is to have convinced millions of them that they are not under God's covenant, despite their own baptisms, which are the sign of God's covenantal relationship with individuals and the church in New Testament times. Satan has convinced them that no covenant exists today, despite the clear testimony of the New

Testament writers. If there is no covenant, then there is no treaty of peace between men and God. If there is no treaty of peace, there are no terms of peace. If there are no terms of peace, then God's covenantal law structure no longer applies. All of these conclusions are taught in many modern churches today. But if such a negation of the covenant has taken place, then the dominion covenant is gone, and men no longer have guidelines from the law: moral, judicial, and dominical guidelines. Without God's law, we have no tool of dominion. Without a tool of dominion, Satan's earthly kingdom doesn't face the same sort of pressure that it would face if men were actively seeking to subdue the earth to the glory of God, but in terms of His law-order. This has been the sad story of the church over the last century. **Having lost the doctrine of God's covenantal peace treaty, His people have lost the vision of victorious conquest.** His people have not acted like ambassadors of peace coming to inhabitants of a rebellious kingdom whose monarch has received a mortal wound. They have come more as Pied Pipers who would lead people out of a supposedly powerful, visible kingdom headed by a victorious monarch, and into the powerless, pitiful kingdom of a distant monarch who will not return in triumph to build up his visible kingdom until the day of final judgment. It is as if the spies sent by Israel into Canaan had been instructed to find people like Rahab, in order to convince them to leave their homes and to come to dwell in the wilderness with Israel, until the day of final judgment. You would conclude from modern Christianity's version of Christ's kingdom that God wanted His people to dwell in the wilderness permanently. Without a doctrine of the covenant—a peace treaty with specific terms of surrender, imposed by an absolute sovereign who controls all of history—the modern churches have lost the faith of pre-Christ Israelites. Yet it was Christ's ministry which was supposed to **improve** men's comprehension of God and God's dominion assignment. He established a **better covenant**, we read in Hebrews 8 and 10; He didn't abolish the concept of a covenant and a covenantal law-order. But you wouldn't know this from the bulk of the sermons preached in 20th-century churches.

Sacraments

Baptism is the church's sign of the covenantal relationship between God and man. Most of the references to baptism in the

New Testament refer to the baptism of John the baptizer, who was Jesus' second cousin, or at least close relative, through his mother's side of the family (Luke 1:36). His ministry preceded Jesus' ministry, and it was he who baptized Jesus at the beginning of Jesus' ministry (Matthew 3:13-16). The Bible does not say specifically that baptism was by total immersion. It can mean immersion, but it can also mean "to dip" and "to wash." Different churches place different interpretations on the meaning of baptism.

Most churches believe that baptism is the New Testament's version of circumcision. We know that Abraham circumcised every male in his household (Genesis 17:23). We also know that whole households were baptized by the apostles in the New Testament era (Acts 16:33). This indicates that baptism, like circumcision, is a visible token of God's covenant, that the baptized person is ritually placed under the terms of the covenant, God's peace treaty. He benefits from God's protection, but he acknowledges that any rebellion on his part against God and God's law will bring judgment.

The reason why whole households were circumcised in the Old Testament was not because every person in the house was regenerate. It was because **the head of the household had placed himself under the terms of the covenant,** and since he was responsible for exercising dominion over his household, **every member had to acknowledge his indirect subservience to God.** God's law reigned in the household through the head of the household. It was a **personal covenant with each member,** yet it was imposed because of the **collective responsibility of all members** in the household under the master.

As we have seen before, God's treaty is two-edged: unto **blessing** as a result of obedience, and unto **destruction** as a result of rebellion. The man under the terms of the treaty is **sanctified.** He is protected. He may not be born again. He has been **set apart** because of God's external relationship with him as a result of his position under the covenant.

We have a New Testament example of just this kind of **non-regenerating sanctification.** It is a marriage between a believer and an unbeliever. Paul wrote: "For the unbelieving husband is sanctified by the wife, and the unbelieving wife is sanctified by the husband: else were your children unclean; but now they are holy" (I

Corinthians 7:14). Does this mean that God automatically regenerates a pagan husband because of his wife's regeneration? Did Paul preach "salvation by marriage"? Obviously not. Then what did Paul mean? This sanctification is God's way of placing a man or wife under the benefits of His covenant, treating them differently from those not under any acknowledged covenantal administration. Likewise, their children. They are **holy**. They are **set apart**. They are singled out by God to be dealt with in a special way. They are not guaranteed a place in heaven because of a parent's justification by grace through faith. **They are put under the terms of the peace treaty**, like the citizens of Nineveh, when Jonah preached to the king, and he repented (Jonah 3:5-10). They believed that collective judgment was imminent, and they put on sackcloth as a sign of humility.

Churches today say that baptism is the New Testament's version of circumcision, but none of them truly believes this, as far as we can tell. Churches do not insist on baptizing every member of a newly converted man's household—wife, children, relatives living under his authority—since they simultaneously argue that baptism is also a sign of regeneration. What they really believe is that baptism is a sign of the spiritual new birth. But circumcision was not restricted to spiritually regenerate people. It was administered to all those under the family authority of a leader who was visibly subjecting himself to the covenant. An entire city-state was circumcised in the Old Testament when the son of the king of a Hivite city wanted to marry Jacob's daughter, Dinah, and the sons of Jacob told the king that every man in the city had to be circumcised (Genesis 34).

Paul dealt with the meaning of Abraham's circumcision. "And he received the sign of circumcision, a seal of the righteousness of the faith which he had yet being uncircumcised: that he might be the father of all them that believe, though they be not circumcised; that righteousness might be imputed unto them also. And the father of circumcision to them who are not of the circumcision only, but who also walk in the steps of that faith of our father Abraham, which he had being yet uncircumcised" (Romans 4:11-12). Abraham's circumcision was a seal of the faith he possessed prior to his circumcision. We are the spiritual sons of Abraham, Paul wrote: "Neither, because they are the seed of Abraham, are they all children: but in Isaac shall thy seed be called. That is, They which are the children of the flesh, these are not the children of God: but the children of the promise are counted for the seed'' (Romans 9:7-8). Who are the children of the promise? All believers in Christ. ''Now to Abraham and his seed were the promises made. He saith not, And to seeds, as of many; but as of one, And to thy seed, which is Christ'' (Galatians 3:16).

Circumcision was a seal of faith's righteousness for Abraham. Nevertheless, Abraham circumcised his first son, born of his wife's bondwoman, Hagar. Ishmael was not part of the covenant line (Isaac, Jacob, Judah), although he may have demonstrated saving faith. Isaac presumably circumcised the twins, Esau and Jacob, yet God hated Esau from the beginning, before he had been born or done good or evil (Romans 9:11). In other words, with respect to circumcision, **it served as a seal of faith to those who believed, but it also was administered to infants and household servants who did not believe.**

Why is baptism any different? **It is a sign of God's covenantal dominion over man.** The baptized infant grows up under the sign of that covenant. He faces the reality of God's promises: **blessings** to those who abide by the terms of His covenant, through faith in Jesus Christ; **cursings** to those who do not. No more, but no less, than circumcision, baptism testifies to a holy God who **separates** the sheep from the goats, the saved from the lost.

With respect to the administration of baptism, what was crucial in the New Testament era was the **speed** of baptism, not the mode. Philip baptized the Ethiopian eunuch immediately, as soon as they drew near to a body of water (Acts 8:36). The Philippian jailer was baptized before the night was over. He washed the bruises of Paul and Silas, who had been beaten by the magistrates, and he and his whole household were baptized (Acts 16:33). They were baptized ''straightaway,'' or as the Greek word can be translated, ''at once.'' It is doubtful that his house contained a pool for a full immersion. The Ethiopian eunuch may have been immersed. But both men were baptized immediately after making a profession of faith.

Oddly enough, modern churches never baptize people immediately. Whether they pour (rare), sprinkle, or dunk, they baptize on Sundays, at a prescribed service, having made the new professors of faith wait for days or weeks. Strange, isn't it? Churches cannot agree on the mode of baptism, which is understandable, since no mode seems specifically to be required in the Bible, but they do agree on the one point that has no support whatsoever in the New Testament: **delayed** baptism. They think they need a formal service, all nicely bureaucratized, all nicely official. And Monday through Saturday, they might as well hang this sign on their doors: "Busy Ethiopian eunuchs on a tight schedule need not apply."

What most Christian churches formally state, but do not really believe, is that baptism is the New Testament's version of circumcision. The meaning of the two sacraments is the same, they say, but they cannot seem to agree on what the meaning really is. From what we have seen, the meaning should be clear: **a sign of God's peace treaty with men, to be adhered to or broken**. Adherence to it, through faith in Christ and outward conformity to its provisions, brings blessings. Rebellion against it brings judgment, sometimes on earth, but always on the day of judgment. It is a **seal of the faith** of the righteous, and a **seal of doom** for the rebels. Because circumcision was administered to households and even whole societies, baptism should also be administered to households. (We no longer have kings who represent a whole nation covenantally, so national baptism today would not apply. If, however, a majority of voters covenanted themselves with God, and agreed to conform the nation's laws to God's laws, citizens who intended to remain citizens could legitimately be required to be baptized, since their leaders had agreed to submit the civil government to God.) And it should be **administered speedily**. To delay the administration of baptism symbolizes a man's delay in placing himself and his family under the care of God, a delay in signing the peace treaty. There is no New Testament evidence supporting the legitimacy of delaying baptism, whatever the mode.

Why water baptism? Because water symbolized both **cleansing** and **judgment**. Prophesied Ezekiel: "For I will take you from among the heathen, and gather you out of all countries, and will bring you into your own land. Then will I sprinkle clean water upon you, and ye shall be clean: from all your filthiness, and from all your idols, will I cleanse you. A new heart also will I give you, and a new spirit will I put within you: and I will take away the stony heart out of your flesh, and I will give you an heart of flesh. And I will put my spirit within you, and cause you to walk in my statutes, and ye shall keep my judgments, and do them" (Ezekiel 36:24-27). This prophecy was fulfilled with Christ's death, resurrection, and the sending of the Holy Spirit, the Comforter. He has placed a new heart in His people (Hebrews 8:10). As for water as a symbol of judgment, we have the testimony of the Red Sea, in which perished Pharaoh and his army, not to mention the great water judgment of the flood in Noah's day. Jonah's three days in the sea monster is also representative (Matthew 12:38-41).

But what of the second sacrament, **the Lord's Supper**, also called communion? What are its origins? The origins of the Lord's Supper are simpler to trace. Jesus met with His disciples in the upper room the night before He was captured (Luke 22:12). Chapters 13 through 17 of the Gospel of John are devoted to a summary of Christ's words to His disciples at this feast. It was the Passover feast, the night that the sacrificial lamb was to be slain. Instead of celebrating the Passover feast with their families, the disciples celebrated it with Christ, the head of a new family. The symbolism is obvious. As Paul wrote, "Christ our passover is sacrificed for us" (I Corinthians 5:7b).

At the original Passover, held the night of Israel's release from Egyptian slavery, the men were required to stand, "your loins girded, your shoes on your feet, and your staff in your hand; and he shall eat it in haste: it is the Lord's passover" (Exodus 12:11). God would pass over their homes, sparing the firstborn, because of the blood sprinkled on the doorposts of every home (Exodus 12:13).

The Lord's Supper was different. They ate and drank sitting down. No longer were they a people about to escape the bondage of Egypt. Christ's sacrifice was about to bring victory over Satan. Now they would go into foreign lands as God's ambassadors, bringing His peace treaty to the nations. They sat. Why? Christ informed them of a new era: "And I appoint unto you a kingdom, as my Father hath appointed unto me; that ye may eat and drink at my table in my kingdom, and sit on thrones judging the twelve tribes of Israel" (Luke 22:29-30). They were now Christ's **judges**. They would bring the law to the nations as ambassadors who were already appointed judges. The war against Satan was about to be won, in time and on earth, at Calvary. God's institutional kingdom was about to burst the bottles of national Israel.

One of the strangest aspects of modern Christianity is that this passage from Luke's gospel, which gives us Jesus' explicit words concerning the meaning of His supper, is virtually never cited by pastors who lead communion services. The words of Christ point directly to **conquest and dominion**. Christ appointed His people a kingdom, and a table, and thrones of judgment, but all we ever hear about the Lord's Supper is the section from Paul's first letter to the Corinthians, where he warned against taking part in the service unworthily. In other words, as the modern churches have interpreted the meaning of the Lord's Supper, it is a moment of great fear, a time of silent self-examination. Christians haven't the slightest indication that it is a celebration of victory, the launching of a new kingdom, and the transfer of the power of judgment to His people.

We have very little information on the nature of the early church's communion services. At Pentecost, when the Holy Spirit appeared in power, Peter preached to the assembled masses. "Then they that gladly received his word were baptized: and the same day there were added unto them about three thousand souls. And they continued stedfastly in the apostles' doctrine and fellowship, and in breaking of bread, and in prayers" (Acts 2:41-42). Here was the first celebration of the Lord's Supper. It was obviously performed in households, and it is doubtful that there was a church officer present in every household, given the huge number of new converts. **Like baptism, the focus of the Lord's Supper was the household**.

We know from Paul's warnings that there were some who were misusing the Lord's Supper. We know that it was a meal, since some people were bringing food, some were drinking themselves into drunkenness, and others had no food and were hungry (I Corinthians 11:21). They were being disorderly. Paul told them to eat at home, so they could then come to celebrate the Lord's Supper. But that supper was a real one, for Christ had celebrated the Passover meal with the disciples. So Paul was appealing them to come with stomachs full enough not to be growling, but not so filled with wine that they were drunken. He wanted an orderly, meaningful celebration.

In the early church, people got together to celebrate the Lord's Supper. They met in homes, or possibly in some hired room. They were supposed to recognize the religious nature of the celebration. Nevertheless, it was a **celebration**. If you look at a modern church's celebration of the Lord's Supper, it looks like a funeral. Silent, solemn people grimly swallowing token bits of bread or unsalted crackers, then swallowing a thimble full of wine, or even less realistically, grape juice. (Were people leaving the Corinthian church drunk because they had consumed too much grape juice?) This is a celebration? More like a cerebration. The modern Lord's Supper is a symbol of a symbol of a symbol: a symbolic meal (a wafer and a thimble full of wine) which symbolized the Passover meal, which in turn symbolized Christ's sacrifice. But where is the **meal** in the Lord's Supper? And where is the celebration? Why eat crumbs and not loaves?

The head of the household directed the Passover meal. He was to answer the questions of the children concerning the meaning of the meal (Exodus 12:26-27). The children participated in the meal. They participated, and so they asked questions about it. In today's churches, the father says nothing. The children are often not allowed to participate. The excuse is given that the children will not be able to "discern the Lord's body" in the bread. What does this mean? Paul warned, concerning the disorderly nature of the Corinthian church's celebration, that they ought to recognize the Lord's body in the church. Paul taught that the church is Christ's body, and he used this analogy to defend the idea of the division of labor within the church. He taught this immediately after he had dealt with the subject of the Lord's Supper (I Corinthians 12). This is what he meant when he wrote: "For he that eateth and drinketh unworthily, eateth and drinketh damnation to himself, not discerning the Lord's body" (I Corinthians 11:29). This is too often interpreted to mean that children do not recognize the symbolic nature of the Lord's body in the bread. But Paul was not talking about people's failure to recognize symbolism in the bread when he warned them about not discerning the Lord's body, since he never mentioned the danger of not discerning the Lord's blood (the symbolic nature of the wine). He wasn't talking about the theological weaknesses in the children; he was talking about **the sins of their disruptive parents**.

The fathers in the Old Testament served as household priests, celebrating the Lord's Supper with their families. It is true that there was a centralized priesthood that cooked the lamb, but this doesn't mean that they replaced the celebration within the family (Leviticus 3). If they had replaced the father's role, they would never have had time to answer the questions of the children, which was the whole idea behind the ceremony of the Passover. Today, the local ministers have replaced the fathers in this celebration, despite the fact that all believers are referred to as priests (I Peter 2:9). The children are often not permitted to eat the Supper, yet the Passover had been instituted by God to serve as an instruction device for children. The celebration has become the emotional equivalent of a wake. Would the early disciples recognize today's version of the Lord's Supper? It's doubtful.

Should the children participate? What did Paul say the celebration referred back to? The deliverance of Israel! "Moreover, brethren, I would not that ye should be ignorant, how that all our fathers were under the cloud, and all passed through the sea; and all were baptized unto Moses in the cloud and in the sea; and all did eat the same spiritual meat; and did drink the same spiritual drink: for they drank of that spiritual Rock that followed them: and that Rock was Christ" (I Corinthians 10:12-14). Did the children pass through the sea? Did the children eat meat? Did the children drink from the rock Moses' rod tapped? (Numbers 20:7-11). Of course! Yet the children of today's churches are frequently prohibited from participating in the celebration that points back to the experience of the Hebrew children—the sons and daughters who conquered the land of Canaan, after their parents had died in the wilderness because of their slave-like fearfulness.

Perhaps some day we will have churches that eat real bread, and drink real wine, and invite children to participate. (Those who may be horrified by the suggestion that wine, being an alcoholic beverage, should ever be served in church, because liquor is always forbidden, should reconsider Deuteronomy 14:26, which enjoined upon every family in Israel the celebration of the tithe, a community celebration: "And thou shalt bestow that money for whatsoever thy soul lusteth after, for oxen, or for sheep, or for wine, or for strong drink, or for whatsoever thy soul desireth, and thou shalt eat there before the Lord thy God, and thou shalt rejoice, thou, and thine household." And the next verse required the Hebrews to invite the Levite priests to the celebration. Maybe some commentators think they can turn wine into grape juice, the way that Christ turned water into wine [John 2], but there is no way on earth that any commentator can legitimately turn "strong drink" into grape juice.) Perhaps these churches will allow fathers to take part in the celebration, as they did in Israel. Perhaps the children will be allowed once again to enter into the festivities, as they did in Israel. Perhaps. But I wouldn't spend a lot of time trying to locate such a church today. Time is too valuable to waste in fruitless searches.

Discipline

God's law applies to all spheres of life. No area of life can stand up and proclaim its independence from God's law—or if it does, it has made a false claim. The church is an agency of dominion. It has a law structure. It stands or falls in terms of its commitment to God's law.

One point must be stressed: government is first of all **self-government**. No human institution can succeed in bringing its own members into conformity to God's law by means of coercion alone. There are too many decisions to be made by participants that are outside the view of a church officer. Whether in the family, the church, or the civil government, **the goal is to substitute self-government for bureaucratic government**. What is needed is self-governing individuals who stand in fear of God, and who devote personal resources to subduing the law of sin in their own lives. As Paul cried out: "But I see another law in my members, warring against the law of my mind, and bringing me into captivity to the law of sin which is in my members. O wretched man that I am! Who shall deliver me from the body of this death? I thank God through Jesus Christ our Lord. So then with the mind I myself serve the law of God; but with the flesh the law of sin" (Romans 7:23-25). In every institution, Christians must devote their efforts to discovering God's laws, and then to disseminating their findings, so that self-disciplined men can begin to subdue their own members, and then their environments.

The church's primary means of discipline is the preaching of the whole counsel of God. Nothing of any lasting value can be accomplished by formal church courts if the ministers are not constantly preaching the whole Bible, from Genesis to Revelation, helping each member of the congregation aware of his own personal responsibilities, before God, to conform his life to God's revealed and concrete standards. The word of God is the most effective means of eliminating sin from the daily lives of the members.

Nevertheless, preaching is not sufficient to govern the life of any church. God has established **ministers of justice** in the church. Paul warned members of the church at Corinth—a sin-burdened church in a corrupt city—that they should not take their disputes with one another in front of civil magistrates. "Do ye not know that the saints shall judge the world? And if the world shall be judged by you, are ye unworthy to judge the smallest matters? Know ye not that we shall judge angels? How much more things that pertain to this life?" (I Corinthians 6:2-3). Here we have a recapitulation and extension of Christ's announcement to His disciples at the Passover that they would sit on thrones of judgment in His kingdom. Christians are to become instrumental in handing down godly judgment, in time and on earth, as well as in heaven. The exercise of godly discipline in the institutional setting of the church is one means of gaining the necessary training.

Paul continued: "Is it so, that there is not a wise man among you? No, not one that shall be able to judge between his brethren?" (I Corinthians 6:5). The church members, Paul reported, were constantly going to law against each other, and before unbelieving magistrates. Isn't it better to be defrauded? (I Corinthians 6:6-7). In other words, the Corinthian Christians were subordinating themselves to the judgments of pagan representatives of a pagan State. They were supposed to subordinate themselves to God's law, as administered by another Christian who was wise in the law. They were supposed to bring themselves under God's administration, in order that they might expand their influence and eventually judge not only men but angels.

The first step in initiating lawful church discipline is a personal confrontation with the individual who initiated the wrong. "Moreover if thy brother shall trespass against thee, go and tell him his fault between thee and him alone: if he shall hear thee, thou hast gained thy brother" (Matthew 18:15). If a dispute is worth a trial by the church, then it must be worth a preliminary confrontation. That way, sin can be bottled up very early. The problem can be solved before it clogs up the court's machinery.

Sometimes men refuse to listen to a complaint against themselves. "But if he will not hear thee, then take with thee one or two more, that in the mouth of two or three witnesses every word may be established" (Matthew 18:16). This is simply a recapitulation of the Old Testament's provision: "One witness shall not rise up against a man for any iniquity, or for any sin, in any sin that he sinneth; at the mouth of two witnesses, or at the mouth of three witnesses, shall the matter be established"

(Deuteronomy 19:15). **The New Testament law structure is the same as the Old Testament law structure, so the criteria of evidence are the same.**

The next step is the church's court: "And if he shall neglect to hear them, tell it unto the church: but if he neglect to hear the church, let him be unto thee as an heathen man and a publican" (Matthew 18:17). To be as a publican! What a fearful punishment. A publican was a tax collector in Jesus' day. Whether in Corinth or Jerusalem, whether among Greeks or Hebrews, there was no public official more despised, more resented, and more looked down upon than a tax collector. And that's all an excommunicated church member could compare himself to: the bottom of the social barrel.

So the basis of church discipline is this. First, personal self-discipline. Second, personal confrontation with the initiator of the wrong. Third, a second confrontation in the presence of witnesses. Fourth, a consideration by the church of the formal charges being brought against a man. Fifth, judgment by the church. By adhering to this simple procedural outline, the church is supposed to minimize such confrontations. It is assumed that the early steps will remove the problem before it becomes a public disgrace and a matter of public censure by the church.

In modern times, it is difficult to understand the threat of excommunication. The idea that "there is no salvation outside the church" is not taken seriously. Even the Roman Catholic Church has generally downplayed this venerable doctrine since about 1950. There was even a priest in the United States, Father Feeney, who continued to preach this old doctrine so enthusiastically that the hierarchy put pressure on him to stop. He refused, and the church excommunicated him in 1953. The irony is obvious: by Feeney's standards, this was the worst thing possible, but by the Church's new theology, it didn't really mean that much. He established a new church, the Slaves of the Immaculate Heart of Mary. In 1958 he established a religious commune west of Boston, Massachusetts. In 1972, the excommunication was removed. The Church had not been converted back to its old doctrine, however. Perhaps its authorities just wanted to be merciful to an aging heretic whose heresy had been initiated by his total commitment to a traditional doctrine which had begun to be an embarrassment to the Church after 1950. (Feeney died on Jan. 30, 1978).

In ancient Israel, excommunication was feared. "Seven days shall ye eat unleavened bread; even the first day ye shall put away leaven out of your houses: for whosoever eateth leavened bread from the first day until the seventh day, that soul shall be cut off from Israel" (Exodus 12:15). Again and again, this punishment was threatened, one which was considered almost equivalent to execution, since God would Himself deal with the offender. To be cut off from the congregation meant social separation from the institutions of life.

In modern times, with a church on every corner, men have felt free to leave any church threatening them with discipline. They are able to walk across the street and be welcomed with open arms. The concept of the majesty of God's law has been abandoned. The ideas of the sovereignty of God, the threat of excommunication, and the concept of meaningful church discipline, have all been forgotten. The church has become a social club, a friendly lecture society, a place for making business contacts, a dating service for teenagers, a free nursery for parents who want Sunday morning off, and a refuge from the conflicts usually associated with the world's affairs. The preaching of the modern church has become a pale imitation of the prophets of Israel, who challenged the culture of their day, from the king down to the lowliest prostitute. Our churches have begun to resemble the mealy-mouthed centers of status quo propaganda that the court priests of Israel and Judah created in order to remain in favor with the people and the kings.

While it may be possible to gain membership which enforces a lowest-common-denominator ethic, if it enforces any ethic at all, **this kind of membership is worthless on the day of judgment.** Such membership only deludes men into thinking that they are in peaceful fellowship with God. It keeps them from facing the magnitude of their own transgressions and the magnitude of God's promised judgment. **Churches that do not pay attention to God's law also ignore their responsibilites in extending God's dominion covenant.** They may be large churches, popular churches, and churches of high repute. They will not be effective churches in fulfilling God's dominion asignment.

Restitution rules church law, as it rules civil law and criminal law. When the crime is so great that no restitution will suffice, then excommunication is the **church's death sentence**—not physical death, but **the second death** of eternal punishment (Revelation

20:14). Only repentance will suffice, and public humility before the church's lawful authority.

Membership in a church is serious business. It should not be undertaken lightly. Like marriage, it is a permanent commitment. Man puts himself under God in a covenantal relationship. Like any covenant, it has terms of obedience. It has a mechanism of enforcement. Just as a single woman must consider carefully whether she wishes to place herself under permanent subordination to a particular man in marriage, so should a prospective church member consider carefully the terms of the church's covenant and the consequences of affirming his commitment to it. Churches offering **minimal covenants** and **numerous members** are dangerous to the soul.

Kingdom

The institutional church is **not** to be equated with the kingdom of God. It is an agency of the kingdom, but it is not identical to the kingdom. The kingdom of God is as broad as the world. The kingdom of God is the goal of God's dominion assignment. It is the reign of Jesus Christ, under God the Father, by means of the Holy Spirit's action in regenerating men. It is the reign of Christ in terms of the law of God, imposed by individuals and institutions.

The extent of the kingdom can be seen in Satan's temptation of Christ in the wilderness. "Again, the devil taketh him up into an exceeding high mountain, and sheweth him all the kingdoms of the world, and the glory of them; and saith unto him, All these things will I give thee, if thou wilt fall down and worship me. Then saith Jesus unto him, Get thee hence Satan: for it is written, Thou shalt worship the Lord thy God, and him only shalt thou serve" (Matthew 4:8-9). Satan had offered Christ what was already His, in principle: the kingdoms of this world. Satan could not grant them to Christ. He is not the Lord of creation; God is. Satan held them all as stolen property. And he was about to lose them all to Christ anyway, for with Satan's judgment at the cross, he was cast out of heaven and down to the earth. No longer can he accuse us before God, as he did in Job's day. The twelfth chapter of the Book of Revelation shows us that it was Christ's resurrection and ascension into heaven (vs. 5) that led to Satan's eviction from the face of God (vv. 7-9). "And I heard a loud voice saying in heaven, Now is come salvation, and strength, and the kingdom of our God, and the power of his Christ; for the accuser of our brethren is cast down, which accused them before our God day and night. And they overcame him by the blood of the Lamb, and by the word of their testimony; and they loved not their lives unto the death. Therefore rejoice, ye heavens, and ye that dwell in them. Woe to the inhabitants of the earth and of the sea! For the devil is come down unto you, having great wrath, because he knoweth that he hath but a short time" (vv. 10-12).

The ascension of Christ to the right hand of God sealed Satan's defeat, and it launched the **internationalization of Christ's kingdom**. It is extended by Christ's ambassadors. The church institutional is one training center for this conquest. Another is the Christian school. The kingdoms of Satan are being brought under the dominion of God. Of course, Satan wages fierce battle against Christ's ambassadors. He rages, for he knows his time is short. The point is, the institutional church is not to be identified with the kingdom of God, for it was **the world's visible kingdoms** that Satan offered to Christ. Satan's forces are losing the battle to maintain control over these visible kingdoms by means of Satan's human followers. They claim sovereignty over the whole world, so **the struggle between the two kingdoms is for the whole world**. Christ told His disciples: "But seek ye first the kingdom of God, and his righteousness; and all these things shall be added unto you" (Matthew 6:33). What things? Food, drink, and clothing (Matthew 6:32). We will have all we need, for the kingdom of God will be co-extensive with the world, Satan's former possession by default, but now under attack throughout the world. That's why he is fighting for his life and his kingdoms here on earth: he has lost the battle in heaven. **This is Satan's last stand**. Christ will be victorious in **every** stronghold Satan now temporarily holds. "Then cometh the end, when he shall have delivered up the kingdom to God, even the Father; when he shall have put down all rule and all authority and power. For he must reign, till he hath put all enemies under his feet. The last enemy that shall be destroyed is death" (I Corinthians 15:24-26). It is a struggle to the death for Satan; it is a struggle to the death for death. Whose is the rule, the authority, and the power the Bible is speaking about? Obviously, someone other than Christ. Where is this rule, authority, and power being exercised? Obviously, no longer in heaven. What was the extent of this kingdom geographically when Christ came to earth? All the earth except Israel. What, therefore, will be the geographical extent of God's kingdom on that final day of judgment? The whole earth.

The kingdom is more than the institutional church. It is every nook and cranny of Satan's present and past reign. It is all of Satan's earthly strongholds. **It is every sphere of life.** The institutional church isn't co-extensive with every area of man's dominion assignment. It is, however, a training center for dominion, for it is the source of God's ordained sacraments: baptism and the Lord's Supper. The church as an institution exercises monopoly control over the use of these sacraments. It also ordains elders to exercise church discipline and preach the word of life.

Conclusion

The church invisible (eschatological) must be distinguished from the church visible (historical). There is also a church triumphant: those in heaven. The church invisible is broader than the church visible in its spheres of influence, but narrower in membership than the visible church. Christians are responsible for exercising universal dominion, whereas the institutional church is responsible for preaching, the sacraments, and institutional discipline. It is not the sole authority on earth: families, businesses, civil governments, educational institutions, and other godly organizations also possess limited, but legitimate authority. It unquestionably has a monopoly over spiritual affairs because of its right of excommunicating members. God honors the excommunication by a law-abiding church against an ethical rebel (Matthew 18:18).

Chapter 6

STATE

The best place to begin a study of the Christian view of the civil government is Paul's letter to the church at Rome. The first principle Paul laid down was that it is not the responsibility of the individual citizen to exact vengeance. "Dearly beloved, avenge not yourselves, but rather give place unto wrath: for it is written, Vengeance is mine; I will repay, saith the Lord" (Romans 12:19). Does this mean that all punishment must wait until the day of judgment? Not at all. God has established an **ordained ministry of vengeance**, the civil government.

"Let every soul be subject unto the higher powers. For there is no power but of God: the powers that be are ordained by God" (Romans 13:1). While this statement introduces a consideration of the civil magistrate, its frame of reference is broader than the civil magistrate. Paul spoke of "powers." These powers are lawful authorities over us. But the word is plural, not singular. Paul did not limit his concept to the civil government alone. He was not even speaking of the Roman State, as such. He was speaking of the **pluralistic authorities of all kinds over each man**. There is no single human authority over man which can claim final sovereignty. There is no absolute and final court of appeal in time and on earth. There are **multiple authorities** that must be respected, each bearing its authority from God.

Men are not to resist higher authorities. To do so is to be damned (Romans 13:2). This is extremely strong language. Paul laid down a fundamental principle of Christian social thought: a revolution against **all** constituted authority, meaning the "powers" of government (including, but not exclusively, civil government), is rebellion against God.

The third verse of Romans 13 is the transition: from authorities in general to the civil government in particular: "For rulers are not

129

a terror to good works, but to the evil. Wilt thou then not be afraid of the power? Do that which is good, and thou shalt have praise of the same." Rulers are a threat to Satan. The very existence of rulers points to a **hierarchy of power and responsibility** in the affairs of men—a structure created by God. Then Paul turned to the institution of civil government: "the power." This singular noun reveals a narrowing of focus: the institution which bears the sword. Paul wrote of the civil magistrate: "For he is a minister of God to thee for good. But if thou do that which is evil, be afraid; for he beareth not the sword in vain: for he is the minister of God, a revenger to execute wrath upon him that doeth evil. Wherefore ye must needs be subject, not only for wrath, but also for conscience sake. For this cause pay ye tribute also: for they are God's ministers, attending continually upon this very thing. Render therefore to all their dues: tribute to whom tribute is due; custom to whom custom; fear to whom fear; honour to whom honour" (Romans 13:4-7).

Paul actually spoke of the civil magistrate as "a minister of God." This is a crucial concept. The word "ministry" is normally associated only with the institutional church. Paul argued that **the minister of justice,** meaning the minister who bears the sword, is also **a minister ordained by God.** In a very real sense, the minister of justice is as important to the life of a godly society as the minister of the gospel is. He has a different function, but he is entitled to tribute, meaning tax payments. In no way are these tax payments considered theft, as such. Undoubtedly, the messianic State can demand tribute at levels that are confiscatory. A monopoly of the sword empowers the State at times to become tyrannical. But taxation as such should not be designated as theft, any more than the tithe to God is theft. **Men are paying for vital services received:** suppression of violence, suppresson of fraud, suppression of Satan's evil works.

In the days before the people of Israel demanded a human king, God was their sovereign ruler. Therefore, when they came to the prophet Samuel, he warned them against the consequences of raising up a human to rule them in the kingdom. We have in I Samuel 8 as fine a summary of the aggrandizing State as there is in ancient literature. Here is what your future kings will do, Samuel announced. The king will take your sons and assign them to the armed forces (vv. 11-12). He will draft your daughters and make them cooks (v. 13). He will confiscate the finest of your fields (v. 14). He will extract ten percent of your agricultural produce (v. 15). He will draft the labor services of your own servants, as well as your beasts of burden (v. 16). "He will take the tenth of your sheep: and ye shall be his servants. And ye shall cry out in that day because of your king which ye shall have chosen you; and the Lord will not hear you in that day" (vv. 17-18). He will not listen to you, Samuel said, because He had told Samuel, "they have not rejected thee, but they have rejected me, that I should not reign over them" (v. 7b).

What was the nature of their sin? **They had substituted an earthly king for a heavenly King.** They wanted to be as the nations around them (vv. 5, 20). In other words, they wanted to elevate a man to the position of honor and power that God had exercised over them. They wanted to be known among the nations as **just another kingdom of man.** They wanted to remove God's name as their ruler and defender, and to substitute the name of mighty men. They wanted to live in the kingdom of man, and not the kingdom of God. God granted them their wish.

We know the mark of tyranny, the mark of man's kingdom. It is **a kingdom which refuses to recognize the sovereignty of God.** This is manifested by **a level of taxation that equals or exceeds the tithe,** meaning ten percent of one's production. The 20th century is the age of the universal humanist kingdoms, for all the messianic states, since World War I, have imposed levels of taxation far beyond Israel's prophesied level of judgment. In fact, there is not a Western nation (let alone one in the Communist camp), that would not have to roll back taxes by at least 50% in order to reach the "mild" taxation of Egypt under the Pharaoh of Joseph's day, who extracted 20% of the national product (Genesis 41:34; 47:24). Yet Egypt is regarded as one of the most powerful dynasties in the history of man. Egypt was a kingdom based on the supposed divinity of the ruler, Pharaoh. Egypt possessed the most comprehensive bureaucracy in the history of man, at least until the advent of modern national bureaucracies, which began to take shape in the late nineteenth century.

Sovereignty

Should Christians regard the civil government as the final court of appeal? Not according to the testimony of the apostles. The incident in the early church recorded in the fifth chapter of the Book of Acts presents us with a basis of legitimate resistance to unwarranted State power. The high priest and chief priests complained to the Roman authorities concerning the continuing preaching by Peter and the apostles. "Then went the captain with the officers, and brought them without violence: for they feared the people, lest they should have been stoned. And when they had brought them, they set them before the council: and the high priest asked them, saying, Did not we straitly command you that ye should not teach in this name? And, behold, ye have filled Jerusalem with your doctrine, and intend to bring this man's blood upon us. Then Peter and the other apostles answered and said, We ought to obey God rather than men" (Acts 5:26-29).

We ought to obey God rather than men. Is this in opposition to Paul's doctrine? Paul's instruction said: "If it be possible, as much as lieth in you, live peaceably with all men" (Romans 12:18). **As much as possible,** be willing to submit to others. **As it lies within you,** be peaceable citizens. Render tribute, custom, fear, and honor **to whom it is due** (Romans 13:7). Paul's injunction concerns powers and power, the entire system of legitimate institutional authority, including the authority of the civil magistrate. If this interpretation of Paul's message is incorrect—if Paul was not speaking of the **many** (all institutional authorities) as well as the **one** (the civil magistrate)—then it appears to be impossible to reconcile Paul's teaching with the response of the apostles. If he was enjoining total obedience to the civil magistrate, to the neglect of other legitimate authorities, then he was establishing a theology for the messianic State, which would save men through law (legislation). But Paul was the great theologian of salvation by grace, not by works of law.

Paul's general principle is that the **autonomous human conscience**—the independent and undisciplined human conscience—is **not** sovereign above **all** the authorities. "Wherefore ye must needs be subject, not only for wrath, but also for conscience sake" (Romans 13:5). But this does not imply that the human conscience cannot legitimately rebel against the dictates of **one** of these established authorities, **if** conscience is supported by one or more of the other lawfully constituted authorities. **To make the dictates of any single human institution the final voice of authority, in time and on earth, is to divinize an aspect of the creation.** It is to substitute human authority for God's authority. **The Protestant Reformation was a revolution against this very doctrine**. It was a rebellion against the Roman Catholic Church's doctrine that the institutional church can speak infallibly and with God's authority, irrespective of the opinions of any other authority or group of authorities. The Roman Catholic Church had arrogated unto itself a monopoly of authority, not because it said explicitly that there are no other lawful authorities, but because it said there was no earthly court of appeal beyond the Pope when he spoke on moral or religious issues. Yet because all issues are at bottom moral and religious issues, the doctrine of papal infallibility was, in fact, an assertion that in principle, all other authorities are under the final sovereignty of the Roman Catholic Church.

In modern times, almost nobody believes in the infallibility of the institutional church, including most Roman Catholics. The Pope certainly has hesitated to enforce his own pronouncements, let alone the pronouncements of all of his predecessors, by means of the church's bureaucracy. What modern men **do** believe in, however, is the infallibility of the State, or the Communist Party, or the latest reigning bearer of power. And even when they have become totally cynical, believing in the sovereignty of no social institution, they retain faith in the sovereignty of some other aspect of man: the hydrogen bomb, the technology of man, the evolution-directing power of modern biological science, the man-occult link, the genius of the lonely artist, the power of reason, the power of feeling, etc. Men seek salvation by their own hands.

Because in our day the political order has the ability to concentrate the greatest earthly power on any single aspect of human life, the messianic State has attained a God-imitating power. Since there is no earthly court of appeal beyond the State, according to modern humanism, there can be no God to bring judgment on the State. A few rebels think that the inevitable forces of history can judge the bourgeois states (Communist doctrine), or that some other factor in the creation can sit in **impersonal** judgment on the State. They do **not** believe that a personal Creator God can or will bring judgment on the various institutional kingdoms of man.

The State, however, is man's most powerful single entity, and it exacts tribute from its servants in the form of taxation, regulation, and an endless stream of new legislation. It is therefore, **de facto**, the highest court of appeals, the sovereign power which **most** men must placate **most** of the time. A growing number of people throughout the worldwide kingdom of humanism may well reject the theology of the State, but they don't agree on any theology to replace it. The theology of the messianic State is slipping in the last decades of the 20th century, but it has not yet been replaced by any other universally agreed-upon theology. It remains supreme by default.

Welfare

The modern State has advanced its claims of total sovereignty by two strategies: war and welfare. The most crucial institutional aspect of the welfare strategy has been the government education system. By requiring people to educate their children, and by establishing State-financed schools, the State has created a **priesthood**, the State-certified teachers, and an **established church**, the public school system.

Welfare in the Bible is almost invariably private in nature. The few cases that indicate the presence of the civil government are ambiguous with respect to penalties, the agency of enforcement, and whether the replacement of the Old Testament kingdom in Israel by the New Testament's decentralized, international kingdom has transferred enforcement and responsibility to another agency.

Perhaps the most effective example of the function of the civil government in the Old Testament—where the specifics of political responsibility are spelled out in greater detail—is the case of **leprosy**. The civil government had the responsibility of preventing the spread of disease. It did **not** do this by means of a massive public health program. On the contrary, the Old Testament spelled out a system which made a public health program financed by taxation virtually impossible to establish. What the Old Testament civil authorities were required to do was to proclaim a **quarantine**. The civil government's function was entirely **negative**.

The laws governing leprosy are found in Leviticus 13 and 14. The sick man was to be brought before the priests and examined thoroughly. The signs are detailed in Leviticus 13:3-44. "And the leper in whom the plague is, his clothes shall be rent, and his head laid bare, and he shall put a covering upon his upper lip, and shall cry, Unclean, unclean. All the days wherein the plague shall be in him he shall be defiled: he is unclean: he shall dwell alone; without the camp shall his habitation be" (Leviticus 13:45-46). The man or woman was cast outside the city's gates. He could not come into the congregation, his home, or his place of employment. He became an outcast—**the** outcast in Israel, if we don't count religious rebels.

Garments worn by lepers or showing the signs of leprosy had to be examined. Except for those actually being worn by the leper, they had to be burned (Leviticus 13:57). He could not sell them to raise money for his own support. Even a house could be condemned. The priests were required to make a careful inspection of a house that was suspected of leprosy. The owner of the house was required to report any signs of leprosy to the priests (Leviticus 14:35). Any house that gave signs of leprosy after the priests' examination was torn down, and its remains were carried outside of the city and tossed into a place reserved for unclean (polluted, defiled) things.

What was the responsibility of the priests, as agents of the civil government, in compensating the victims? **Nothing.** There is not one word about any form of economic compensation. The authorities came into a man's house, inspected it, and tore it down. The family was left without a home. Yet the civil government was not required by biblical law to pay the victim anything. Or consider the leprous man. He lost his occupation. He was separated from his family. He had to spend his days wandering outside his city, shouting "Unclean, unclean." He became a social outcast. All he could do was beg in the area outside the city, or start a small garden for his food. He could not produce anything for sale in the market, since all the works of his hands were unclean. This was quarantine on a total basis. The lepers had to be separated from all healthy people. The role of the civil government was entirely negative.

Given the defenseless position of the leper, we would think that if the Bible required public assistance, it would be in this instance. The victim faced a disaster that was no fault of his own. He was not lazy. He may have been a property owner. In the case of king Uzziah, whose rebellious act of burning incense upon the altar of incense God judged by making him leprous (I Chronicles 26:16-19), he was quarantined, cut off from the Temple, forced to live in a specially built house (v. 21). Even the king was not exempt from the regulations. In other words, the most influential people in society, the decent citizens, could be cut down by leprosy, but the civil government did nothing for them. If the civil government was not required to give assistance to **these** victims of uncontrollable forces, how in the world can a coherent case be made for "Christian" socialism?

Welfare is to be a product of private decisions. The State is to be kept out of the welfare area because it has a monopoly of tax collection. By providing programs of tax-financed assistance, the messianic State transfers wealth by force from some people to others. It transfers sovereignty from private citizens and voluntary agencies to itself. It consolidates power in the name of necessity. It is forever seeking out new beneficiaries of other people's productive efforts, in order to consolidate raw political power over people. **The welfare function, when centralized and made compulsory, leads to the creation of a messianic State**, and this State becomes arrogant.

With responsibility must come authority in human institutions. With the responsibility to help the poor comes power and influence. The Bible makes it plain that **centralized power is a threat to human society**. Uzziah was not allowed to act both as priest and king; God cursed him with leprosy and separated him from the Temple in order to separate the institutional powers of church and civil government. By transferring welfare functions to the State, voters have established a centralized agency bearing a monopoly of power through compulsory taxation. Local, voluntary countervailing powers suffer a reduction in power, for they suffer a reduction in responsibility. People in a crisis look to the modern State for their healing (another use of the word "salvation," just as a salve heals a burn). The **countervailing power** of private welfare agencies is steadily removed by the increasing welfare functions of the State.

Because the modern State is innately bureaucratic, **charity then becomes a matter of public law**. Bureaucratic rules are established governing the use of public funds. This **bureaucratic procedure** is necessary in order to insure that funds extracted by the public are used by bureaucrats in ways approved by the political representatives of the people. But this means the creation of **a vast system of rules, regulations, forms in triplicate, and investigating teams**. Charity is removed from the scrutiny of those who are providing it, and who must give account to donors who can turn off the funds. The personal judgment of the administrator is hemmed in by legal restrictions, since the State must limit the "arbitrary" decisions of local bureaucrats. The criteria of poverty are centralized, reducing the importance of local conditions, and local judgments by charity providers concerning the needs of recipients. And all the while, the State is expanding its power by creating **a permanent welfare class** which owes its survival (it thinks) to the continued "generosity" of the State.

A universal responsibility for providing welfare will eventually bankrupt the State. Like the continual wars of an expanding empire, the continual "wars on poverty" carried on by messianic States will destroy them. There is never sufficient productivity in the private sector to redress all imagined wrongs, or to compensate all conceivable victims, within a society. Capital is limited. Nature is cursed. There is universal scarcity. But the messianic State refuses to acknowledge the limits on nature. It locates endless cases of poverty, distress, and crisis, but it doesn't have access to resources sufficient to remove these instances of poverty. **What the modern welfare State does is to assert its own divinity**. It comes before men and promises them a universal insurance policy against failure, crisis, and God's judgment. It tells men that nature can be redeemed from the limits of scarcity by the fiat word of the State. **The State becomes an order of salvation**. It promises to roll back the curse of the ground, not by means of biblical law, but by **overcoming the restraints** imposed by biblical law on civil governments.

Is it any wonder that we should witness the rise of the welfare State in the same era that we have witnessed the decline of biblical faith? Men must worship something. They cannot escape their own nature. They are under a sovereign God's power, and when they rebel against this form of subordination, they necessarily substitute another authority, another source of sovereign power, so that they can serve it. **They need power to attempt their rebellion against God's power**. In other words, **you can't fight something with nothing**. You can't fight absolutely sovereign power unless you claim for yourself, or your representative, absolutely sovereign power.

The welfare State is an aggrandizer. It is a self-proclaimed divinity. It tries to become a substitute family, and a substitute church. It tries to provide men with institutional defenses against all disasters. A local private charity can legitimately admit that it doesn't have the resources to solve every problem, but it can concentrate its assets in an attempt to mitigate the effects of **some** problems. A division of labor in combatting disasters can then flourish. But the modern welfare State cannot admit defeat. Defeat is only for private, limited, non-saving institutions. Any defeat suffered by a messianic State is blamed on its enemies: foreign devils, domestic saboteurs, selfish taxpayers, "loopholes" in the tax laws, or whatever. The messianic State must attribute its own failure to inaugurate the millennium, its failure to establish heaven on earth, its failure to overcome scarcity, to the **moral rebelliousness of its political enemies**. The messianic State also has a doctrine of the Fall of man, and it is an ethical Fall at that. Its opponents are stubborn, or crazy, but in any case they need treatment. Men have transgressed the legislation of the State. Men have not turned over all the assets necessary to insure everyone against disaster. Men are in rebellion against the well-intentioned salvation of the politicians and the unelected bureaucrats.

It is sad to say, but there are sympathetic defenders of the programs of the welfare State who also claim to be Christians. They tell us that the Bible teaches that the poor and defenseless must be defended by the efforts of a welfare State, with its programs of compulsory wealth redistribution. But as the hardest case known in the Bible demonstrates, the case of the leper and his household, **the welfare function of the civil government is exclusively negative, the protection of life and property**. In the case of the leper, the protection of the lives of those around him must be the foremost concern of the civil magistrate. The fact that he suffers doubly, from both the dreaded disease and the destruction of his capital, is not to deter the civil authorities. In short, there is no biblical case for the construction of a hypothetically Christian welfare State. The "Christian socialist" is a self-deluded (or demon-deluded) individual. Like the leper, he is infected. In his case, he is infected with a false theology, the religion of humanism.

The fact that there are so many "Christian" socialists in the world today testifies to the failure of orthodox, Bible-believing Christians to take seriously the concrete revelation of the Bible, especially Old Testament law. They have few answers for the "Christian" socialists because they have such a defective version of the Bible. The translation is not the problem; **the unwillingness of modern conservative Christians to accept as binding the whole**

of the Bible is the problem. The existence of so many "Christian" socialists also testifies to the success of the humanists in getting the Christians to send their children to State-certified, tax-supported, humanistic schools. When will Christians learn their lesson?

Discipline

Every law-order must rest primarily on self-government. No law-enforcement agency can possibly afford to trace down every violation of the law, or provide for perfect justice. Certainly, no agency can do this in the midst of a loss of faith in the law-order which that agency seeks to defend. In an age of lawlessness against all authorities—which Paul said would lead to damnation—law enforcement must be limited.

The messianic State cannot admit this. Every wrong must be made good, every crime must be punished: this is the official position of the messianic State. But since this goal is impossible in a world of sin, limited resources, and rebellion, the State's officials must pick and choose. Which laws will be enforced, which violators will be prosecuted, which crimes are intolerable? These questions must be asked by every agency of government, private or civil. Some law-order must be imposed, yet no law-order can be imposed by an outside authority against the wishes of the "protected" citizens. **If a law-order is not enforced by self-government first and foremost, then it cannot hope to persevere.**

Any law-order which has no **enforcement mechanism** isn't a law-order. The family has a means of enforcing the decisions of the sovereign agent, the father. The church has a mechanism for enforcing the decisions of the church's authorities. The civil government also has mechanisms of enforcement. In all cases, the first means of enforcement is **self**-discipline. The Bible provides us with the first principle of a law-order: "The fear of the Lord is the beginning of knowledge: but fools despise wisdom and instruction" (Proverbs 1:7). Again, "Behold, the fear of the Lord, that is wisdom; and to depart from evil is understanding" (Job 28:28). "Fear God, and keep his commandments: for this is the whole duty of man" (Ecclesiastes 12:13). **The first step in government is God-fearing self-government,** meaning **commandment-abiding self-government.**

It is the moral obligation of parents to teach their children the whole of God's revealed law (Deuteronomy 6:6-7). It was also required in Israel that once every seven years, the whole law was read before the assembled congregation of Israel (Deuteronomy 31:10-13). **The terms of God's peace treaty with men are to be universally known.** This, in fact, will mark the external victory of God over Satan, in time and on earth, when no man will need to teach his neighbor the law of God, because the law of God will be universally understood (Hebrews 8:11). Because of the spreading of the gospel into every nation, in principle this prophecy of Jeremiah is fulfilled in our age (Jeremiah 31:34). **The knowledge of God's law is the starting point of every system of government, including civil government.**

The enforcement of God's law is necessarily **decentralized.** In the church, an offense against an individual must be taken by the victim to the guilty party; from there, the complaint, if unsatisfied, is carried up the church's institutional chain of command (Matthew 18:15-18). The same pattern is supposed to be adhered to by the civil government. When the burden of providing personal judgments for all the people of Israel in the wilderness grew too great for Moses to handle effectively, his father-in-law, Jethro, came to him and suggested an alternative. Teach them the ordinances of God, he said, and "shew them the way wherein they must walk, and the work that they must do" (Exodus 18:20). This is the **first** step: convincing the people of their responsibility before God, and giving them the standards of self-evaluation, God's law. **Second,** said Jethro, appoint honest men over the people to try the cases, so that the whole population doesn't have to come to a single man for judgment (Exodus 18:21-22). Get the **division of labor** operating in the field of judicial law. Moses agreed with Jethro, and the system of hierarchical judges was established (vv. 25-26). Here is the biblical pattern of discipline: **the law at the top, self-disciplined men at the bottom, and a system of appeals courts in between.**

The whole system rests on the assumption that men fear God, that they are striving to subdue themselves and their immediate environment by the law of God, that they are essentially self-governed, and that the courts are not clogged with endless appeals. It assumes that men are willing to accept the judgment of other men because both the judges and the judged are striving faithfully to conform to the requirements of biblical law.

Obviously, pagan States are not striving to impose biblical law.

What is the Christian to do when a command of the pagan authority comes into flagrant conflict with the commandments of God? Peter laid down the basic principle: **obey God rather than men**. What a Christian must determine is whether a particular law of the State is directly threatening his position as an ambassador of God's invading kingdom. This is where the other authorities are important. The Christian needs to be able to appeal to the Bible, to elders in the church, and to magistrates at the local level who will recommend resistance to the central government. But when all authorities agree, or at least all of those willing to take a specific stand agree, then the Christian must obey the civil magistrate. Paul's words in Romans 13:2 are too clear. **The individualistic, autonomous resistance to the civil magistrate by the Christian is prohibited**. He must conform to the authorities, and if they are agreed, he has no valid alternative, except to leave the jurisdiction of the civil government under which he lives. **The Bible does not advocate anarchy**.

Modern governments attempt to prejudge the courts. Regulatory agencies operated by tenured bureaucrats are not a valid biblical substitute for the hierarchical system of appeals courts. The central government is not to issue endless regulations so complex that even specialized lawyers cannot decipher them. The idea is to issue **laws that all men can understand** and then **hold each man responsible** for obeying them. The Bible teaches us that **self-government** is the only way any civil government can expect to retain order and freedom at the same time. When central governments become too powerful, when they attempt to redeem every area of life by means of complex formal laws, then they produce a combination of **paralysis and anarchy**. The central government cannot understand the society, nor can the members of that society understand the State's legislation. **Both order and freedom are destroyed**, for the State becomes tyrannical, unpredictable, and arbitrary, while its citizens become hostile, lawless, and rebellious to all constituted authorities.

The State unquestionably has the power of execution. Capital punishment is demanded by the Bible, and the State has no options, once the crime has been determined and the criminal convicted. The fundamental principle of biblical law, however, is **restitution**. The victim is to be compensated. The goal is full restoration, plus a penalty to compensate the victim for his trouble, and also to serve as a deterrent against future criminal behavior. **The State is not to save men from damnation; it is to make possible godly behavior in a world in which the criminal element is restricted and almost completely eliminated.** (The goal of absolute perfection, in time and on earth, must not delude us into believing that it will be attained, nor should men attempt to achieve perfection by constructing a massive State which promises perfection. We may aim at the goal of perfection, but not at the expense of biblical law, which warns against the total sovereignty of any human institution.) Biblical social peace reduces the law-abiding man's costs of dominion.

Conclusion

The civil magistrate is an office established by God for the restriction of evil. The proper standards of the civil law are found in the Bible. Men are to obey the civil magistrate except in cases where it would be immoral to obey, and where support for resistance has been obtained from other ordained officials, meaning lower civil magistrates, or elders in the church. Anarchy is forbidden. Men are to obey for conscience's sake.

Proper civil government is hierarchical. A system of courts must enforce the law by trying specific cases brought to them. The civil magistrate is supposed to proclaim the terms of biblical law to all men, so that they may strive to conform themselves to its standards. The political goal should be **self-government**, not the rule of bureaucrats. The goal should be **universally proclaimed and universally understood law**, not the rule of incomprehensible regulations. The goal is not the creation of an army of lawyers, but of the rule of law in men's hearts. The State is not to become an agency of salvation. It is not to proclaim salvation by law or salvation by works. Its function is to restrain evil, to provide justice, to provide a system of law in which acting men can work out their salvations or their damnations with fear and trembling. The civil magistrate is to suppress evil, primarily violence and fraud. He is to enforce God's peace treaty with men, or God's judgment will be visited upon the city of man. The State's function is **ministerial**, not salvational. It is to **restrain evil**, not create good men. When the State seeks to become an order of salvation, it produces an imitation of hell on earth.

As societies become larger and more complex, the civil government must remain decentralized in order to achieve its goal of creating social peace. The familiar argument of the socialists and interventionists that complex societies require more centralized State intervention is ridiculous. The more complex a society becomes, the less able the State's officials are to direct the society. They are like jugglers who are trying to juggle an ever-growing number of pins, balls, oranges, plates, and other items. It is only by means of **self-government under God's law** that a complex and developing society can regulate itself. As the French social philosopher Lamennais said in the 1830's, **centralization produces apoplexy at the center and anemia at the extremities.** The pyramid society is the society of Satan. It cannot succeed. It will inevitably destroy the social stability necessary for continuing economic development, for the principle of political centralization inevitably comes into conflict with the complexity of a developing economy. The apoplexy at the center cannot effectively maintain a healthy development of the increasingly anemic extremities.

The use of pyramid structures by pagan cultures in the ancient world is no accident. The great Cheops pyramid of Egypt was a representation of the whole world—an almost inconceivable precise mathematical monument. (The best book on this subject is Peter Tompkins' *Secrets of the Great Pyramid.*) A basic principle of occultism and magic is this: "As above, so below." The occultist searches for a "handle" on the universe. He wants power over the external world. He searches for mystical illumination, or some other means of transforming himself and his environment, but through ritual, or special exercise, or secret initiation. The quest is for a magical talisman, or some other device for the representation of the cosmos. If you can manipulate a microcosm (model) of the world, you can achieve power over the world. The most familiar device for most of us is the voodoo doll: stick a pin in the doll, and the person who is represented by that doll is supposed to be harmed.

The tower of Babel (Genesis 11) was another representative pagan architectural structure. It was probably something like the Babylonian ziggurat, a tower made up of concentric circles which resembled a ladder to heaven from whatever direction an observer approached it. Here is the theology that Satan offered to Adam: autonomous man's way to heaven. The tower was a link between heaven and earth, but one which men built, not God. The pinnacle of the tower represented the seat of power, the link between evolving man and the gods. Mankind, or at least representatives of mankind, would bridge the gap between man and the divine. The earliest pyramid in Egypt was a step pyramid, a transitional structure between the tower and the familiar Cheops-type pyramid. Like the Mesopotamian tower, the pyramid was a symbol of the link between heaven and earth. It is not surprising, then, that the pyramid has long been a popular symbol for many occult organizations throughout history.

When we find hierarchical secret organizations—circles within circles, secret initiation rites, secret passwords, arcane symbols—we should be aware of their theological and philosophical origins. When these organizations are invested with power, especially political power, we are face to face with the society of Satan. The biblical principle is the very opposite of the one governing secret societies: "Ye are the light of the world. A city that is set on a hill cannot be hid. Neither do men light a candle, and put it under a bushel, but on a candlestick; and it giveth light unto all that are in the house. Let your light so shine before men, that they may see your good works, and glorify your Father which is in heaven" (Matthew 5:14-16). The single hierarchical power structure, the secret handshake, the inner circle, the system of initiation: here is Satan's rival program to God's system of multiple hierarchies, revealed law, and open evangelism. Christians should understand the difference.

Chapter 7

ECONOMY

The English word, "economy," is derived from the Greek word, *oikonomia*, meaning management. It comes from two other Greek words, *oikos*, meaning household, and *nomos*, meaning law. An economy in this limited sense is the management of a household. An *oikonomos* was a **steward** (Luke 2:2-4). *Oikonomia* also refers to God's divine training of His people, as in I Timothy 1:4, where the King James Version translates it as "edifying": "Neither give heed to fables and endless genealogies, which minister questions, rather than godly edifying which is in faith: so do." (The last two words, "so do," are not in the original Greek; they were added by the translators.).

The steward is a manager of an owner's resources. He is responsible to his employer for all the assets which he manages. This is the biblical doctrine of stewardship. "The earth is the Lord's and the fulness thereof; the world, and they that dwell therein"(Psalm 24:1). "Who am I, and what is my people, that we should be able to offer so willingly after this sort? For all things come of thee, and of thine own hand have we given thee" (I Chronicles 29:14). Men are God's appointed representatives on earth, but Jesus' parables of stewardship indicate that the true owner will not delay forever in His demand for a full accounting from His stewards (Luke 12:42-48; 16:1-8). In fact, the parable provides us with the most important and clearest instruction in the Bible concerning God's final judgment and its eternal consequences, and it lays down the fundamental principle: **from him to whom much is given, much is expected**. "But and if that servant say in his heart, My lord delayeth his coming; and shall begin to beat the menservants and maidens, and to eat and drink, and to be drunken; the Lord of that servant will come in a day when he looketh not for him, and at an hour when he is not aware, and will cut him in sunder, and will appoint him his portion with unbelievers. And that servant, which knew his lord's will, and prepared not himself, neither did according to his will, shall be beaten with many stripes. But he that knew not, and did commit things worthy of stripes, shall be beaten with few stripes. For unto whomsoever much is given, of him shall much be required: and to whom men have committed much, of him will they ask the more'' (Luke 12:45-48).

This doctrine of **full personal responsibility before God** is crucial to our understanding of the Bible's message of salvation. All men are sinners. No sinner can stand before God alone and expect to survive God's eternal wrath. Without Jesus Christ as a man's sin-bearer, meaning a man's **redeemer** (a person who buys another person out of bondage), no man can survive.

Consider yourself. You have read this book this far. You have more knowledge about God's plan of salvation, not to mention man's subordinate plan for damnation, than most people have ever possessed. Not that many people have ever read a whole book on Christ's work and its implications for this world. You are far more responsible before God right now than you were before you picked up this little book. You will have to give an account of your response to the information in this book. You will also have to give an account to God of your handling of all your personal financial assets, from this point forward, in terms of the message of this book. **There is no escape**. You now have the information, and it is your personal, inescapable task for the remainder of your life to work out the implications of your faith, in terms of the information this book has supplied, in fear and trembling (Philippians 2:12).

Ownership

The Bible says that God owns the entire creation, including all the souls in the universe. He proposes and disposes. None can resist His will. But man, who was made in the image of God and who still has a twisted image of God as his very being, has been appointed to be God's steward. Every man is an **economos**, or an economist. Every man makes decisions concerning the resources under his administration. He chooses what things to do with these assets. He says "yes" to one possible use of any given resource, and "no" to all other uses. We are responsible for every single decision we ever make, and this includes our economic decisions.

All economic resources are inescapably **personal**. Ours is a universe of cosmic personalism. There are no impersonal historical forces guiding our decisions. The world is governed by a personal God. All assets must be personally owned, for God owns them all. He may delegate the control over an asset to a man, or to a family unit, or to a unit of the civil government, but men are involved in the allocation decisions at every level, including collective administrative units.

God is both one and many. He is a Trinity. Therefore, responsibility can be both individualistic and corporate. God holds individuals responsible to His laws, but He also holds whole societies responsible, which is why He wiped out the Canaanites. The pure collectivist, who believes that all property should be collectively owned, that the State or the Party should own all scarce economic resources, is denying one aspect of lawful economics, for he is denying one aspect of man's reflection of God's very nature, the individualistic. At the same time, the pure anarchist or individualist who denies the lawfulness of the State as a property manager also denies an important aspect of human society, the collective, for he also denies one aspect of God's being, the collective sharing of decision-making responsibility. The question for any economic order, is where the proper balance is. What is the **proper allocation of responsibility** between the State and the individual, or among the collectives like the family, church, and corporate business, and the individual economic actors?

We need biblical revelation to guide us. This should be the **first principle of Christian economics**. Men will rely on God's testimony concerning Himself and His social creation, or else they will rely on their own rebellious fantasies, their own ideas of where the balance should be.

What we must start with is **the sovereignty of God**. He is the owner of all the creation. Second, all ownership must be **personal**. Third, all men are fully **responsible** for their economic (and all other) decisions. Fourth, as we learn in Genesis 3:17-19, the earth is **cursed**. It now brings up thorns and thistles to interfere with man's stewardship, which is a dominion stewardship. In short, God has imposed **scarcity**.

What is scarcity? The best definition that economists have come up with is this one: "**At zero price**, there will be more demand for an economic good than supply of that good." Air is not an economic good in most cases. At zero price, there is more supply

of it than demand for it. This is not true in a submerged sub-
marine, or on top of a tall mountain, or on the back of a scuba
diver in tanks. It is also not true of cooled air in summer, or warm
air in winter. It is not true of filtered air in a city filled with air
pollution, or a farm area filled with dust. But for staying alive in
most instances, there is no price tag necessary on air. We don't
need to allocate air to the highest bidder. Such a good is not an
economic good. It may well be useful. It may even be life-
sustaining. But it is not an economic good. **It is not a subject of
human choice**. It is not a resource which requires man's decisions
in order to allocate it.

This seems simple enough, but you'd be surprised at how many
people have never thought about it, and how many have come up
with definitions that are just plain stupid. The most influential
economist of the 20th century was John Maynard Keynes, and in
the concluding notes (chapter 24) of his most influential book, *The
General Theory of Employment, Interest, and Money* (1936), he
announced: "The owner of capital can obtain interest because
capital is scarce. But whilst there may be intrinsic reasons for the
scarcity of land, there are no intrinsic reasons for the scarcity of
capital" (p. 376). But capital is simply the combination by man of
land (which he admitted may be intrinsically scarce) and **labor** (including intellectual labor) over **time**. But if one aspect of capital is
scarce—at least one aspect, when in reality all three are
scarce—then inevitably capital must also be intrinsically scarce.
Keynes was a logician; he knew this. Economists are students of
scarcity; they know this. How, then, could Keynes have said what
he did? Because his humanistic system was a defense of the State as
savior, the State as **messiah**, the State as **magician**. As he said on
the very same page, "it will still be possible for communal saving
through the agency of the State to be maintained at a level which
will allow the growth of capital up to the point when it ceases to be
scarce." He knew exactly what he was saying.

Here is the perpetual theme of all socialists and communists: **the
creation is not permanently cursed**. Nature is naturally abundant,
but man's institutions have restrained this natural productivity. If
we only destroy private property, we will be able to live once again
(as our ancient forefathers did) in totally abundant communism.
This is the communist's version of Eden, the return to a golden
age, and in the case of Marxism, a return initiated by bloodshed

and revolution—the theology of human and social sacrifice, as an alternative to Christ's sacrifice. They expect the regeneration of man and the regeneration of nature through the establishment of the collective ownership of property. **Man will regenerate himself by uprooting his present social and political institutions**. This is an ancient heresy, going back to the chaos festivals of the ancient world, where annual ritual law-breaking festivals were supposed to put life back into society. These festivals served as symbols of the coming chaotic revolution which would eventually return society to the lost Age of Gold. (Mardi Gras in the United States and Carnival in the Caribbean are festivals that are remnants of the older chaos festivals.) It is not by the imposition of God's revealed law-order that socialist revolutionaries will progressively bring dominion over the earth, and progressively reduce (though never completely eliminate) the effects of God's curse on the creation. It is by the abolition of God's law-order, the coming revolution against all "bourgeois" institutions, that Marxists believe we will eliminate nature's scarcity. The socialists may forego the use of violence, but they expect the increase of State ownership to bring forth total abundance. They rely on the expansion of State power, and the elimination of private property, to bring in paradise. The State, as the highest and most powerful representative of man on earth, becomes the source of personal regeneration and social transformation.**The State, in short, becomes the modern god.** In the ancient world of paganism, the State was seen as the link between heaven and earth. Modern pagans officially deny the existence or relevance of the gods, but because they deny the existence of any sovereign agency above the State, the effect is much the same: the State is man's only available god walking on earth.

In biblical revelation, the sovereign owner is God. He sets forth laws of administration by which responsible men, both as individuals and as members of collective agencies, are to allocate the resources of their employer, God. Because of man's continuing tendency to elevate himself into the position of ultimate sovereignty over the creation, the Bible consistently **decentralizes** responsibility. The State is drastically restricted by biblical law. It announces God's law, enforces God's law, and adjudicates disputes among men in terms of God's law through a hierarchical appeals court system. But its function, as we have already seen, is almost wholly **negative** in scope. The State is not the initiator. It is rather the **adjudicator**. It provides the institutional support for preserving peace; and men, acting as responsible stewards, both as individuals and as members of **voluntary** collective associations, allocate the scarce means of production.

Discipline

By now, you can probably guess what I'm about to say. The primary form of discipline of God's law-order is **self**-discipline. This is true in the family household, the institutional church, and the civil government. It is also true of the economy. It is the individual worker who is to exercise dominion. He is **called** to his work by God. This is why we refer to a man's job as his **vocation** (the same Latin root underlies **vocal**) or his **calling**. Man is subordinate to God, ultimately. This is why Paul's command is the central command for all economic activity: "...work out your salvation with fear and trembling" (Philippians 2:12b).

Accompanying this subordination to God, which also exists in the family, the institutional church, and the civil government, the economy provides **intermediate levels of responsibility**. Like the other major human institutions, there is a human **hierarchy**, which in turn reflects the hierarchy of the Trinity itself in God's relationships with the world. We have separate tasks as laborers. There is a **division of labor** in the world, just as there is inside the other spheres of human existence. And where there is a division of labor, there must also be a hierarchy of command, since each laborer is responsible for his work. He must answer to somebody on earth, as well as to God. **Whenever a person claims that in his own capacity he answers only to God, and to no other man or institution, he is asserting his own divinity in history.** Like the misused doctrine of the divine right of kings in the early modern period of European history, the doctrine of **unmediated authority** between God and man is an assertion of an individual's independence from earthly judgment, an assertion of personal autonomy, an assertion of **antinomianism** (that is, anti-law). It means that an individual is free to rebel against any authority and all authority, in time and on earth, in the name of his sole allegiance to God. It means that the individual doesn't have to answer to anyone until he is in his grave. It means he is a king on earth, for no person stands above him, in the name of God, to call him to account. Whenever we find this doctrine—against the family, against the institutional church, or against the civil government—we find lawlessness, arrogance, and the scent of revolution, if **individuals** are declaring the doctrine. If a particular **institution** is making use of the doctrine, then we find tyranny, arbitrariness, and centralization, for the director or directors of that institution are saying that they, as representatives of this institution, are beyond criticism from other men or institutions. Such a claim is also an assertion of divinity in history. Orthodox Christianity rejects the doctrine of unmediated earthly authority, whether used by anarchistic individuals or power-seeking institutions. **Orthodoxy rejects the "divine right" of anything or anybody, in time and on earth, except Jesus Christ,** who humbled himself before God and man in order to bridge the ethical gap between God and man. Christ has a monopoly of divine right.

One of the greatest difficulties in describing the workings of a free market is the **apparent anarchism** of market relationships. Defenders of the market order have been generally unsuccessful in explaining to people why such a seemingly anarchistic system should possess any order at all. The defenders have failed to convince men that the market system is, in fact, a system. Socialists and economic interventionists constantly want the State to operate the economy, since there appears to be no man-serving system of discipline in market relationships.

Nevertheless, there must be discipline for any system to operate. We know that the free market has paralleled the greatest growth of human economic welfare in the recorded history of man. Defenders of the free market argue that this free market order has produced the prosperity; socialists deny this assertion, but they have to admit that free market economies have paralleled prosperity chronologically. So it is illegitimate to argue that there is no discipline in market operations. The free market couldn't have survived for two centuries if there had been no institutional discipline, no hierarchy.

What we find in the free market is a **two-way hierarchy**. Because it is a true two-way system, men have overemphasized one side or the other. There is a **hierarchy downward**, from the consumer to the owner of the profit-seeking business. Yet there is also a **hierarchy upward**, from the owner to his managers and then to the sales force. The man caught in the middle is the manager. He must translate the signals sent to him by the **consumers** through the sales force, so that the owners or central managers can make accurate assessments of market demand. At the same time, he must transmit the wishes of the **central managers** to the sales force, advertising force, or research and development team.

Socialists emphasize the power of large-scale corporations to determine what they will produce and then manipulate the consumer, forcing him to buy what they have produced. Free market economists emphasize the sovereignty of the consumer, and the impotence of the central managers to force the consumer to buy anything. They tend to de-emphasize the power of the modern corporation. Who is correct?

No one is absolutely correct in every instance. There are monopolies that can, for a time, impose their will on consumers. They can set high prices for their products or services, and consumers think they have to pay. Of course, the consumers must then restrict their purchases of other goods and services. This means that other corporations lose business. They begin to go out of business. Capital is shifted to serve the desires of those persons who have achieved the monopoly.

The defenders of the market point out that **in almost all known instances of monopoly, the State is the creator**. The State uses the threat of violence to keep competitors out of the market. States grant licenses, or tariffs, or import quotas, or special loans, or other forms of assistance to certain large companies, and the consumer winds up paying a tax to these companies. The tax is imposed by these firms through the coercion of the State. The consumer has his choices restricted by law, and the seller who has the monopoly can then extract a price higher than the market would have permitted, had open competiton been permitted by the State.

Consider **labor unions**. How do the unions "defend the workers" from the "exploitation" of the owners? How can they possibly increase the share of the product going to labor? After all, if someone who sells a service to a buyer of that service starts charging more than the buyer wants to pay, won't the buyer search elsewhere for less expensive services? So how do the unions do it?

It's simple, really. They get the State to make it illegal for competing laborers to offer their services to businessmen who are buying labor. Or more precisely, the State makes it illegal for a buyer of labor services to make the offer to buy at a price below that arbitrarily determined by the union. The union can extract higher prices for its services for its own members, but only by **limiting the membership,** and by **making it illegal for other workers who are not members to sell their services.** The union benefits its members at the expense of non-members.

What labor union supporters never, ever admit is that **the labor unions provide a huge subsidy to businessmen who are not in the unionized sectors of the economy.** You see, all those workers who would like to sell their services to businessmen in the unionized sectors now have to seek employment in the non-unionized sectors. They don't really want to work here, since they really wanted to work in the unionized sectors for higher pay or better working conditions. But the unions got the State to freeze them out. The businessmen in the unionized sectors are not permitted to hire them. So they have to sell their services to businessmen in the non-unionized sectors. These businessmen can then offer lower wages to these workers, since the other businessmen in the unionized sectors are not permitted to hire these "surplus" workers. Their competitors—unionized buyers of labor services—are not allowed by the State to bid for labor services in an open, free market.

What is the economic basis of all trade unions? **Exploitation.** The unions get together with the State. They get a law passed which benefits their memberships at the expense of other workers—the **majority** of workers—who are not union members. They exploit these other workers, and they exploit those businessmen who would have hired these other workers, but who are prohibited by law from doing so. And the indirect result is a transfer of wealth to businessmen in non-unionized sectors. The **exploiters** are the State, the unions, and (indirectly) the non-unionized businesses. The **exploited** are the non-unionized workers who must now seek to sell their services to lower-paying businessmen; also exploited are those potential buyers of labor services who are forced to pay higher-than-market wages to union members. **The majority of workers are exploited by a minority of workers,** and indirectly, also by the majority of businesses that are doing the hiring but which are not yet unionized. In the United States, for example, only 25% of all workers are unionized, a figure which has remained constant for decades. This means that up to 75% of the labor force is being exploited. The 75%, who can vote, continue to vote against their own freedom, their own self-interest, because of their envy against "big business" and their ignorance of economic cause and effect. **Envy plus ignorance** is a catastrophic equation in political life.

Does this mean that all labor unions are immoral? In the 20th century, yes, that's exactly what it means. However, there could theoretically be unions which do help workers without using the coercion of the State to exploit competing workers—the majority of workers. The unions could serve as information gatherers, informing their members of better job opportunities at other plants or in other locations. This would tend to feed labor into those markets in which the highest pay is available. Furthermore, the unions could serve as **voluntary** charity societies, helping members who face disasters. **But in the modern world, where the State is used by special-interest groups to exploit the majority, the compulsory labor union is one of the great offenders. The modern trade union movement is unquestionable, categorically immoral**. Christians should not come to any other conclusion. Those who do are envy-dominated, or ignorance-dominated, or both. Or worse, they may be members of coercive unions who are self-consciously "milking" the system.

Where is the discipline of the market? In the wallets of the consumers. If the consumers refuse to buy from a particular seller, that seller loses income. If the seller continues to offer goods or services at prices the buyers are unwilling to pay, he will eventually go bankrupt. This threat of bankruptcy, or at least reduced sales, is what keeps the businessman alert to the desires of the consumers. He must subordinate **his** estimations of what the consumers ought to want to the **estimations of the consumers,** who tell businessmen daily what they want. The market is merciless. Consumers are sovereign. They decide what they are willing to buy, and from whom, and on what terms. Businessmen can work to convince consumers to buy what they are selling, but that's only a hope. The consumer makes the final deal. He is the responsible agent.

Of course, every consumer is simultaneously a buyer, and vice versa. The producer is **buying money**, while the consumer is **buying goods or services**. A man goes to work in order to "buy money," so that he can later buy goods and services. We labor in order to become future buyers. We sell our resources in order to buy other people's resources. The system is **mutually hierarchical**.

It depends on whether we are entering the market to buy money (as sellers of goods) or to buy goods (as sellers of money).

Each party in a transaction is **legally sovereign**. Nobody has to buy or sell. Each man is fully responsible for his actions. Each person is a **steward before God** over the resources, including his intellectual and labor skills, under his authority. He has sovereignty over the disposal of his goods or services. He can use them up himself, or give them away, or trade them, or loan them. It is his responsibility to make this decision. What the rest of us have the right to do is to approach him with bids. "Give them to me! Loan them to me! Sell them to me! Please. I'll make you a fabulous deal. . . !" And even when someone refuses to listen to us, he suffers the consequences. He forfeits the goods, money, or services we would have provided him if he had only traded or sold to us. Or he forfeits the good feelings he might have had if he had given us the goods. He bears the costs of his decision. He also reaps the benefits (if any).

What the market allows us to do is to make our own decisions about the allocation of our own resources. We seek the benefits. We pay the costs. We make the evaluation of benefits versus costs. We are responsible before God and men for our personal economic decisions. **The genius of the market system is this personal equation between costs and benefits.** The person who is morally responsible before God for the stewardship of God's goods (including the person's life) is the same person who reaps the rewards of any decision, while bearing the costs of that decision.

The free market is the most remarkable institution men have ever developed for making accurate cost estimates. Nothing ever developed historically even comes close. This is very important, given Jesus' warning on making accurate cost estimates. "For which of you, intending to build a tower, sitteth not down first, and counteth the cost, whether he have sufficient to finish it? Lest haply [it happen], after he hath laid the foundation, and is not able to finish it, all that behold it begin to mock him, saying, This man began to build, and was not able to finish" (Luke 14:28-30). Jesus was illustrating a spiritual principle. He warned men to count the costs of discipleship, which is the major theme of Luke 14. He illustrated His warning, however, by means of a situation which was familiar to His listeners, namely, a construction project. The man runs out of money (resources) before he brings it to completion. He estimated the benefits, but he failed to estimate accurately the costs. Men are not supposed to make this mistake in spiritual affairs, nor are they to make the mistake in economic affairs.

The free market imposes a **rigid discipline of costs** on every action. There can be no escape. Each man must make constant cost-benefit estimations. Each man must face the collective bids of all competing sellers when he sells, and all competing buyers when he buys. This is a fundamental premise of a developed free market: **buyers compete against buyers**, while **sellers compete against sellers**. Only in those relatively rare instances (in a developed market, anyway) where a single seller of goods or services (buyer of money) faces a single buyer of goods or services (seller of money) that we find competition between the two. The competiton is based on comparative knowledge of the market (competing buyers for the buyer, competing sellers for the seller), and one of the parties may know more. Or the competition is based on competing sales skills, with the buyer dangling money in front of the seller, and the seller dangling goods or services in front of the buyer. But the broader the market—the more sellers competing against sellers, the more buyers competing against buyers—the fewer cases there are of buyers competing directly against sellers. Sellers establish relatively fixed prices, and then say "Take it or leave it." The consumers then decide which to do.

We usually think of consumers as consumers of goods and services (sellers of money), and we think of sellers as sellers of goods and services (buyers of money). In such a framework, the discipline is that of an **auction**. Buyers and potential buyers bid up the money prices of those items that may interest them. Sellers of such items are also in the auction, and they compete by offering lower prices. When the buyers purchase all the goods that sellers want to offer at a given price—when there are no additional sellers or buyers—we say that the market has established a **clearing price**. It is **the search for this clearing price** by all potential buyers and all potential sellers that constitutes the great discipline of the market. This is the very essence of the **market process**. It is always an **uncertain search**.

Let's take a very simple example. Say that you own a theater. You buy the talents of some performer, or some moving picture, and then you try to sell seats at the theater. You hope to make more money from the sale of seats than it costs you to rent the performer, pay the electricity bill, hire ushers or ticket-takers, and pay for the advertising. Simple enough? Fine. Now here's the big question: **What should the selling price of each ticket be?** The seller of tickets wants the largest income possible. Does this make him an exploiter? Hardly. He just wants to compensate himself for the expenses of putting on the performance, including a return for the **risks** he has taken. He really isn't certain what the proper price is. This is what so few critics of the free market ever understand. **The seller can't be sure.** What should he aim at? That is also simple. He wants to price each seat so that on the night of the performance, **every seat is filled,** and **there is no one waiting in line to buy a ticket.** If he can figure out the "clearing price" of his theater's seats for that performance, he will make his maximum income.

The discipline of the market is merciless. Consumers expect sellers to make accurate estimations of what they **will** be willing to pay for goods and services. The entrepreneurs (forecasters) who want to serve the desires of consumers then have to **estimate** what consumers **will** want in the future, what it **will** cost to get what they want into their hands, what they **will** be willing to pay for these goods and services, and what **will** be left over for himself after all expenses are paid. **The future is uncertain.** The Bible warns us about this. Man cannot know everything perfectly. He cannot know the future perfectly. Yet he has to deal with the future in terms of his knowledge and his resources today. Men must count the cost of reaching goals in the future. And what we all know is that we, and others, **constantly make mistakes** when we try to estimate future costs and future benefits.

We are stewards. We are not to waste the resources entrusted to us by our Master. We are to increase the value of the assets that are under our administration, as Jesus warned us in the parable of the talents. Jesus said that the kingdom of God is like a man who is planning a journey to a far country, and who selects several subordinates in terms of their varying abilities, and he gives each one some coins. One man receives five coins, another two, and another only one (Matthew 25:15-16). **This parable absolutely denies the concept of equality of opportunity,** if by this doctrine we mean equal starting positions in the race of life, for the men have varying skills and varying initial capital bases. So influential is this parable in Western thought that we refer to a man's talents when we speak of his skills, but the **talent** of the parable was a coin: the initial capital, not the initial skills, of each steward. (The "talent" was a unit of weight in the ancient world, one used in weighing coins.) Upon his return, the master calls each man to give an account of his stewardship. He expects each steward to have increased the number of talents in his possession (Matthew 25:20-23). The skills of each man are different, the initial capital is different, and the ultimate rewards are different. The only equality in the parable is the **equality of the law** under which each steward operates. None can escape the final day of reckoning. In fact, the very term, "day of reckoning," means a day of giving an account, a final counting.

Here we find the familiar themes of the whole Bible: the sovereignty of God, who is the Creator and therefore the owner; the assignment of dominion to individual men, for which they are held fully accountable; the provisioning of them with resources, including the most critical resource of all, **time**; their efforts to increase their assets, as a sign of their successful dominion; and a day of final judgment, when the Master returns in power to judge every man's performance. And it is **the free market**, as a system of making accurate estimations of costs and benefits, through its system of freely fluctuating money prices and open competition, which provides man with **a crucial tool of dominion**. It is man's **counting system**. It disciplines each man, forcing him to keep accurate records and make accurate predictions.

The free market provides us with **mutual discipline**, for we are all both producers and consumers. There is a **hierarchy**, with consumers sovereign over the assets entrusted to them. There is a system of **consumer sovereignty**, which is of course a system of delegated sovereignty from God, one which is implied by His granting of resources to His people and even to His enemies, in time and on earth. At the same time, the division of labor has led to the creation of **organizations of production**, in which rulers and subordinates cooperate in order to meet consumer demand. The factory is a **hierarchy**, while the market is a system of **mutual discipline**. But the factory, the sales force, and corporate management must be subordinate to the market if the business is to prosper, unless it is able to get the State to step in and protect the firm from consumers' sovereignty, by substituting **State sovereignty** and **bureaucratic sovereignty** in place of consumers' sovereignty.

Intervention

No earthly institution is absolutely sovereign. We have to understand this principle if we are to understand the Bible's view of God, man, law, and human institutions. Therefore, **the free market isn't absolutely sovereign**. There are areas for legitimate intervention by the State. We have already seen one of these: quarantine in the case of leprosy (Leviticus 13 and 14). Another area is the right of the civil government to establish minimum safety standards. In ancient Israel, the Israelites were required to put safety railings on all **new** homes built in the land of Canaan (but not on the homes which had belonged to the Canaanites), because in those days, flat roofs were used for entertaining guests (Deuteronomy 22:8). The courts also assigned full responsibility for damages to a man who started a fire on his property, which then spread to a neighbor's property (Exodus 22:5-6). This, by extension, would include other types of damage, such as air or noise pollution. In other words, the civil government can step in and prohibit certain types of **actions that injure innocent bystanders**, even though such actions allow producers to produce less expensively. There are certain kinds of costs that can be passed onto other people (smoke, noise, etc.) who are not beneficiaries. Costs then rise, but the beneficiaries (producers) don't bear all these extra costs. The equation of costs and benefits that the individual producer must make as a steward before God (and as a profit-seeking actor) becomes unequal: the producer (seller of goods) becomes the total beneficiary, but he passes on some of the costs of production to innocent bystanders. The civil government is empowered to step in and assess costs, imposing these extra costs on the potential beneficiary of the production process, namely, the producer-seller. The civil government can therefore act to reduce these "spillover effects" by requiring **restitution** on the part of the guilty party to the victims. The threat of making restitution thereby increases the likelihood that producers will bear a larger proportion of the total production costs.

It is simply impossible to make a biblical case for a zero-civil government society. **There can never be a valid case for "Christian" anarchism, any more than a valid case for "Christian" socialism**. But a careful reading of the Bible reveals that the civil government is basically an institution for establishing God's justice by means of courts of law. The principles of biblical law are to be imposed on the market: restitution, prevention of coercion, prevention of fraud (false weights and measures: Leviticus 19:36), national defense, law enforcement, enforcement of contracts (including marriage contracts). The Bible rejects the socialists' utopia of a **caretaker State**. The Bible's description comes far closer to the traditional free market ideal of a **night-watchman State**.

The State is to prevent moral evil. The Old Testament is only too clear on this point. Sexual deviation is prohibited: homosexual acts (Leviticus 20:13), prostitution (Leviticus 19:29), beastiality (Exodus 22:19). adultery (Leviticus 20:10), and incest (Leviticus 20:11). **The State is not creating good men** by enforcing such laws; it is merely **preventing evil acts** between consenting, but deviant, adults. These laws protect the family, and the holiness of God demands that the State enforce such laws. The anarchist would not allow the State to punish a homosexual adult who solicited sexual favors from 8-year-old boys in exchange for heroin. Those who proclaim a zero-State society, whether in the name of Christ or the name of reason, are forced by the logic of their position to come to just this conclusion. The Christian doesn't have to accept this conclusion. Pure anarchism (anarcho-capitalism) is unbiblical.

Why should the State prohibit sexual acts by consenting adults? Who is hurt? Outside parties are hurt. Innocent bystanders are hurt. Why and how? Because **God promises visible, external, national judgment on whole societies that violate His moral laws**. The anarchist assumes that there is no God, or that God will not bring judgment to a whole society because of the flagrant and public sexual rebellion of some members of that society. The Bible tells us specifically that God has, does, and will bring judgment on sexually deviant societies, and that it is the sign of a society's respect for God—men's fear of God—that the civil government be empowered to punish sexual deviation.

Obviously, such sins must be public acts. The Bible does not teach that the **secret** acts of a **minority** of citizens will bring God's judgment on the nation. The Bible does not sanction an army of inquisitors who knock down doors and break into bedrooms. The "night-watchman State" of the Bible does not grant to the bureaucrats that many economic resources. They cannot afford to hire such a standing army of inquisitors. But if the sins are public and flagrant, if other members of the household call in the authorities to suppress the sin, or if the evidence of the sin becomes available to law-enforcement officials in the normal course of investigation, then the State must deal with the crime. Even if the free market's mechanism produces profit for sellers of moral evil, the State is empowered to prohibit it. The market is not absolutely sovereign. We must not defend the idea of the "divine right of the free market." The Bible tells us that there are limits on the market, as there are on every human institution. But it also tells us that there aren't as many limits as modern socialists would like us to believe.

It is also interesting to note that John Maynard Keynes, the 20th century's most influential economist, and a defender of increased economic intervention by the State, was a homosexual. His associates in Britain's so-called Bloomsbury Group were notorious sexual deviates. He did appreciate the free market in one respect, however: his ability to travel to Tunisia on homosexual quests with his friends, where they would purchase the favors of boys. Keynes was perverse in more areas than just economic theory. (For a thoroughly documented account of the Bloomsbury Group, see Michael Holroyd's two-volume biography of one its most notorious members, *Lytton Strachey: The Years of Achievement, 1910-1932* [1968]). Keynes favored State intervention into economic production, not sexual morality. He favored controlled markets and uncontrolled debauchery. The Bible almost exactly reverses this perspective.

Economic Development

Deuteronomy 8 and 28 lay down the fundamental principles of a growing economy. That principle is simple: conformity to the laws of God, by individuals and also by the civil government. Welfare is to be voluntary; poverty is to be eliminated steadily by advancing per capita wealth. **The economic argument for creating a welfare State is negated, since increasing personal wealth throughout the covenantal society is sufficient to alleviate the major causes of poverty.** There will always be poverty, Christ said. The poor shall always be with us (Matthew 26:11). The question is, rather: What will the **relative poverty** be between godly societies and ungodly societies? The poor man in a godly society will enjoy external blessings greater than those in poor, backward societies. The funds available for charitable giving are also greater in advancing economies.

We know that we cannot expect economic growth forever. In a finite universe, nothing can grow forever. After all, if the four billion people in the world in 1980 were to reproduce so that the total population increased at 1% per year for a thousand years, there would be 83 **trillion** people in 2980. Obviously, this won't happen. But the very fact that God promises compound economic growth to His people in response to their obedience to His law indicates that **we live in a world that is going to come to an end**. We cannot experience economic growth forever. The Bible says we will have compound economic growth in response to our faithfulness. Therefore, we can conclude that if we are faithful, we will have economic growth, and this points to the day of judgment, which will cut time short.

The zero-population growth advocates and the zero-economic growth advocates are humanists who want to believe that there will not be a day of judgment. They recognize that we live in a world of finite resources, and they don't want to admit that time is in very short supply. So they conclude the obvious: we cannot hope to have compound economic growth forever. But this is the wrong conclusion. Instead of arguing for the State to cut short all economic growth, they should argue for God's cutting short of man's time on this cursed earth. They should argue for the new heavens and new earth (Isaiah 65; Revelation 21, 22).

The Bible calls for us to pursue economic growth. **Long-term economic growth is a sign of God's blessing on His people**. True, it should not be pursued as such. "But seek ye first the kingdom of God, and his righteousness, and all these things shall be added unto you" (Matthew 6:33). **All these things**: here is the promise of economic growth and prosperity in response to covenantal obedience. It also includes large families, since both sickness and miscarriages will be eliminated (Exodus 23:25-26), and large families are recommended (Psalm 127:3-5), and long life is promised (Exodus 20:12). If you have a high birth rate, and the children survive, and people live longer, you will have a massive population explosion. **The population explosion is a means of dominion**. We will have both growing per capita wealth **and** rapidly increasing numbers of people. This can't go on forever, of course. It goes on until the day people rebel against God, or until the Day of Judgment comes. **Rapid growth is a blessing of God which points to our final deliverance from sin and bondage.**

Economic growth comes to societies that respond to God's call to repentance. This doesn't mean that every single redeemed man will become rich, or that all the sinners will go broke. What it means is that **as a general phenomenon, those living under the rule of God's law-order will prosper, and that those living in societies that are in rebellion to God will not prosper.** Long-term economic growth for an entire nation is a sign of God's blessing. Long-term poverty for an entire nation is a sign of God's wrath. Of course, in a **transition stage** between faithfulness and arrogance, wealthy societies can continue to experience external economic growth. We find this in Deuteronomy 8:10-17. A rebellious society can be lured into total destruction by its own external blessings. **But long-term poverty is always a sign of God's curse.** The so-called under-developed societies are underdeveloped because they are socialist, demonist, and cursed. **Any attempt to blame the poverty of the underdeveloped world on the prosperity of the West is absolutely wrong.** This is the old Marxist and socialist line. It blindly fails to acknowledge the wrath of God on demonic, tyrannical, and socialist tribal cultures. There are too many books being written by ostensible Christian scholars, who are in fact outright socialists and Marxists hiding behind a few out of context Bible quotes, that attempt to make Christians feel guilty for their prosperity in the face of the "Third World's" poverty. In fact, the Bible tells us that **the citizens of the Third World ought to feel guilty**, to fall on their knees and repent from their Godless, rebellious, socialist ways. **They should feel guilty because they are guilty, both individually and corporately.** As God warned the Israelites: "And it shall be, if thou do at all forget the Lord thy God, and walk after other gods, and serve them, and worship them, I testify against you this day that ye shall surely perish. As the nations which the Lord destroyeth before your face, so shall ye perish; because ye would not be obedient unto the voice of the Lord your God" (Deuteronomy 28:20).

Guilt-manipulation by misguided or in some cases unscrupulous scholars should be seen for what it is. The blood of Jesus Christ has removed our guilt. Our adherence to biblical law, with its requirement of the tithe, is sufficient to remove the power of the professional guilt-manipulators. This is one reason why tithing is so important for the kingdom: it removes the psychological leverage that "Christian" socialists have over modern Christianity, especially over the Christians who have subjected themselves intellectually to the socialistic, Marxian, and Keynesian humanisms of the modern university.

The call for "economic justice," meaning socialist programs of wealth redistribution, with the civil governments of the West financing the socialist tyrannies of the Third World, is a sham. It is a lie. It blames the West for the generations and even millennia of perverse wickedness on the part of the Third World's demon-worshipping tribes. When the socialist-Marxist government of Zimbabwe (formerly Rhodesia) elevated witch doctors back into a position of prominence in the summer of 1980, those leaders helped to seal the doom of Zimbabwe. We should not be deluded about who is responsible for the lack of economic growth in the Third World. **They** are responsible. Their abject poverty **is** economic justice: God's economic justice. He promises that same poverty for all nations that rebel against Him. Poverty is exactly what they deserve.

Did Israel send foreign aid to the Canaanites? Was Israel to be burdened by guilt feelings because Jericho residents had lost their housing? Did God tell Israel that the nation should be taxed, especially the rich, so that Israel could launch a program of international foreign aid? Yet Christians who ought to know better have swallowed this socialist propaganda because a group of socialists parading under Christ's banner have written books telling them that they're guilty, and that we need more socialism, more confiscatory taxation, and more State-to-State foreign aid schemes. Christians who fall for this nonsense are helpless to defend themselves because they simply don't know what the Bible says about economics, poverty, and the messianic socialist State. They are **easily manipulated** because they are **wilfully ignorant**.

Men don't want to believe that there is a relationship between moral rebellion and economic crises. Even free market economists refuse to consider such a possibilty. Almost all modern economists, for example, look at the Great Depression of the 1930's and conclude that capitalism was a failure, that it collapsed, that statist intervention was needed to save the capitalist system. Yet what preceded the Great Depression? The "Roaring Twenties," with its debaucheries, its moral rebellion, its erosion of the family, its revolutionary art, its humanism, its ridicule of

Christianity. All over the West, the nations turned from God to man as the source of prosperity. Man couldn't be stopped. Man was on the way to Easy Street. Man was now the king.

Then there were the massive war debts from World War I. All the nations had floated huge loans to finance the war. Their central banks had printed up billions of dollars or pounds or francs or marks to finance the war. Inflation became a way of life in the West when the War broke out. The gold standard was abandoned. Credit was extended everywhere. Market speculation was rampant—a rational, if dangerous, response to the inflationary policies of the State. Then, when the monetary inflation led, as it always does, to contraction bankruptcies, bank holidays, and depression, the various governments intervened to pass tariffs, legislate fixed prices (when prices should be falling to clear the market of unsold goods), and fix wages (when wages ought to be falling to clear the labor market of unemployed men). Men grew despondent. Pessimism overtook the capitalist system, precisely because men had worshipped mammon, had inflated their nations' currencies, and had made debt a new way of life. Was this the fault of capitalism? Or was this the fault of wartime economics, domestic monetary inflation, the arrogance of man, and a moral rebellion against God? And more to the point, was the modern humanist State any better able to solve economic problems than the humanistic free market? Is the market as such a failure, or the humanists who buy and sell in that market, financing the system with government-created fiat money?

Conclusion

The Bible teaches that by **service to men** a man becomes a leader. Jesus told His disciples: "And whoever will be chief among you, let him be your servant: even as the Son of man came not to be ministered unto, but to minister, and to give his life a ransom for many" (Matthew 20:27-28). The theme of the suffering servant who later triumphs, who serves faithfully and then succeeds economically, is a familiar one in the Bible. Jacob served his lawless uncle, Laban, under difficult conditions, but then became rich (Genesis 31:1, 36-42). Joseph served faithfully in Potiphar's house, only to be cast into prison on false charges (Genesis 39). But from the prison, Joseph rose to the second in command of all Egypt (Genesis 41:38-43). David served king Saul faithfully, in war

(I Samuel 17) and in peace (I Samuel 16:15-23). Yet Saul turned on David and sought to kill him, again and again (I Samuel 18:10-11; 19:10; 23:7-8,15). Saul had to admit that David had served him faithfully, and that David was more righteous than he was (I Samuel 24:17-19). And Saul also recognized what David's service had won him: "And now, behold, I know well that thou shalt surely be king, and that the kingdom of Israel shall be established in thine hand" (I Samuel 24:20). David became the king. **Service leads to successful dominion**.

The market encourages men to serve their fellow men if they wish to increase their own wealth. Each man faces market demand. Consumers are bidding against each other constantly in order to buy what they want. These signals in the form of prices tell potential producers what the costs of any action are. They tell entrepreneurs that there are potential profits available to those who successfully **forecast** future demand, and who recognize an opportunity for profitable sales that competing entrepreneurs fail to recognize. That's where profits come from. Entrepreneurs who think they see an opportunity for future sales to consumers go into the resource markets and buy up scarce economic resources—raw materials, capital equipment, labor services, etc.—at low prices. The prices of these resources are low because other entrepreneurs have failed to see the potential for future sales to consumers. So entrepreneurs buy low and sell high, but not at the expense of consumers. They are selling consumers the goods they want at prices they are willing to pay. **The profit comes from the other entrepreneurs**, who failed to recognize an opportunity, and who therefore hesitated to buy up the producers' goods earlier. **The consumers are benefited**. After all, what if even this entrepreneur hadn't seen what they were going to want to buy in the future? Then consumers would have been forced to select from even fewer of these now-demanded products. The consumers have been helped; the profit comes from the successful entrepreneur's ability to **forecast** the consumers' desires, and then to **organize production efficiently** and profitably.

In short, **profitable stewards on a free market are faithful servants**. They need not be suffering servants. Perhaps they make continual profits by their continuing ability to forecast the future. After all, that's how Joseph was able to benefit Pharaoh: he knew the future state of supply and demand. But he had received God's revelation which informed him of the coming bountiful harvests and the seven years of famine that followed (Genesis 41). He knew the future, and he gave sound advice to Pharaoh about how to deal with the predicted future conditions. But you and I aren't like Joseph. You and I don't know the future that perfectly. You and I must bear the risks of uncertainty—the unknown future which we all must deal with, one way or another, as long as we're still breathing and making decisions.

What the free market does is to establish a close relationship between **personal costs** and **personal benefits**. What it also does is to establish **a system of money calculations,** whereby we can make more accurate estimations of costs and benefits. What the market does is to process everyone's best efforts in predicting the future, and the result is today's array of prices. What the market does is to force each man to bear the costs of his own efforts. It weeds out those who waste scarce economic resources, who fail to serve consumers at the least expenditure of resources. What the market does is to provide the **personal freedom** for each man to work out his calling before God with fear and trembling. What the market has produced is the **greatest output of goods and services in the recorded history of man**.

The market is nonetheless despised by socialists, Marxists, and other defenders of salvation by statist action. They worship the State. They see the concentrated power of the messianic State as mankind's one hope of justice. They reject the notion that **personal economic freedom is among the most important freedoms that a political order can offer to its citizens**. They call for ever-more intervention, ever-more regulation by the central government. And some of them do so in the name of Jesus. They conclude that Jesus wanted us to establish a statist order because there is injustice in the world. Conclusion: the State is the source of justice, the only means of righting the wrongs produced by the market. The result, all over the world? A rising tide of statism, and a rising tide of resentment, envy, and revolution. God will not be mocked. The whole world faces a series of potential economic catastrophes.

The market provides discipline: mutual discipline of buyers and sellers, with buyers competing against buyers, and sellers competing against sellers. It also provides a **measure of success** for serving consumers faithfully: **profit**. It provides a **hierarchical**

enforcement system, with consumers on top, signaling their desires to middle and higher management by means of buying or refusing to buy from any given company. The higher managers must tell the lower managers what to do, generally, though not in the details, and middle managers must carry out these general guidelines. The consumers then vote for or against the products.

The market is no better than the consumers. If they want evil things, the market will provide them efficiently. This market should not be autonomous. Just because selling some product or service may produce a profit doesn't mean that the State should permit it to be sold without the threat of punishment. But for **most** of our needs, **most** of the time, the market provides the **finest integrating device** known to man, a system which allows producers and consumers to mesh their individual plans by means of a competitive price system. The **harmony of humanity** is fostered by the competition produced through the free market. By serving his own interests, the profit-seeking producer must seek the good of others. Here is Jesus' golden rule in action: do unto others as you would have others do unto you (Matthew 7:12). And the marvelous feature about the free market is this: if you do it well, you may make a very handsome profit. You can do very well by doing good.

Nevertheless, perhaps the most important feature of the free market in the final decades of the 20th century is this: **its success makes unnecessary the messianic State.** When men's incomes are growing, and their personal responsibility is increasing, and their range of choices is increasing, they have even less excuse for calling on the god of the State to save them, protect them, care for them, and bear all responsibility for them. **The market renders Satanic man with even less excuse.** For dominion men, it provides the economic framework for long-term economic growth and long-term cultural dominion. The socialists will fail, massively, when the socialist system paralyzes the productive, dominion-oriented producers. And when it does, statism's intellectual defenders will be recognized finally for what they are, namely, defenders of the economics of Satan.

SUMMARY OF PART II

Society entails **responsible cooperation** among men. It relies on the concept of **self-government**. Any social order which minimizes self-government, substituting the rule of any single policing institution, is doomed to failure. God has established **multiple institutional authorities**, and these lawful institutions restrain individuals, as well as restrain each other. The idea of **checks and balances** is implicitly Christian. Such a concept of social order stems directly from the Bible's doctrine of the total depravity of man. Man has rebelled against God; therefore, no man and no human institution can be fully trusted. Since man was unwilling to subordinate himself to God, he is therefore unfit to rule absolutely as a pseudo-God.

Even in Eden, the Bible indicates, no single institution was absolutely sovereign. **Only God is absolutely sovereign, even when man is ethically perfect.** The presence of the family in Eden was inescapable, but before there was a family, Adam had an assignment. This assignment was intellectual in nature, but it also involved the idea of choice and allocation. So there was an economy in Eden. Adam was a ruler as a husband, but he would have been a ruler as a father. He was also a priest, and as a priest, He owed God full worship. This implies the existence of a church, a community of worship. It is most difficult though not impossible to make a case for the civil government in Eden, and it is indicative of the nature of paganism, ancient and modern, that the State becomes the primary institution in society.

Any attempt on the part of rebellious man to eliminate the family, or to subordinate the economy to the State, or to rule the State by the institutional church, or to abolish all institutions except the family and the market, or any other combinations or permutations of rebellion, cannot hope to survive in the long run. There are times when any one of these institutions is subordinate to another (in wartime, for example, the State might be seen as temporarily dominant), but no institution is absolutely subordinate. Even in wartime, the Bible says, newlywed husbands cannot be drafted into military service for twelve months, for the sake of the wives (Deuteronomy 24:5).

What we have in the biblical social structure is **balance**. What we have is both **social order** and **personal freedom**. What we have is **self-government under God**. What we have is full responsibility of men and institutions under the law of God. What we have, in short, is **biblical covenantalism**.

What we don't have is bureaucratic stagnation. What we don't have is a social pyramid, with a single human institution on top, and with all other institutions dependent on that one institution for guidance and support. What we don't have is the unitary State. The unitary bureaucratic State is implicitly demonic, for it is Satan's rule of top-down power, not God's system of upward responsibility, where those on the bottom are the initiators, and those on the top are adjudicators.

The pyramid system is evil. It is the tower of Babel. It is the Pharaoh's architecture of the divine-human link. Wherever it exists, human freedom is stamped out. What is needed to counteract the pyramid society is a system of **multiple hierarchies**, none of which is absolutely sovereign over the others.

Consider the problem of adultery. Obviously, the family is involved. The whole authority pattern of the family is shattered by adultery. The law of God has rules dealing with adultery for the family. It has ways for solving the problem. But adultery also has implications for the institutional church. The church's government structure steps in and begins to bring solutions to the problem, as a lawful institution exercising authority over family members. But the civil government also has partial authority over the family in this case. A covenant has been made between two parties, and this is a civil covenant. Who is to gain custody of the children? Who is to be judged the victim of the adulterous partner? Who is to be given alimony, or assessed some sort of damages? The State intervenes to provide legal answers that are binding on the partners. Then, too, the economy is affected. Will both parents enter the labor force? Will one of them wind up on the charity rolls? Will the children be able to go to college? Who will finance their educations? What consequences will there be for the economic structures of any new families that are formed by the divorced family's original partners? The economic consequences of adultery cannot be avoided.

This is what a system of multiple hierarchies is all about. No institutional structure has absolute and final sovereignty in handling the problem. At the same time, all may have lawful authority to take steps to deal with the problem, insofar as God's law reveals the specific areas of responsibility to the administrators of each governmental unit. All of them involve government or rule. The State, meaning the **civil** government, is not "**the** government." It is only one governing body among many.

This is what biblical social order is all about. Where we find the pyramid structure instead of multiple hierarchies, we know we are entering the society of Satan.

PART III

EXPECTATIONS

INTRODUCTION TO PART III

By now, you are becoming aware of the remarkable alternative that Christianity offers to the modern humanist cultures. It offers **stability**, with the promise of **growth**. It offers law, but with full personal responsibility for responding to it. It rests on the idea of **self-government under God**, by means of God's law, rather than conformity to a massive messianic State, with its endless regulations, tyrannies, and arbitrariness. It offers **increasing wealth** for the vast majority of those who live under its laws. It offers **freedom of choice** on a scale never dreamed of by ancient man, or even man in the 1930's. It offers **meaning in history**, for it proclaims an absolutely sovereign God who brings all things to pass—all things, not just some things. It puts us in communication with a God who knows everything, controls everything, and reveals Himself to us. We deal with **a God of absolute justice**, and who enforces the terms of His law to the last jot and tittle, yet **a God of absolute mercy**, who spared not His only begotten Son, that whosoever shall believe on Him shall have everlasting life.

Christian social theory offers us a doctrine of the Trinity which tells us much about our social institutions. We learn that God is both **one** and **many**, that He is fully personal. This God employs the **division of labor**, with each Person of the Godhead performing separate functions with respect to the creation, yet with each Person equal in majesty to the other two. The creation reflects this arrangement. Man lives in a social world which imposes full personal responsibility on the individual, yet at the same time imposes responsibility on the collective associations of mankind. **Society is therefore one and many.** Neither anarchic individualism nor collectivistic holism is biblical. At the same time, God has revealed through His law the standards of responsibility, so that a **proper balance** between the one and the many can be established in

175

human society.

We therefore avoid the twin pitfalls of total decentralization (fragmentation) and total centralization (statism). We achieve **a balanced social order**, in which neither of the extremes of power-seeking and judgment-avoiding rebellious men can be established.

But it isn't enough to proclaim the foundations of a godly society, nor is it sufficient to describe some of the institutional arrangements of such a society. What is needed is a **dynamic**, a psychologically motivating impulse to give godly men confidence that their efforts are not in vain, and that their work for the kingdom of God will have meaning in the future, not just in heaven, but in time and on earth. We need a goal to sacrifice for, a standard of performance that is at the same time a legitimate quest. What is needed is confidence that all this talk about the marvels of the kingdom of God becomes more than mere talk. What is needed is a view of history that guarantees to Christians **external, visible victory, in time and on earth**, as a prelude, a down payment, to the absolute and eternal victory which Christians are confident awaits them after the day of judgment.

Here is where most attempts at sketching a Christian social order break down. Some Christians, of course, reject the whole notion of a distinctly Christian social order, even as a hypothetical ideal. Others think that this ideal is closer to humanistic socialism, or perhaps medieval guild socialism, than it is to the decentralized social order described in this book. Others may believe in the kingdom blueprint described here, but they have concluded that the church will fail, in time and on earth, to institute the reign of God through his people and their construction of law-honoring, decentralized institutions. Still others who say they agree with the blueprint think that Christians will reign, in time and on earth, but not before Christ comes physically to set up His earthly kingdom, which Satan and his troops will rebel against just before the day of judgment, a thousand years after Christ returns physically to set up His kingdom. Until He returns in power to smash His opponents, however, the church will become more and more impotent, more and more persecuted, and we can expect no victory as a result of our efforts, but only by means of a great discontinuous event, the second coming of Christ. Until He returns, our lot will be progressive defeat, in time and on earth. There is no relationship between what the church accomplishes in history and what

Christ will inaugurate immediately after He returns.

But what if these opinions are totally incorrect? What if the following scenario were the case? First, God saves men through the preaching of the gospel of Jesus Christ. Second, these men respond in faith to God's dominion assignment, given to us through our fathers, Adam, Noah, and Christ in the great commission (Matthew 28:18-20). Third, these regenerate men begin to study the law of God, subduing their own hearts, lives, and areas of responsibility in terms of God's comprehensive law-order. Fourth, the blessings of God begin to flow toward those who are acting in His name and in terms of His law. Fifth, the stewardship principle of "service as a road to leadership" begins to be acknowledged by those who call themselves Christian, in every sphere of life: family, institutional church, schools, civil government, economy. This leads to step six, the rise to prominence of Christians in every sphere of life, as Satanists become increasingly impotent to handle the crises that their world-and-life view has created. Seventh, the law of God is imposed progressively across the face of each society which has declared commitment to Christ. Eighth, this provokes foreign nations to jealousy, and they begin to imitate the Christian social order, in order to receive the external blessings. Ninth, even the Jews are provoked to jealousy, and they convert to Christ. Tenth, the conversion of the Jews leads to an unparalleled explosion of conversions, followed by even greater external blessings. Eleventh, the kingdom of God becomes worldwide in scope, serving as a down payment by God to His people on the restoration which will come beyond the day of judgment. Twelfth, the forces of Satan have something to provoke them to rebellion, after generations of subservience outwardly to the benefits-producing law of God. Thirteenth, this rebellion by Satan is immediately smashed by Christ in His final return in glory and judgment. Fourteenth, Satan, his troops of angels, and his human followers are judged, and then condemned to the lake of fire. And finally, fifteenth, God sets up His new heaven and new earth, for regenerate men to serve in throughout all eternity.

If men really believed that this scenario is possible—indeed, inevitable—would they redouble their efforts to begin to subdue the earth? If they knew that their every effort would be credited not merely to their account in heaven, but to the account of God's historical church, and also to the person's account here on earth, would they work to subdue the earth? If they knew that **God's plan for history is cumulative**, and that each effort by His saints adds up, building the foundation for the institutional reign of Christ, in time and on earth, would they redouble their efforts? If they believed that no great cataclysm is going to bail them out, that no miraculous return of Christ physically to pull their chestnuts out of the fire is going to happen, would they work more efficiently to get their lives in order, their zones of responsibility in order, and their children better trained to fight Satan's lies? If they believed, in short, in the **continuity of victory**, in time and on earth, precept by precept, line upon line, here a little, there a little, until the people of God will stand victorious, having subdued most of the earth by means of God's regenerating grace and God's sanctifying law, would they begin to work in world-subduing ways? Or would they wait passively, for better, stronger, and more committed Christians to establish their piece of the kingdom, committed Christians like Caleb—85-year-old Caleb (Joshua 15:6-15)—when he and his family entered the land of Canaan?

We need to know what the Bible says about God's kingdom. We need to know if we are expected to bring the kingdom into visible power by our own efforts, under God's directing sovereignty, or whether we are to expect continual failure, until some sort of discontinuous event breaks through history, overcomes our failure, and elevates us to seats of power despite our demonstrated weakness and incompetence. We need to know whether God really expects us to win, just as He expected and commanded the Israelites to win, when they entered Canaan. We need to know whether we can expect failures as great as those suffered by the Jews, even though we preach the gospel of Jesus Christ, and Him resurrected. We need to know whether the gospel of Christ is no more powerful as an historical force than the shadows possessed by the Jews in the years before Christ's death and resurrection.

And when we know, and believe, and proclaim the truth, the world won't know what hit it.

Chapter 8

THE KINGDOM OF GOD

The best place to begin a study of the kingdom of God is to go to the parables and analogies regarding the kingdom which Jesus gave to His disciples. Some of them are what we might call "pocketbook parables," dealing with economic analogies. The parable of the talents is an example (Matthew 25:14-30), or the parable of the clever steward (Luke 16:1-11), or the parable of the unjust servant (Matthew 18:23-35), or of the field in which a treasure is buried (Matthew 13:44), or of the analogy of the pearl of great price (Matthew 13:45-46). Others are "agricultural parables," such as the parable of the four seeds (Matthew 13:3-23), or the parable of the mustard seed (Matthew 13:31-32). But one of the most illuminating is **the parable of the wheat and tares.** "Another parable put he forth unto them, saying, The kingdom of heaven is likened unto a man which sowed good seed in his field. But while men slept, his enemy came and sowed tares among the wheat, and went his way. But when the blade was sprung up, and brought forth fruit, then appeared the tares also. So the servants of the householder came and said unto him, Sir, didst not thou sow good seed in thy field? From whence then hath it tares? He said unto them, An enemy hath done this. The servants said unto him, Wilt thou then we go and gather them up? But he said, Nay; lest while ye gather up the tares, ye root up also the wheat with them. Let both grow together until the harvest: and in the time of harvest I will say to the reapers, Gather ye together first the tares, and bind them in bundles to burn them; but gather the wheat into my barn" (Matthew 13:24-30).

This parable confused His disciples. It was deliberately intended to confuse the masses who came to listen to Him, as He explained: "All these things spake Jesus unto the multitude in parables; and without a parable spake he not unto them: that it might be fulfilled which was spoken by the prophet, saying, I will open my mouth in parables; I will utter things which have been kept secret from the foundation of the world" (Matthew 13:34-35). When the disciples asked Him why He spoke always in parables, He told them: "Because it is given unto you to know the mysteries of the kingdom of heaven, but to them it is not given" (Matthew 13:11). He spoke in parables, citing Isaiah 6:9-10, in order to keep the listeners in darkness: "For this people's heart is waxed gross, and their ears are dull of hearing, and their eyes have closed; lest at any time they should see with their eyes, and hear with their ears, and should understand with their heart, and should be converted, and I should heal them" (Matthew 13:15). There have always been people who haven't liked the idea that **God deliberately hides the saving grace of the gospel from some rebellious men**, but He does. Isaiah said so, Christ said so, and Paul said so (Acts 28:27).

So the disciples were confused by the parable of the wheat and tares. Christ explained it to them. "He answered and said unto them, He that soweth the good seed is the Son of man. The field is the world; the good seed are the children of the kingdom; but the tares are the children of the wicked one. The enemy that sowed them is the devil; the harvest is the end of the world; and the reapers are the angels. As therefore the tares are gathered and burned in the fire, so shall it be in the end of this world. The Son of man shall send forth his angels, and they shall gather out of his kingdom all things that offend, and them which do iniquity; and shall cast them into a furnace of fire: there shall be wailing and gnashing of teeth" (Matthew 13:37-42). And the crowning triumph: "Then shall the righteous shine forth as the sun in the kingdom of their Father. Who hath ears to hear, let him hear" (Matthew 13:43).

The tares and the wheat continue to grow together in the field. **There is no rooting up of either tares or wheat until the final day of judgment.** This is extremely significant as an insight into God's plan for history. History unfolds as a field planted with two kinds of seed. One seed grows unto righteousness, and the other seed grows unto perdition. But the two grow side by side in the world. Neither is rooted up before its time, and both are rooted up on that final day. Each seed works out its particular destiny, and each type of seed develops according to its inherent characteristics. This is a parable describing the **continuity of history,** on earth. There is no discontinuity in the development of the two kinds of seeds. There is no premature rooting up of the wheat. From seeds to full-grown plants: there is no break in the process. Then comes the day of harvest, which is the day of burning for the tares.

If anyone looks at the parables of the kingdom, he finds this concept of historical continuity repeated. The parable of the talents teaches that each man develops his capital, working out the implications of his faith, in responsible or irresponsible steward-ship. Then comes the day when the Master returns. Again and again, the parables point to the continuity of history, with good men and bad men working side by side in the same world, until the return of God in final judgment. There is only one return. There is only one judgment. There is only one period of rewards and punishments. **There is no great intermediate discontinuous break in the development of the two principles, good and evil**. The evil seeds have no warning of the impending judgment. They have no period in which the wheat is pulled up, and then replanted after a period of time, testifying to the tares of what is coming at the end of the age.

Speaking of the final judgment, Christ instructed His disciples: "But as the days of Noah were, so shall also the coming of the Son of man be. For as in the days that were before the flood they were eating and drinking, marrying and giving in marriage, until the day that Noah entered the ark. And knew not until the flood came, and took them all away; so shall the coming of the Son of man be" (Matthew 24:37-39). There was no break with history prior to the great Flood, Christ said. There was no warning that a mighty change was almost upon them. There was no warning. They couldn't look back and see that something like the Flood had hap-pened before. Nothing like the Flood had ever happened, and nothing quite like it will ever happen again, as the rainbow testifies to us (Genesis 9:15-17). But the day of judgment is analogous to the Flood, in this sense: it is a mighty dividing point, in which the sons of Satan will perish utterly, and the sons of God will not. The natural sons will perish, and the adopted sons will not. And the point of Christ's words dare not be missed: **there will be no warning, no discontinuous event** which breaks with the familiar patterns of life, to sound the alarm for the ethical sons of Satan to hear.

This is what the Bible teaches about the kingdom of God. For many of you, it will seem very peculiar. Perhaps the idea of the day of judgment sounds too impossible to believe, and you will point to the continuity of history to make your point. I can well understand this approach to such a message of the coming perdition. It's the same response the people of Noah's day made to Noah. But what astounds me is that there are literally millions of Christians who don't believe what these parables teach about the development of good and evil. They believe that there will be a massive discontinuous event, possibly more than one, in which Christ will come first for His people (the wheat), gather them up into the sky, and keep them suspended there for up to seven years. Then He will replant them, except that they will be fully grown and already harvested, right next to the tares, and to make things even more complicated, He will sow the field again with another batch of wheat seeds. How in the world could the tares miss the significance of events like these? What a warning of the radically discontinuous event to come, namely, the last day! Yet Christ pointed out that at that final day, people will go about their business as they did before the Flood in Noah's day—not after the Flood, not after a great warning had been sounded, but before. If a great historical discontinuity in between the planting of Christ's kingdom and the final harvest is actually coming, why didn't any of our Lord's parables or analogies so much as mention such an event or events to come?

If we are to take the parables seriously, then we have to begin to think about **the continuity of history in between Pentecost and the final judgment**. If there is no great break coming which will divide this period into two or more segments, then whatever happens to the world, the flesh, the devil, and the church (institutional) must happen without direct, cataclysmic intervention, either from God or Satan. The process will be one of growth or decay. The process may be an ebb and flow, heading for victory for the church or defeat for the church, in time and on earth. But what cannot possibly be true is that the church's victory process or defeat process will be interrupted and reversed by the direct, visible physical intervention of Jesus Christ and His angels. **No discontinuity of history which overcomes the very processes of history in one cataclysmic break will take place.** Christians must not base their hopes for collective or personal victory on an historically unprecedented event in history which is in fact the destruction of history. They will sink or swim, win or lose, in time and on earth, by means of the **same sorts of processes as we see today**, although the speed will increase or decrease in response to man's ethical conformity to God's law, or his rebellion against that law.

Growth

"Another parable put he forth unto them, saying, The kingdom of heaven is like to a grain of mustard seed, which a man took, and sowed in his field: which indeed is the least of all seeds: but when it is grown, it is the greatest among herbs, so that the birds of the air come and lodge in the branches thereof" (Matthew 13:31-32). From something tiny to something substantial, from something almost invisible to something that gives support and shelter: here is the way that the kingdom operates in time and on earth. It is a growth process—continuous, not cataclysmic—which leads to its visibility among men, and its support for men.

"Another parable spake he unto them; The kingdom of heaven is like unto leaven, which a woman took, and hid in three measures of meal, till the whole was leavened" (Matthew 13:33). First of all, before anyone jumps to conclusions, **leaven is not a symbol of sin.** The Hebrews were not permitted to eat leavened bread at the Passover, but leavened bread was used in the sacrifice of the peace offering (Leviticus 7:13). The leavened bread was offered as the first-fruits of the Lord, meaning the **best** of a family's productivity: "Ye shall bring out of your habitations two wave loaves of two tenth deals: they shall be of fine flour; they shall be baked with leaven; they are the first-fruits unto the Lord" (Leviticus 23:17). **Leaven is the best man has to offer, the bread he eats with pleasure**. It is man's offering to God. The Passover avoided leaven. In the Passover, people also ate bitter herbs with their unleavened bread (Exodus 12:8). This bread and bitter herbs symbolized the hard times in Egypt, the world out of which God had delivered them. Unleavened bread avoided the additional **time** necessary for yeast to rise—a symbol of a major historical discontinuity, for God delivered them from Egypt overnight. Unleavened bread symbolized God's overnight deliverance, since it was not the best of what man had to offer God. God broke into the daily affairs of His people and delivered them from bitter herbs and unleavened bread. He delivered them into a land flowing with milk and honey, a land in which men have the wealth and time to bake and eat leavened bread. They were to offer this bread to God in thankfulness. **Leaven is a symbol of time, of continuity, and of dominion**.

But what was the meaning of unleavened bread? Why were the Hebrews required to eat it at the Passover? Why were they required to get rid of all leavened bread in the land for a week before the feast? (Exodus 12:15). Because the original Passover was celebrated in Egypt. It was **Egypt's** leaven which had to be purged out of their midst, before they left the land. It was a symbol of Egypt's culture, and therefore of Egypt's religion. Leavened bread was representative of the good life in Egypt, all of those benefits in Egypt which might tempt them to return. So God required them to celebrate a **discontinuous event**, their overnight deliverance from bondage. They were to take no leaven with them—none of Egypt's gods, or religious practices, or culture—to serve as "starter."

Once they entered the land of Canaan as conquerers, they were **required** to eat leavened bread and offer it as a peace offering to God. This was the leavened bread of the first-fruits offering. This is why Christians are supposed to eat leavened bread when they celebrate Communion (the Lord's Supper). It is a symbol of conquest. **We are now on the offensive, carrying the leaven of holiness back into Egypt, back into Babylon**. We are the leaven of the world, not corrupting the unleavened dough, but "incorrupting" it—bringing the message of salvation to Satan's troops, tearing down the idols in men's hearts. **God's holy leaven** is to replace **Satan's unholy leaven** in the **dough of the creation**. Leaven is therefore not a symbol of sin and corruption, but a symbol of growth and dominion. It's not a question of an "unleavened" kingdom vs. a "leavened" kingdom; it's a question of **which** (whose) leaven. It's not a question of "dominion vs. no dominion"; it's a question of **whose** dominion. The dough (creation) is here. Whose leaven will complete it, God's or Satan's?

The kingdom is like leaven. Christianity is the yeast, and it has a leavening effect on the pagan, satanic cultures around it. It permeates the whole of this culture, causing it to rise. **The bread which is produced by this leaven is the preferred bread**. In ancient times—indeed, right up until the 19th century—bread was considered the staff of life, the symbol of life. It was the source of men's nutrition. "Give us this day our daily bread," we are to ask God (Matthew 6:11). The kingdom of God is the force that produces the fine quality bread men seek. The symbolism should be obvious: Christianity makes life a joy for man. It provides man with the very best. It is what all men really prefer, when they have the time and money to obtain it. Leaven takes time to produce its product. **Leaven is a symbol of historical continuity**. Men can wait for their leavened bread, for God gives them time sufficient for the working of His spiritual leaven. They may not understand how it works, how the spiritual effects spread through their culture and makes it a delight, any more than they understand how yeast works to produce leavened bread, but they can see the bread rising, and they can see the progressive effects of the leaven of the kingdom. They can look into the warming oven and see the risen bread. If we really push the analogy, we can point to the fact that the dough is pounded down several times before the final baking, almost as the world pounds the kingdom; but the yeast does its work, **just so long as the fires of the oven are not lit prematurely**. If the full heat of the oven is applied to the dough before the yeast has done its work, both the yeast and the dough are burnt, and the burnt mass must be thrown out. But given sufficient time, the yeast does its work, and the result is the bread men prefer.

What a marvelous description of God's kingdom! Christians work with the cultural material available, seeking to refine it, to permeate it, to make it into something fine. They know that they will be successful, just as yeast is successful in the dough, if it is given enough time to do its work. That's what God implicitly promises us in the analogy of the leaven: **enough time to accomplish our individual and our collective tasks**. He tells us that His kingdom **will** produce the desirable bread. It will take time. It may take several poundings, as God, through the hostility of the world, kneads the yeast-filled dough of man's cultures. But the end result is guaranteed.

But what about the terrible things that the whole world suffers? What about bloodshed, chaos, fear? Christ's words are familiar to many Christians: "And ye shall hear of wars and rumours of wars: see that ye be not troubled: for all these things must come to pass, but the end is not yet" (Matthew 24:6). The words may be familiar, but are they really understood? Jesus has announced a remarkable prophecy: there shall be wars and rumors of wars. We should expect this. We should not be troubled. Why not? For the end is not yet. But how are we to know for certain that the end is not at hand? Precisely **because** there are wars and rumors of wars.

Why can't modern Christians understand this? Because we hear of wars, and because they keep breaking out, we know that the end is not yet. We need not be troubled, for this, too, shall pass. What shall pass? Wars and rumors of wars. What Christ told His disciples in no uncertain terms is this: **there must come an era in which Christians shall not be besieged with wars and rumors of wars.** And this period is not on the far side of the day of judgment, for the end is not yet. When shall the end come? **After** a period in which men do not make war, and the rumors of wars finally cease. What else could Christ's words mean? **The sign to His people that the end is not imminent is the very existence of wars and rumors of wars.** For as long as they exist, the end is not yet. After they cease, we can start thinking seriously about the possibility of the end of this fallen world. When the world is subdued to the glory of God, **then** we face the increasing possibility of the end. When the yeast has done its cultural work, and men are at last eating the fine leavened bread that the Christian yeast has produced, **then** they can contemplate the final judgment. When all men have before their eyes the testimony of God to the success of His law and the success of His ambassadors in bringing peace and justice to the world, **then** the rebels will have something to rebel against in that last desperate act of Satan and his host (Revelation 20:7-9a). That rebellion will be immediately crushed (Revelation 20:9b-10).

It is one of Satan's most successful lies that Christians look at their defeats on the battlefield of faith, that they listen to rumors of wars, and see wars on their television screens ("Live and direct by satellite: nuclear holocaust! Full details at eleven."), and they conclude that Jesus is coming soon. But Jesus is **not** coming soon, if we accept His words at face value. We are still besieged by wars and rumors of wars. God's kneading process is still going on. The yeast has not done its work yet. The dough is not ready for the oven. The time has not come for eating the leavened bread. There are still wars and rumors of wars; therefore, **the end is not yet.**

Now it might be possible to argue that Christ meant that wars and rumors of wars will continue, and that Christians will be pounded down, until the hypothetical first return of Christ, when only His people will be raptured into the sky, after which He shall return with them (now fully transformed, possessing their perfect bodies) in power to set up His earthly kingdom. This could be interpreted as the era of the oven, when God's leavened bread will be baked, and men will love one another and eat the bread of righteousness in peace. Wars and rumors of wars could then be seen as pointing to the first return of Christ, and therefore our end—our preliminary end—does draw nigh in the midst of wars and rumors of wars. But this interpretation is in flagrant opposition to Christ's parables of the kingdom, which rely on the idea of **continuity in history**, the unwillingness of God to separate the wheat from the tares until the final judgment, when the tares will be burned. According to this misinterpretation, the tares are not burned at the hypothetical first return of Christ in power, which is to be followed by a thousand-year direct reign, in time and on earth. The tares remain in the field, along with a mixture of fully redeemed Christians in their new, perfect humanity (I Corinthians 15:52), side by side new converts to Christ, in their normal bodies— the kind Christians presently battle with—and side by side the tares. What kind of agriculture is this? What kind of agricultural parable can be conformed to this sort of discontinuous agriculture, an agriculture of **premature uprooting**?

What modern Christians have abandoned is the concept of slow but steady growth. Christians sometimes want victory for the church, in time and on earth, prior to the final judgment. They believe in it. But they are so discouraged by the signs of the church's present impotence, and the visible power of Satan's troops, that they conclude that they need a divine miracle, a radically discontinuous intervention in history, in order to bring them the cultural and political victory they long for. This was the error of the Hebrews in Jesus' day: they expected the messiah to set up an instantly successful Jewish kingdom in tiny Palestine. That's why the crowds rushed to welcome Jesus to Jerusalem at the beginning of the Passover week, and that's why they crucified Him at the end, when He failed to give them what they wanted: a miracle elevating them to total power, despite their own failure to exercise power on earth in terms of God's law. They had rejected the primary tool used in God's dominion assignment. They had broken the terms of His peace treaty. They had violated His revealed law continually, having substituted the words of men. Yet they expected the messiah to place the keys of dominion right in their laps. Christ rejected their offer of an earthly kingship on their lawless, treaty-breaking terms. They crucified Him.

Isn't this basically what the modern church wants? Don't Christians expect God to promote them overnight from buck private at least to captain? Some of them are corporals, and they expect to become field grade officers, preferably bird colonels, in one move. Christians want to become field marshals, just like the native corporals in Africa became field marshals once the British and French pulled out. But what kind of field marshals should we expect on this basis? We have seen the "field marshals" in the African "democracies." A hundred years ago we would have called them tribal tyrants. Men who have no idea what a kingdom is elevate themselves from "President for Life" to "Emperor for Life" in Africa. And a few years later, or less, they are assassinated. A short reign indeed. But Christians expect Christ to bail them out of their present troubles, and to stand behind them, like a cosmic big brother, in the coming kingdom where He shall rule directly on earth. He will tell us exactly what to do, and He will back us up, day by day, moment by moment. He will give us a totally centralized political system, and we will be obedient bureaucrats, initiating nothing, rescinding nothing, making no mistakes, and making no responsible progress. We shall serve in a real kingdom as play-pretend rulers. We will carry out our orders. We shall not mature personally. God will subdue the earth using us as crude tools, since we have failed to subdue it as maturing stewards. We are perpetual failures.

Such a view is a counsel of defeat. It means that God's plan in Eden has been successfully overthrown by Satan. God's hope to have man, specifically created to exercise dominion, actually exercise dominion as a faithful, fully responsible subordinate, has been destroyed. God finally calls the experiment to a halt. "Get down there, Son," He says to Jesus, "and clean up this mess. They can't rule, they can't build anything permanent, they're a bunch of foul-ups, and you're going to have to get in there and fix it up. Don't give one of them an ounce of personal responsibility. Don't let one of them make an independent decision. No mistakes, from now on. I'm tired of their mistakes. They're a wash-out. Give them their officers' epaulets, make every one of them at least a second lieutenant, but You give every command. They couldn't tie their own shoelaces without making a mess of it."

And Satan's reponse? "It's just what I told you. I told you so about Job, and I told you so about them. They ignored your law. They wouldn't bear any serious responsibility. They were culturally impotent. Your kingdom plans are a shambles. Sure, You're a Big Shot. You can always get in there and straighten things out. Everyone knows that. But Your plan was a failure, your hopes for man an illusion, for You didn't plan on me. I stopped you. I messed them up. I may not be the Almighty, but I sure am pretty mighty. I was mighty enough to thwart the very definition You gave to man, the very being You made him: **dominion** man. He's no dominion man. He's nothing but a rotting robot. That's it, God, your great work of art, the capstone of creation, the being who possesses your very image, is nothing but a breathing robot. Personality? Nonsense. He's a robot. You're right, man can't tie his own shoes; not even Your adopting can change that. I may be going into the lake of fire, but I proved my point. Your second lieutenant, redeemed man, is no more a second lieutenant than some brand-new recruit. And I'm the one who did it to You!''

Christians believe this all too often. Maybe they haven't thought through the implications of their hope in a premature rapture into the clouds, and their hypothetical return in glorified bodies to rule the earth as robot bureaucrats, but they ought to think about it. They have denied the reality of the parables of growth. They have denied the reality of God's dominion assignment. Millions of them explicitly deny their obligation to use God's revealed law as a tool of dominion, or in any other way. Yet they hold out hopes for a promotion. They all want to become officers, but few of them want to attend officers' candidate school. Boot camp, they believe, is just about all they can handle. That's what the generation of the exodus thought, too, and they died in the wilderness, all except Joshua and Caleb. They died in boot camp.

The parables of growth point to a fulfillment of God's plan, in time and on earth. They point to **a steady expansion of the leaven of the gospel.** They point to an expansion of God's kingdom, in time and on earth, as the leaven makes something edible of the **fallen dough** of creation. **The fallen dough will rise.** It takes leaven. It takes kneading. It takes time. But the fallen dough of the cursed creation will rise. God promises this. But Christians still refuse to believe it. When Christ announces "The kingdom of God is like unto . . . ;'' they reply, "Oh, come on, it couldn't be like that. No, it's really like this. . . '' Some Christians substitute a parable of uprooted wheat, which is then replanted, though fully mature, alongside of the still-maturing tares, and alongside of

newly planted wheat. Others, who do believe in historical continuity, have rejected this vision of a premature uprooting. But they
have no confidence in Christ's earthly leaven, either. They wind up
arguing for the triumph of Satan's earthly leaven. Satan's leaven
will steadily push out the few remaining traces of Christ's cultural
leaven. Only at the final judgment will Christ return in power, in-
stantaneously remove Satan's leaven, and instantly fire up the
oven, leaving His earthly leaven, the church, to do its work instantly, raising the dough in the midst of the oven. In other words,
their view of the leaven of the church violates the whole analogy,
that is, the steady rising of the dough before the oven's final baking.

Both approaches are popular. Whichever of these two substitu-
tions a man accepts, he has abandoned the analogy of the leaven.
He has abandoned the principle of godly growth over time. He has
abandoned Christ's explicit teaching concerning the true nature of
His kingdom. He may deny the continuity of growth (uprooted
wheat). He may deny the continuity of victory (Satan's leaven
wins). Christ's dominion man must fail, in time and on earth. In
the second view, Satan's leaven triumphs, and God doesn't even
bother to go through the "breathing robot" stage, with the direct
rule of Christ, in Person, through His robots. God just scraps
history, wiping out Satan. God redeems the earth in an instant,
makes His people into fully redeemed, perfect dominion men, who
now can exercise dominion over a fully redeemed creation. The
garden of Eden was a failure as a training camp for dominion; the
land of Canaan was equally a failure as a training ground for
dominion; and finally, the church of Jesus Christ, the New
Jerusalem, winds up an historical failure as a training ground for
dominion. Nothing worked, so God will scrap the whole program
in an instant and intervene graciously to give us the victory on a
platter. Here is a revised version of the parable of the mustard
seed: just add instant judgment (since time, God's law, and the
ethical subordination of Christ's church to the Master obviously
failed, and since the preaching of the gospel failed, and since
Christian institutions failed), and presto: **an instant mustard tree.**
So much for continuity.

What does God expect to accomplish, total victory? Yes. Does
He expect to achieve total victory, in time and on earth? No. He
doesn't offer total victory to cursed mankind. Paul's first letter to
the Corinthian church spells this out in considerable detail. We

must be changed, in the twinkling of an eye (I Corinthians 15:52). The final discontinuous event, the ascension of the saints (sometimes called the "rapture") and their instant transformation, brings the final judgment and the creation of a new world, **that final oven in which the leaven-filled, risen kingdom is baked**. Peter wrote: "But the day of the Lord will come as a thief in the night; in the which the heavens shall pass away with a great noise, and the elements shall melt with fervent heat, the earth also and the works that are therein shall be burned up. Seeing then that all these things shall be dissolved, what manner of persons ought ye to be in all holy conversation and godliness, looking for and hasting unto the coming of the day of God, wherein the heavens being on fire shall be dissolved, and the elements shall melt with fervent heat? Nevertheless we, according to his promise, look for new heavens and a new earth, wherein dwelleth righteousness" (II Peter 3:10-14). The whole earth is going to be burned up, producing a new loaf. The whole earth is subject to that final transformation. This implies that the whole earth shall have been filled with the leaven of the gospel—not perfect, but ready for the oven. Then our bodies will be transformed, glorified, for "flesh and blood cannot inherit the kingdom of God; neither doth corruption inherit incorruption" (I Corinthians 15:50). The continuity of history is finally interrupted. This is the end of the world.

But that's the point: it's the end of the **whole** world. What area of life will avoid this final conflagration? Which part of the leavened dough will be untouched by the blinding heat of the oven? Which part of the loaf will be left unbaked? None of it. The boundaries of God's kingdom are the boundaries of the whole earth. It is the task of every Christian to serve as yeast for a fallen world. It is a task that cannot legitimately be avoided. Can we point to whole portions of the unleavened dough and say: "Well, that's not the responsibility of Christians. The law of God doesn't apply there. The dominion assignment doesn't cover that zone. Satan owns that section, lock, stock, and barrel"? What does Satan own? Why, the very gates of hell cannot prevail against the church (Matthew 16:18). Satan doesn't hold title to anything. He lost title at the cross. Or better put, **his lease was cancelled**. Jesus announced in the vision given to John: "I am he that liveth, and was dead; and, behold, I am alive for evermore, Amen; and have the keys of hell and of death" (Revelation 1:18). **Satan is a lawless squatter.** The world belongs to God, and He has designated it as our inheritance. But we need to **subdue** it, to lease it back from God by demonstrating our commitment to the terms of His peace treaty with us. We conquer by the preaching of the gospel. Out sword is the **sword of the gospel**. It is still our assignment to subdue the earth, and by the sword of the gospel we will conquer.

The Last Outpost

There are too many Christians who have read Christ's statement about the gates of hell not prevailing against the church. They have interpreted these words as if Christ had said: "...and the gates of the church shall prevail against hell." They think of Satan as a captain of an invading army, and we are faithfully defending God's fortress. We expect to see our supplies cut off. We expect rationing of water. We expect to see our comrades picked off by the sharpshooters in Satan's vast army. But at the end, we know that the gates of the church shall prevail. The shrinking boundaries of Christ's kingdom shall not be reduced to nothing. We know that at the moment when all seems lost, Christ will come riding up on a white horse, with the main army. We will hear the trumpet sounding "Charge!" just before the satanic invaders bash down the gates. That will show them! They will snatch defeat from the jaws of victory, while we will snatch victory from the jaws of defeat.

Who is "we" in this reworked parable? What have "we" accomplished? So we have held the fort. The little piece of earth that flies the flag of Jesus will have been defended. Big deal. What God told Adam to do, and what He told Noah to do, was **to extend His kingdom over the face of the earth**. He announced our full responsibility in this dominion assignment. Christ came down as our Supreme Allied Commander and announced: "All power is given unto me in heaven and in earth. Go ye therefore, and teach all nations, baptizing them in the name of the Father, and of the Son, and of the Holy Ghost, teaching them to observe all things whatsoever I have commanded you: and, lo, I am with you alway, even unto the end of the world. Amen" (Matthew 28:18-20). So what are we so proud of? That we defended the outpost? That we were willing to fight to the last man? That we kept Christ's flag from being torn down by Satan's host? We, meaning Christians living in time and on the earth, are the victors? In what sense? We stood firm, of course, and were almost wiped out. We advanced nothing, extended nothing, and were nearly overrun. Why, we didn't even do as good a job as the Israelites did in Canaan. They were told to wipe out the Canaanites, but were only able to drive out some of them. But we will supposedly be found on that final day as the Hebrews found the Canaanites: holding down the fort, with our feet planted by the walls of the tiny town, doing our best to keep from being overrun, and praying fervently for God's supernatural troops to show up and deliver us from imminent defeat—the last defeat. "But let's not give up! The gates of the church will prevail against hell! To the ramparts boys, and don't fire until you see the whites of their eyes! Don't give up, boys, there'll be medals of honor for us all when Jesus comes with the main army!''

Medals of honor, indeed. For whom? For a bunch of insubordinates? For a bunch of fearful incompetents who shoot themselves in the foot every third volley? For defending the last outpost from an attack from all directions, when they were ordered to advance in all directions?

The modern church sees itself as the reserves. The main army is in heaven, and we're the reserves, fighting to defend Christ's fort. Why Christ is waiting to send in the main troops isn't quite clear. Reserves are notoriously incompetent. The army calls them up and sends them in to hold on until the main troops can be assembled, armed, and sent into the fray. The reserves have to hold on until the main army comes. You can't expect much from the reserves, after all. Nobody ever does. All they can do is hold out until relief comes.

This picture is all wrong. The church, since the day of Pentecost, has been the invading army. **The church is the main army**. The reserves are in heaven, waiting to deliver the final, crushing blow to Satan's forces. Angels serve men. We shall judge the angels (I Corinthians 6:3). We are made in the image of God; the angels aren't. We were assigned the dominion work, not the angels. We are attacking Satan's territory, not the other way around. Satan is trying to hold down the fort, not us. We know his fort will not prevail in that final day. We will have Satan's troops bottled up inside that fort just before Satan tries one last counterattack, when the angels come to bring final judgment on this world. **God's angels do the final mopping-up operation**. The basis of victory will already have been established: the preaching of the saving grace of Jesus Christ, and the enforcement of His kingdom's peace treaty, nation by nation, one by one.

Christians have to rid themselves of Satan's lie, namely, that the church isn't the main army during its stay on earth. The "church triumphant" in heaven can't help those of us who remain. All the church in heaven can do is praise God, and cry out: "How long, O Lord, holy and true, dost thou not judge and avenge our blood on them that dwell on the earth?" (Revelation 6:10). **Christ is waiting for His church to surround Satan's last outpost. Christ is waiting for the work of the leaven to replace Satan's leaven in the dough of creation**. But the modern church can't believe this. They see themselves as surrounded, outpost by outpost, denomination by denomination. Each outpost has seen others fall to Satan: to theological liberalism, to evolutionism, to Marxism, to "liberation theology." The few outposts remaining are filled with discouraged troops. "Christ just has to come soon with the main army. We don't believe that we can win now. We've spread our forces too thin." Each little band is surrounded. "They've cut us off from each other, and now they're going to pick us all off, one by one." The best each little garrison hopes to accomplish is to be the last outpost standing when Christ finally sends in the main force. Each one wants to be the last little band still on its feet. For today's Christians, that's considered a major victory. This is the mentality of the reserves, and "green" reserves at that.

Christians give far too much credit to angels. Angels are powerful, and God's angels protect us from the devil's angels, and sometimes from the devil's earthly troops (II Kings 6:15-20). But they aren't that important in human history, or else God's word would have revealed more about them. What God's word **does** warn us against is sin, to serve the evil purposes of Satan, to worship gods other than the God of the Bible. What is central to man's history is not the comparative power of angel armies, but the **ethical decisions of men**. Satan only pulled a third of the angels with him (Revelation 12:4), so if it were a question of the comparative strength of the two armies, the issue would have been settled in Christ's day, or even before man was created. This should tell us that the angels are secondary. **What is primary is the war between the kingdom of Satan and the kingdom of God, in time and on earth**. The angels are **our** reserves; we're not the angels' reserves. Satan's men have fallen angels to serve them, until the day when those angels attack Satan's own earthly troops (for his is a divided kingdom), as Revelation describes: "And the fifth angel sounded, and I saw a star fall from heaven unto the earth: and to him was given the key to the bottomless pit. And he opened the bottomless pit; and there arose a smoke out of the pit, as the smoke of a great furnace; and the sun and the air were darkened by reason of the smoke of the pit. And there came out of the smoke locusts upon the earth: and unto them was given power, as the scorpions of the earth have power. And it was commanded them that they should not hurt the grass of the earth, neither any green thing, neither any tree, but only those men which have not the seal of God in their foreheads. And to them it was given that they should not kill them, but that they should be tormented five months: and their torment was as the torment of a scorpion, when he striketh a man" (Revelation 9:1-6). Who gets tormented? **Satan's** followers. It reminds us of the plagues of Egypt, when the priests of Pharaoh were successful only in adding to one plague imposed by God, not in removing the plague. Egypt wound up worse off because of the Egyptians priests' connection wth Satan's demonic host: more frogs (Exodus 8:7), rather than fewer frogs. It may have made Pharaoh secretly happy when they tried to demonstrate their equality with Moses and Aaron by adding to the plague of lice, and failed (Exodus 8:18).

By thinking of the angelic host as if they were the critical factors in the development of God's plan, Christians have misled themselves. **The central factor in history is Jesus Christ, the Incarnation**. This shows us where the issues of history and eternity are being fought out: in time and on earth. Skirmishes are fought between the angelic armies, but these are secondary in importance. Satan's kingdom is being conquered by the gospel, not by the sheer force of God's angelic host. **The terms of surrender are ethical**. The offer of salvation is not being made to Satan's angelic host, but to his earthly troops. Christians are steadily seeing the defeat of Satan's human forces, for **Satan suffers continual defections**. As the power of the gospel increases its zone of sovereign mastery, even more will defect. He will have only the remnants of an army when the final trumpet sounds. He will be trying to hold the fort in the last outpost. And the gates of hell shall not prevail.

Stages of Conquest

We know that the **first** step in the transformation of the earth is God's sovereign grace in extending salvation to individuals. He regenerates them, adopts them, calls forth from them an acknowledgment of His lordship. He extracts from them, in principle, their unconditional surrender. By grace are men saved, through faith, and that not of themselves; it is a gift of God, lest any man should boast (Ephesians 2:8-9).

The **second** step is the response of men in acknowledging the assignment of God's dominion covenant. Men are to subdue the earth (Genesis 1:26-28; 9:1-7). This assignment is basic to man's being, and men carry it out, either under the lordship of Satan or the lordship of Christ. The Satanists, having no autonomous law, and therefore no tool of dominion, are unable to carry out this assignment. We know that in hell and then the lake of fire, men are impotent, passively being consumed forever, "where their worm dieth not, and the fire is not quenched" (Mark 9:48). When salt is poured on a city, it is destroyed; nothing will grow in that soil (Judges 9:45). A little salt acts as a savor, which is why Christians are referred to as the salt of the earth (Matthew 5:13), and why salt was required in the animal sacrifices in the Temple (Leviticus 2:13), but too much salt is a sign of God's total judgment, which is why Lot's wife was turned to a pillar of salt (Genesis 19:26). This is the curse of hell: **total impotence**. "For every one shall be salted with fire, and every sacrifice shall be salted with salt" (Mark 9:49). Sin requires a sacrifice, and if man does not choose to cling to Christ's sacrifice, then he shall become the sacrifice. Rebellious man becomes an eternal sacrifice burning before God.

God is using His people as salt. They are the salt of the earth, as a savor, but they also serve as salt to Satan and his kingdom. **Christians are salting over the city of Satan, destroying it, causing it to become impotent.** This is the salt of the gospel. It is **savor to the regenerate,** and **death for the unregenerate.** It is like salt in a man's diet: too little makes for boring foods, and too much can make us sick.

Thus, when men who are regenerate take seriously God's dominion assignment, and they adopt God's law as their tool of dominion, they begin the process of salting Satan's kingdom, which is the other side of the dominion coin. **The flourishing of God's kingdom is the salting over of Satan's.**

The **third** step is the use of the law to subdue one's flesh, and then one's environment. Paul's anguish concerning the war between his flesh and his spirit tells us what we are up against (Romans 7). So does Paul's description of our spiritual warfare in Ephesians 6: "Put on the whole armour of God, that ye may be able to stand against the wiles of the devil" (v. 11). Truth, righteousness, the gospel of peace, the shield of faith, the helmet of salvation, the sword of the Spirit, and the word of God: here is our equipment (vv. 14-17). The word of God provides us with our moral guidelines.

The law of God also provides us with a tool of external dominion. God promises blessings for that society which surrenders unconditionally to Him, and then adopts the terms of His peace treaty (Deuteronomy 8 and 28).

Fourth, the blessings of God begin to flow in the direction of His people. "A good man leaveth an inheritance to his children's children: and the wealth of the sinner is laid up for the just" (Proverbs 13:22). As Benjamin Franklin said, honesty is the best policy. Capital flows to those who will bear responsibility, predict the future accurately, plan to meet the needs of consumers with a minimum of waste, and deal honestly with both suppliers and customers. Again, Deuteronomy 8 and 28 show us the nature of this wealth-transfer process. This wealth-transfer program is through market competition and conformity to God's law. **Satan's kingdom is progressively decapitalized.**

Fifth, the stewardship principle is universalized. God owns the whole earth: "The earth is the Lord's, and the fulness thereof; the earth and all they that dwell therein" (Psalm 24:1). The steward must acknowledge his Lord's total authority over him, yet he is expected to administer this property faithfully, efficiently, and profitably, as Jesus taught in the parable of the talents (Matthew 25:14-30). God finally comes as the owner to **dispossess** those who have not recognized His absolute sovereignty over His own land, as Jesus warned the Jews in His parable of the vineyard (Matthew 21:33-41). **In every institution, God dispossesses Satan's subordinates and replaces them with His subordinates.** To retain derivative sovereignty over the earth, men must honor the original owner. Everything is held by **lease**. This lease has terms attached to it, and the terms are spelled out in God's law. The whole idea of the Jubilee year, where every 50 years the land of Canaan returned to the original Hebrew families, points to a final Jubilee, when God returns the land to His adopted sons (Leviticus 25:8-17). Dominion men purchase back—redeem—every institution that they can afford, steadily, until that final day, just as Jacob purchased his birthright from his older twin brother Esau, even though God had promised Esau's birthright to Jacob (Genesis 25:23, 29-34). As God makes more capital available to His people—more money, more tools, more influence—they can afford to lease even more of Satan's kingdom, which he holds as a squatter anyway. God's law begins to dominate every sphere of life, across the face of the earth.

Sixth, the rise to prominence of those who conform themselves to His law, and who subdue their environments by the appropriate laws. This is what God said would happen to Israel, as nations marvelled at Israel's laws (Deuteronomy 4:5-8). Men who seek responsibility in terms of their faith in God tend to have the responsibility given to them by those who resist taking responsibility. Joseph was master of Potiphar's house, although he was a slave officially (Genesis 39:6). Then he was placed in prison, and soon he was the real keeper of the prison (Genesis 39:22). Finally, he became second in command in all of Egypt (Genesis 41:40-43). Ungodly men can exercise dominion only in terms of power, since they reject God's law, and God steadily removes their power from them. Satan refuses to subordinate himself to anyone or anything, but **dominion is always exercised by those who are subordinate to the One who exercises sovereign power**. Satan becomes wholly subordinate on the last day, but then all power is removed from him. He never surrenders, and therefore he is destroyed. He refuses to surrender to God unconditionally; he is therefore destroyed absolutely.

Seventh, the treaty of peace is extended to all areas of those cultures that surrender to God unconditionally. The whole of society must be put under dominion. Societies can rule under God's sovereign authority, as Israel was called to do, or they can become tributaries to God's conquering kingdom, as the nations far from Israel were expected to do (Deuteronomy 20:10-11), or else they are to be destroyed (Deuteronomy 20:12-15). There is no "King's X," no escape hatch.

Eighth, this provokes the nations to jealousy (Deuteronomy 4:5-8). They see the wisdom of God's law. The church is to be a city on a hill, for we Christians are the light of the world (Matthew 5:14). We are not to put our light under a bushel (Matthew 5:15-16). **People want external blessings.** These blessings are the product of a social order which respects the law of God. They have to get the blessings on God's terms. **They must capitulate.** Any blessings received except in terms of God's law-order are preludes to destruction (Deuteronomy 8:11-20).

Ninth, even the Jews will be provoked to jealousy. Paul cited Deuteronomy 32:21 concerning the Jews: "But I say, Did not Israel know? First Moses saith, I will provoke you to jealousy by them that are no people, and by a foolish nation I will anger you" (Romans 10:19). The Gentiles have received the great blessing. "I say then, Have they [the Jews] stumbled that they should fall? God forbid: but rather through their fall salvation is come unto the Gentiles, for to provoke them to jealousy" (Romans 11:11). This becomes a means of **converting the remnant of Israel in the future**, and when they are converted, Paul says, just think of the **blessings** that God will pour out on the earth, given the fact that the fall of Israel was the source of great blessings for the Gentile nations. "Now if the fall of them be the riches of the world, and the diminishing of them the riches of the Gentiles, how much more their fulness?" (Romans 11:12). When the Jews receive their promise, the age of blessings will come. When they submit to God's peace treaty, the growth of the kingdom will be spectacular. This is what Paul means by his phrase, "how much more." This leads to stage **ten**, the explosion of conversions and blessings. If God responds to covenantal faithfulness by means of blessings, just consider the implications of widespread conversions among the Jews. When the fulness of the Gentiles has come in, then Israel will be converted (Romans 11:25). The distinction between Jew and Gentile will then be finally erased in history, and the kingdom of God will be united as never before.

Eleventh, the kingdom of God becomes truly worldwide in scope. This involves the beginning of the restoration of the cursed world. The curse will then be lifted progressively by God. One result is longer life spans for man. This is a down payment on the paradise to come after the final judgment. God says: "For, behold I create new heavens and a new earth: and the former shall not be remembered, nor come into mind" (Isaiah 65:17). But this process of creation is part of history, to be concluded by the final conflagration. It has preliminary visibilty, in time and on earth. How do we know this? Because of verse 20, one of the crucial teachings in the Bible concerning God's preliminary blessings: "There shall be no more thence an infant of days, nor an old man that hath not filled his days: for the child shall die an hundred years old; but the sinner being a hundred years old shall be accursed." Isaiah 65:20 therefore points to a time **before the final judgment**, when people still die and sinners still operate, but which resembles the **long life spans of those who lived before Noah's Flood**. This passage cannot possibly be referring to the world beyond the final judgment, yet it points to external blessings, namely, long life, that do not exist in our world. These words cannot legitimately be "spiritualized." They refer to life on earth. They refer to a specific blessing on earth. It is a blessing that is a down payment on paradise, a testimony of God that He can deliver this fallen cursed world. This testimony, however, is not based on a radical break with the processes of history, but is instead a testimony that stems from the steady expansion of God's kingdom. There is **continuity** in history, and there is also **progress** in external affairs. This is not some hypothetical internal kingdom, but a visible kingdom of flesh and blood.

Twelfth, the forces of Satan then have something concrete culturally to rebel against. They will have the testimony of the **success of God's kingdom**, in time and on earth, to point to their failure. They will have to conform themselves outwardly, as spies do, in order to retain the external blessings of God. They will be as the foreigners dwelling in Israel were: under the law, protected by the law, and blessed in terms of the law. They will have to become **subordinate** in order to gain access to the **blessings**. Yet ethically, they cannot remain subordinate forever. Satan couldn't in heaven, so he will not on earth. Neither will his followers. But they must rebel **against something**. Their kingdom is being invaded, not Christ's. **They** are fighting the defensive strategy; we aren't. They are headed back toward the last outpost, not us. They will rebel (Revelation 20:7-9a), but they will not succeed.

Thirteenth, Satan's rebellion is immediately smashed by Christ and His angels (Revelation 20:9b-10). Satan tries one last time to defeat Christ, but he rebels from a position of weakness. He sought in Eden to beat God by using His creation, mankind, against Him. God has reversed the tables on Satan. He has defeated Satan's kingdom by using man as His instrument of dominion, exactly as He said he would in Genesis 1:26-28. Satan has no victory to claim. He has been proven wrong about the impotence of Christ's human followers, just as he learned from Job, once God had taught Job what He was all about. **God did not save Job by a miraculous intervention, after all. God saved Job by the testimony of His word, by carefully teaching Job the doctrine of the sovereignty of God.** Then He restored Job's health and wealth. Why should we expect something different on this side of the cross? Why should we expect Satan's victory now, when he was decisively beaten in his challenge against Job? At the end of history, Christ and His angels visibly defeat Satan, where he is trapped in hell, desperately hoping that the gates of hell shall prevail against the church. Yet the history of Christ's victorious kingdom, in time and on earth, will **already** have destroyed the basis of that last hope of Satan.

Fourteenth, the final judgment leads to Satan's confinement to the lake of fire. The contents of hell are dumped into the lake (Revelation 20:14). This is the end of Satan's quest for dominion apart from subordination to God.

Fifteenth, God creates the final version of the new heaven and new earth, wherein grows the tree of eternal life (Revelation 22:2). Men now have access to it. No longer is it in Eden, with a flaming sword to keep men from gaining access to it on the basis of their own works and power (Genesis 3:24). He demonstrates that His down payment on this final dwelling place had been wholly reliable.

It is strange that Christians today cannot envision the program for conquest God has established for His people. They lack confidence in themselves, it seems. They lack confidence in their understanding of their own responsibilities. They have misread the plain teaching of the Bible, finding alternative outlines that remove their guilt for inaction. **They prefer not to acknowledge their personal ethical burden of striving to fulfill the terms of God's dominion assignment.** And even when they admit that this assignment really was given to man by God, and is still in force, they conclude that it's an impossible task, and God never has believed that regenerate men can fulfill their assignment, in time and on earth.

They lack confidence in Jesus Christ.

It would be very interesting to be able to go back to the era of the Judges, in order to discover if theologians and popularizers of the defeatist faith in that era had rewritten God's dominion assignment regarding Canaan. We can imaginatively reconstruct some of the possible arguments. The first approach might have gone something like this: "Well, yes, God told us either to drive the Canaanites out of the land, or to destroy them utterly from the face of the earth. But, of course, His language must be understood as referring to **spiritual victory**. God in fact has allowed us to conquer in His name. We are not to have anything to do with the gods of Canaan. We are to live as though we had successfully driven them out of the land. In principle, we have, since we have driven Canaan's gods out of our hearts, our lives, and our congregations. Of course, we live as strangers in the land which God had promised for our inheritance (Judges 2:34). We are not, however, spiritual strangers to the land of promise. No indeed! We dwell victorious in the land—in the hills, perhaps, since the Amorites won't let us come into the valley, but **victorious in spirit**. And when they finally attack us in our mountain strongholds, as we know they will, and burn our walled cities, as surely they must, we will hold out, praying to God for martyrdom, or else His triumphant return with His angels, which will definitively prove to everyone that we are more than conquerers." This is the "continuity of defeat" version, also known as the triumph of Satan's leaven, in time and on earth.

Another variation might be the "temporary interlude of defeat" version. It might have gone something like this: "Yes, God told the generation which came out of Egypt that they could conquer if they were faithful to His covenant. But they weren't faithful to that covenant. So God abrogated that covenant. He brought our fathers to the very edge of the land (Deuteronomy 34), but they did not pass over. His covenant has been suspended during **our** period of history. He **will** bring His people into the land, driving the Canaanites completely out of the land, but not until He returns in power and might with His angels. **Then** He will re-establish His covenant with His people, and the Canaanites had better look out then! But God did not plan on **our** entry into the land. True, we are here in the land, but God has a new administrative principle for our generation. We are to preach the gospel to the people of the land, but we know that they will not convert in huge numbers, and they will seek to drive us out of the land. But they will not succeed. Just before they try, Christ will appear secretly, and secretly remove us to heaven. After seven years we will return, in our restored bodies, to serve as princes with Jesus, subduing Canaan for a thousand years, fulfilling God's command given to our forefathers in Egypt. So it's not **our** responsibility to drive the Canaanites out of the land. (Besides, those guys are **tough**!)."

Excuses, excuses, excuses: man never runs short of excuses. The problem is, God never accepts them. Adam and Eve didn't escape, just because each of them blamed somebody else for the problem. **God holds His people responsible for laboring continually to subdue the earth to His glory by means of the grace of law**. That responsibility is with **every** generation, and God expects His people to extend the dominion of His kingdom, generation by generation, culture by culture. He had told us that Christians **can** do it, and that eventually His people **will** do it. It may take a thousand years, but they will do it. Man was created for this very purpose, and Satan will not successfully thwart God's plan. Angels will not take the credit for Satan's long-term retreat into his last stronghold; the redeemed adopted sons of God will take the credit, under the sovereignty of God.

Delegating Authority

As we have seen in earlier chapters, God's institutional outline provides for both central and local decision-making. God is both one and many. His rule gives equal ultimacy to the unity and diversity of life. But it should be obvious that God is the head. He is the final authority. He is the absolute sovereign. He is the only true source of commands. **Christ**, as the Incarnate God, who was fully human and fully divine, two natures in one Person, in union but without mixture, is **the only link between heaven and earth**. No other human, no other institution, can legitimately assert a claim to divinity. No other institution is perfect. No other person or institution is infallible. None. Not the family, not the institutional church, not the civil government, not the economy.

Therefore, we have **a system of complementary, competing authorities**. The Bible tells us: "Where no counsel is, the people fall: but in the multitude of counsellors there is safety" (Proverbs 11:14). **In a multitude of lawful sovereignties there is also safety**, in time and on earth. Each authority has its assignments, defined by

God's law, but no single authority has absolute authority in any given sphere of life. Only God has absolute sovereignty. Therefore, the Bible establishes a system of checks and balances, and God's law provides the pivot point.

There must be a major authority in any given institution, but that authority can be challenged by other lawful authorities. A father must rule his household, but a wife can sometimes override him, as Rebekah overrode Isaac's choice of evil Esau as the son to receive the blessing. (She did have God's promise to guide her [Genesis 25:23; 27:1-17].) A father may not murder his children, either. The civil government can legitimately defend them from death. Parents may choose to abort an unborn child, but the Bible says this is murder, and the criminals must be executed, which would include the physician who was a participant (Exodus 21:22-25).

The authority structure in any institution is **hierarchical**, but it is never absolute. It faces awful challenges from other ordained institutions. It also faces the possibility of appeal from one lower on the chain of authority to a higher institutional authority. **The proper structure of responsibility is upward, from the responsible individual to a supervisor.** The man beneath is to exercise self-government, but the man above may establish terms of performance, if they are in conformity to God's law, and he may supervise performance. **Each institution acts as a miniature court.** There is an executive function with the head of the institution to establish general rules, goals, and standards of performance, as well as to establish punishments and rewards. But any functioning system which is top-heavy becomes bureaucratic, lethargic, and unproductive. No man is omniscient. No man is God. Therefore, a wise man **decentralizes authority**, making each subordinate fully responsible for his own performance, and a wise ruler sets up a **reward system** which encourages **self-motivation and self-government**. Since no man can police everything under his authority, the wise ruler acknowledges this fact and delegates authority downward. **He delegates precisely because he wants to extend his own dominion.** Delegating authority is not a retreat from responsibility, but the essence of responsibility. Few decisions in life are more difficult, more laden with responsibility, than the **selection of a subordinate** to take over a particular task. (Selecting a wife is one example.) Yet it must be done if institutions are to grow. Any institution which relies on a central governing committee to achieve its goals is going to be a bumbling, blind, and woefully inefficient organization.

God delegates authority to man. He tells man to subdue the earth. If a sovereign, omniscient, omnipotent God delegates authority to a creature, then it is imperative that men follow God's lead. Most government should be self-government. In fact, **most government is already self-government,** and a system that isn't built on this assumption cannot hope to succeed in the long run.

By creating theologies of despair, men have called for the creation of a huge central government, meaning the State or the institutional church, or a combination of the two. If we insist that God failed in his choice of a competent subordinate when He delegated authority to man, then we become hesitant to delegate authority ourselves. If God Almighty selected man to subdue the earth, and man was not only immediately deflected from his assignment, but was **permanently** deflected, despite the grace of God, then what possible hope can mere men have in locating subordinates who will become dominion-minded and reliable self-governors? If God's plan for man to subdue the earth was permanently deflected by Satan, then only a fool would delegate much authority to a subordinate. A wise man under such a theological assumption would hold onto every shred of power he had, as if his future depended upon it. He would never develop institutional arrangements that foster independence among subordinates. He would delegate only as a man delegates to a machine or a totally submissive servant. He would choose only breathing robots, rotting machines, known as bureaucrats, to fulfill his purposes.

This is basically the kind of blueprint for the millennium that millions of Christians have today. God supposedly chose the wrong being to exercise dominion. Satan rules in power in earth, and poor, pathetic man—even (we might say **especially**) regenerate man—cannot hope to triumph, in time and on earth. So Christ will just have to intervene directly in the historical process, remove man from all ruling authority, and return physically to start giving orders to His servants. If God has to intervene directly in the process of history, and change the rules of history to establish His kingdom on earth (for example, by mixing Christians with transformed bodies with Christians converted after Christ's return, not to mention the devil's servants—tares—who never were removed from history), then we can expect a **bureaucratic kingdom on earth**, the likes of which mankind has never seen. Egypt's bureaucratic consolidation will be a joke in comparison with Christ's supposed coming kingdom. No more delegated authority. No more responsible individualism. No more personal maturity through self-government. Just a massive, unquestionable system of bureaucratic government—the hierarchy to end all hierarchies, the pyramid to end all pyramids.

All this follows directly from a particular theology of despair. This theology of historical defeat, this cosmic pessimism regarding the abilities of regenerate men under God's sovereignty, leads inescapably to the acceptance of bureaucracy. Those who hold this theology of historical defeat and who also belong to some non-denominational church which has no institutional chain of command—none which anyone will admit to, anyway—have become pessimistic with regard to reversing the socialist world's march into bureaucracy. **Satan is a consummate bureaucrat,** who wants direct power, but who has no law structure that is reliable, and no subordinates who can be trusted. Yet his kingdom in this century has pushed around Christian cultures, precisely because the Christians have become reconciled to the idea of the triumph of bureaucracy. They see no defense against it, except a bigger and better bureaucracy to be established by Jesus when He comes to rule in person for a thousand years. "It you can't beat the system, join it. If you can't join it, imitate it."

Because Christians just don't trust God's judgment in selecting them to rule the earth, without God's physical presence, they don't trust themselves. They don't trust in their own judgment. They have no faith in their own dependent and responsible efforts to subdue the earth, under God and by means of His law. They want directions. They want to be told what to do. **They are afraid of responsible self-government.**

We are sheep. The Bible calls us sheep. But we are to be obedient sheep, and we are to strive to become shepherds, as the apostles become shepherds. Because of **self-government under God's law** and **under God's lawfully constituted authorities,** we sheep can become shepherds. We can then become rulers. As sheep, we must never forget the voice of the Good Shepherd (John 10). He is the source of our strength. The means of advancing from sheep to shepherds is through self-government under God and in terms of His law. We are not to become bureaucrats—the ultimate human sheep—but **law-abiding shepherds** (John 21:15-17). We must learn to trust the judgment of those who assign us new responsibilities, just as deacons are supposed to trust the judgment of elders who assign them responsibilities (Acts 6). The way to advance from sheep to shepherds is by continual delegation of responsibility downward, not by the continual expansion of centralized, bureaucratic power at the top.

Confidence and Leadership

For a successful program of delegated responsibility to persevere, the church must become convinced that such delegated authority can produce long-term benefits. **The church must become confident in its own earthly future.** The church must become convinced that it is an honor to bear new responsibilities, in time and on earth, in every area of life. The church—and I mean the multitude of Christians acting as dominion men—must become convinced that we aren't God's cannon fodder, that we aren't destined to defend the last outpost. Who wants to take responsibility for commanding despondent troops who won't take responsibility themselves? Who wants to lead an army of incompetents whose own Supreme Commander has supposedly told them that the army is destined for temporal defeat? Who wants to be a commander in a losing cause? Who wants to command troops when it isn't safe to delegate authority to any of your subordinates—a lesson which you learned from your Supreme Commander, who made this mistake at the very beginning of the war? Nobody sensible would do it. And I submit that this is a major factor in explaining why **Christians have nobody sensible leading them in this century.** Or at least very, very few sensible people.

What should be our first step in locating a generation of competent leaders? Moses selected Joshua to lead Israel into the land because Joshua was one of only two spies who had returned to Israel, 40 years before, to recommend that they march in right then and take the land that had been promised to them (Numbers 14:6-10). Caleb, the only other spy to agree with Joshua, also entered the land, as God had said he would (Numbers 14:24). Only two men were optimistic. Not an auspicious beginning for Israel in the wilderness. But God has all the time necessary to achieve His goals. He simply waited for all of the older ones to die off, except Caleb and Joshua. Then they marched across the Jordan River and began the conquest.

The younger generation took God's word more seriously than their parents had. They entered Canaan believing that God would give all the nations of Canaan into their hands. They didn't remain true to this faith; they were unsuccessful in dislodging several of the tribes (Judges 1). They were, however, far more confident than the generation of the exodus had been, and far more successful.

Therefore, the first step in locating reliable leaders is **to reverse the paralyzing pessimism of 20th-century Christianity**. We must take God seriously. When God gave man his dominion assignment, God meant business. He was serious. He built the dominion impulse into man, and only a progressive demonization of men can begin to thwart that impulse. In hell and in the lake of fire, the dominion impulse cannot find expression. Part of hell's horrors is the eternal thwarting of that impulse. For regenerated men, the adopted sons of God, there can be no question concerning the continuing nature of the dominion assignment. Since it was built into man's very being—the task which defined man's purpose from the beginning—**the progressive ethical untwisting of the presently distorted image of God in man will bring the dominion impulse into the forefront of the life of man**. The kingdom of God is an **ethical** imperative, but since man bears God's image, and his built-in purpose is to exercise dominion over God's creation, the kingdom of God is also an **ontological** imperative—an inescapable aspect of the being of regenerated mankind.

Israel was defined in terms of God's promise to Abraham (Genesis 15:13-16). God would give the seed of Abraham the land. This was an unconditional promise, for Abraham had surrendered to God unconditionally. God had dragged Abraham to Himself. He had dragged Abraham out of Ur of the Chaldees and Haran. He told Abraham what He would do for Abraham's heirs, and He would fulfill His promise (Galatians 3:16-19). Israel would enter Canaan. Israel was **destined** to enter Canaan. Yet Israel was also **commanded** to enter Canaan, and the older generation refused to obey. Their punishment: to die in the wilderness. But Israel did enter the land eventually.

Redeemed mankind must subdue the earth. It is God's dominion assignment. We cannot evade its implications without suffering punishment. Our generation may try to evade its responsibilities in this regard. Our generation may continue to deceive itself, arguing that the Bible's promises of victory, in time and on earth, are to be interpreted as spiritual victories only, the internal victory over sin, but with endless defeat in the external world of culture, until Christ finally returns to deliver us from destruction. Men may try to justify their failure in the external world by pointing to their own hypothetical victory over sin in their spiritual lives. Christians who do this will view the institutional church as a haven of refuge, God's port in the storm, and they will turn inward, concerning themselves with endless bureaucratic ecclesiastical squabbles, signifying practically nothing. Or Christians may take another approach, and try to postpone the establishment of God's visible kingdom until after Christ returns physically to give us total direction, placing us in various bureaucratic positions where we will be allowed to follow detailed orders from the cosmic Command Post. General Headquarters will issue comprehensive orders, and we will obey them to the letter. We won't ever again have to make responsible decisions, fitting the letter of the law to external circumstances without deviating from the spirit of the law—a difficult, though responsible, process. The future external, visible kingdom will therefore not be our responsibility to build, but Christ's.

By using either of these two approaches, today's Christians seek to justify their own cultural impotence, their own lack of dominion. They **internalize the kingdom,** pointing to supposed victories inside their souls—victories that never result in cultural influence. Or else they point to **a coming discontinuous event,** which will bring power to them only in terms of the creation of a massive supernatural bureaucracy. In the meantime, both views preach pessimism concerning this age. **Both views prophesy the defeat of the church externally in this age.** Both views create a desire to escape from the responsibilities of this world—the comprehensive responsibilities of cultural dominion. Both views reinforce our rebellious tendencies to defy God, deny the dominion assignment, and retreat into a closed, isolated society to sing our hymns, pray our prayers for deliverance, and eat our mess of pottage.

We have tried to sell our birthright to the devil. Let **him** exercise dominion! Let **him** bear the responsibilities! Let **him** rule in time and on earth, if only he will give us a little more time to pray and sing. Maybe if we grant him his right to rule temporarily, he'll be nice and let us alone. **Let Satan rule, if Satan lets us alone**: this is the "battle cry" of 20th-century Christianity.

We need to revive our hope in God. We need to revive our hope in His good judgment. We need to revive our hope in ourselves, as redeemed men, so that we can face the dominion assignment with confidence. We need to regain our confidence in the power of God's revealed law as a tool of dominion. We need an eschatology of victory, in time and on earth—an optimism concerning our ability to extend dominion and subdue the earth, making manifest the comprehensive kingdom of God, in time and on earth, before Christ finally comes in victory to remove His people from a world whose potential has been used up because God's people have fulfilled the terms of God's dominion assignment.

This requires unconditional surrender. We must surrender to God's absolute sovereignty. We mustn't mouth the words, "the sovereignty of God," if we really mean, "The sovereignty of God, with a little sovereignty to man." We have to read Job 38-41, Romans 9, and Ephesians 1 again and again, until we recognize **God's total sovereignty**. Then, once we see who is really sovereign, we can have faith in ourselves, as redeemed and progressively restored ambassadors of God on earth. Then, and **only** then, will we bring God's peace treaty before the citizens of Satan's shrinking and defensive kingdom, calling them to sign the treaty now, to submit unconditionally to its terms of surrender, and to make a covenant with the God of the invading kingdom. Those who are **meek before God** shall inherit the earth.

The kingdom of Satan is very much like Jericho in Joshua's early days. The church of God has its marching orders. It is to conquer the land, driving out the inhabitants. This time, we are not to use force, as the Israelites did, but we are to use the sword of the Lord, the preaching of the gospel. We are **ambassadors**, not spies, this time. We announce the coming of the kingdom. We warn the residents of today's cities of the coming judgment. In Deuteronomy 20:10-15, God gave us the command not to destroy a distant city without offering it the opportunity to sign a peace treaty and to become tributaries. This is the same treaty God sends to the nations today. Their time is running short. God's kingdom is coming. They must capitulate now, or else spend eternity as fiery sacrifices to God. It is to their advantage to become members of God's kingdom.

God gave the people of Canaan time to think about His arrival, in the person of His people. They knew what was coming a generation in advance, and they trembled (Joshua 2:9-11). Perhaps they grew temporarily confident when the Israelites of Moses' day grew fearful, and decided to remain in the wilderness, culturally impotent, fed by God's miraculous manna (Exodus 16:15,31-35). **God graciously spoon-fed these pathetic former slaves until they died.** The Canaanites were given an extra generation to fill up their cup of iniquity (Genesis 15:16). But the day God parted the waters of the Jordan River, the manna ceased forever (Joshua 5:12). God would spoon-feed these people no longer. The miraculous manna would never again appear on their land. The land was now permanent land; they would have to subdue it under God's law. That spelled the end of the road for most of the Canaanites, and had Israel been more faithful, it would have been the end for all of them.

This leads us to a crucially important principle: **when God's people seek continual miracles from God, rather than victory by means of labor under God's revealed law-order, they are admitting defeat.** When God's people prefer to be spoon-fed rather than to exercise responsible dominion, the kingdom of Satan is given another stay of execution. It is this continual praying for miracles, for discontinuities in history rather than the **continuity of victory under law,** which has paralyzed the expansion of God's kingdom. **Pessimism** concerning the church's ability to extend God's comprehensive kingdom, coupled with **the slave's hope in miraculous, discontinuous deliverance,** have kept the church wandering in the wilderness for several generations. Should we be surprised at the second-rate officers we have today, given the state of mind of the troops? Should a generation of slaves, who wait trembling for their master to tell them exactly what to do next, expect anything better than third-rate bureaucrats to lead them? When men flee from the burdens of responsible self-government, as men of both kingdoms are doing all over the world today, should we expect to see **God's freedom under God's law** demanded by His people?

Let us flee the wilderness. Let us abandon hope in our daily manna, our daily miracles. Let us abandon the need to be spoonfed by God. Let us begin to act like shepherds. Let us begin to accept the burdens of responsible self-government under the guidelines provided by God's law. Since the law is no longer a threat to us eternally, because we are delivered by Christ from the **curse** of the law, **let us approach God's law as a master craftsman approaches a tool that he understands and respects**, and not as apprentices who are afraid of the tool and the responsibilities of using that tool in their labor. When Christian leaders see that they are called to lead confident troops who understand the responsibilities of self-government, and who are willing to bear these responsibilities because they understand the law of God, their tool of dominion, we will find better quality leaders accepting their positions of responsibility, not just in the institutional church, but in every institution, in every walk of life.

Conclusion

The kingdom of God is comprehensive. It involves the inner life of man, as well as the environment around man. Both social and natural environments are in view. There can be no zones of neutrality. No area of life can be segregated from the rest, and marked as a neutral zone between God's kingdom and Satan's kingdom. Every area of life is going to be part of one or the other kingdom. Therefore, Christians are called to serve as ambassadors of Christ, and as subduers of the earth, throughout the earth. Did Christ exempt any area of the face of the earth from His gospel? Or did He tell His people to preach the gospel everywhere? We are commanded to disciple all nations (Matthew 28:18-20). But this inevitably means that all nations are under the requirements of the law, for they are all in need of Christ's redemption—His buying back from the curse of the law.

Is the law partial? Is the law anything but all-encompassing? Are men not totally in need of spiritual deliverance because of the comprehensive nature of the law's demands? **The law is comprehensive, Christ's deliverance is comprehensive, and God's kingdom is comprehensive, in time and on earth**. If this were not true, then men would not be required to repent, in time and on earth. If they fail to repent before they die, or before Christ returns in judgment, then they must become **permanent salted sacrifices**, burning on God's awful altar, forever (Mark 9:49). The comprehensive nature of God's punishment should testify to the comprehensive claims of God's law, and the comprehensive scope of God's kingdom, in time and on earth. To argue in any other way is to minimize the extent of Christ's sacrifice on the cross, to lessen its significance, and to lessen its cost to our Lord.

Any social movement which is serious about changing the shape of history must have at least two features. First, it must have a doctrine of the possibility of positive social change. If men don't believe that history can be changed through concerted effort, then they are unlikely to attempt to change very much. Second, they need a unique doctrine of law. They need to believe in their ability to understand this world, and by understanding its laws, change its features. They need a detailed program for social change, in other words.

There is another feature of a successful program of social reconstruction which is usually present, and which is undeniable powerful: the doctrine of predestination. The doctrine of historical inevitability strengthens the souls of those who are convinced that "their side" is going to win, and it weakens the resistance of their enemies. A good example in the Bible is the optimism of the Hebrews under Joshua, and the pessimism of the people of Jericho (Josh. 2:8-11).

Where have we seen a fusion of all three elements? Where have we seen simultaneously the doctrine of predestination, the doctrine of the possibility of positive social change, and the doctrine of law? In the 20th century, we have seen all three doctrines espoused by the three most powerful social and religious movements of our time: Marxian Communism, modern science, and (in the final decades of the century) militant Islam. All three have a dynamic of history. All three believe that external affairs can be controlled by elites. All three have a doctrine of world conquest. All three have evangelical wings. All three, therefore, are religions, for they espouse distinct (and morally mandatory) ways of life.

The war is on. The major participants recognize this war. Too many contemporary Christians have not seen it, or else they have misinterpreted its implications for themselves and the church. The war is between Jesus Christ and the more militant forms of anti-Christianity, especially those that proclaim their versions of all three doctrines.

All three doctrines need to be held for maximum leverage in this world of religious conflict. The doctrine of predestination can lead to social impotence if it is coupled with pessimism concerning the long-run triumph of the church, in time and on earth. Those who hold both the doctrine of predestination and an eschatology of earthly, historical defeat have a tendency to turn inward, both psychologically and ecclesiastically. They worry too much about the state of their souls and the state of the institutional church, and not enough about the state of the kingdom of God in its broadest sense. Such a theology is guaranteed to produce defeat, and we should expect such theologies to remain backwater views of backwater groups, as they are today and have been in the past.

The communists have all three doctrines: predestination, inevitable victory, and law. But their law-order doesn't work. It's parasitic. It has produced endless economic disasters from 1917 until the present. It cannot succeed in the long run.

The question is therefore not "predestination vs. no predestination." The question is: "**Which** predestination?" The question is: "**Whose** predestination?" God's? Modern science's? Islam's? Communism's? The battle for world supremacy will be waged among the competing predestinarian world views. Everyone else is simply going along for the ride. Will it be the sovereignty of God or the sovereignty of man?

We must become **optimists** concerning the victory that lies before Christ's people, in time and on earth. We must be even more optimistic than Joshua and Caleb, for they were only asked to spy out the land of Canaan. They were called to give their report prior to Christ's sacrifice at Calvary. Why should we be pessimistic, like that first generation of former slaves? Why should we wander in the wilderness, generation after generation? Why should we despair? Why should we adopt the mentality of slaves, or the mentality of the beleaguered garrison in the last outpost? It is Satan's garrisons that are defending the outposts, and when Christians recognize their responsibilities for building the kingdom, and when they master the law of God as a tool of dominion, and when they gain a vision of freedom through self-government, and when some victory-oriented leaders step forth to lead them into battle in every area of life, then Satan's troops will find themselves defending their last outpost. And the gates of hell shall not prevail against God's church.

Chapter 9

A STRATEGY FOR DOMINION

There is only one Supreme Allied Commander, Jesus Christ. There is only one source of a comprehensive strategy that includes every possible tactic. God has that **integrated strategy-tactical plan**, and He is putting it into operation, moment by moment, across the whole universe.

Satan also has a strategy, and he also has tactics, but he is not omniscient, omnipotent, omnipresent, or omni-anything. He is a fallen creature, a rebellious creature, a creature who has abandoned God's law, the tool of dominion. He has refused to be subordinate to God, and therefore he cannot possibly be successful in subduing the earth. It is impossible to subdue the earth without being subordinate to God. For creatures, **dominion requires subordination**. The only power Satan has is by God's discretion, which is why Satan had to come before God in order to gain God's permission to destroy Job's assets (Job 1). He is under God, so he does have power, but because he refuses to subordinate himself ethically, he has in principle abandoned dominion's first principle. His kingdom cannot succeed. His strategy is negated from the very beginning, for it relies on the doctrine of autonomous power—the power of the independent, self-existent creature—and this doctrine is wrong. **It isn't possible to have autonomous power as a creature**. But Satan wants it, and more important, all his subordinates want it. Nobody wants to be under Satan, but his troops put up with him for the sake of the power he gives them in exchange for their allegiance. But when God reduces Satan's power, what will he possess then to compel, or buy, the allegiance of his troops? Mercenary armies have one thing in common: they never defeat a determined, dedicated home guard. Satan's army is a mercenary army. God's army is a home guard. The only thing that is holding up the victory of God's home guard is the home guard's lack of confidence, lack of training, and lack of tactics.

We have already surveyed our lack of confidence in the chapter on the Kingdom of God. Christians have adopted, almost universally, visions of defeat. Christians have abandoned the responsibilities of God's comprehensive dominion assignment. To gain a true understanding of our assignment and our prospects, we need to re-examine the popular eschatologies of defeat. We need to adopt an **eschatology of victory**—a doctrine of the "last things" that is optimistic concerning the "next-to-the-last things." We have to recognize the **continuity of history**, the **continuity of victory**, and the **continuity of God's law**. We have to abandon our reliance on promises of cosmic miracles—not local miracles, of course, but great, sweeping, cosmic miracles—that are supposed to bail out God's failures, His church. We have to abandon any version of the continuity of defeat, the triumph of Satan's leaven in creation's fallen dough.

But if we do this, what else will we need? If we adopt a **dynamic of history**, as the Marxists have adopted—optimism concerning man's future, in time and on earth—but a better-grounded optimism than the Marxists possess, what else will we need? **A comprehensive, detailed knowledge of God's revealed law.** We need a dynamic of history, meaning a world-and-life view which is promised success by God, but we also need a **tool of dominion**. God made the earth, and He made man in His own image. He established moral and physical laws, and these laws are comprehensible to man, for man is made in God's image. These laws correspond both to the mind of man and the external environment, including man's institutional environment. The **principles of God's law** are found in His **Ten Commandments** (Exodus 20:1-17). The details are God's **case-law applications** of the principles, and these are found primarily in the second through the fifth books of the Old Testament.

We have been given both a dynamic of history and a tool of dominion. We have done our best to ignore them both. We have, especially in the last hundred years, retreated from both in the name of "Christian liberty," or "separation from the world." But such an approach is doomed to defeat. Those who adopt such an attitude will become less and less influential in the world they have abandoned to the devil in the name of God. Those who adopt an eschatology of victory and a commitment to God's law will steadily displace the retreatists. The retreatists get what they expect: **defeat**, both by the devil and by those Christians who have decided to take charge. The retreatists, or as they are also known, the **pietists**, are the modern equivalent of the Israelites of Moses' day. They are not happy with the wilderness, but they know nothing else, and they are convinced that it's not their responsibility to march into Canaan and take charge. They see themselves as ambassadors of a distant kingdom whose Master has kept most of the kingdom's assets and weapons with Him in that distant land. They know He will return eventually, but without warning, without sending in back-up troops until the last moment. Today's Christians are not confident ambassadors for Christ, for they do not recognize the comprehensive nature of their assignment and the incomparable power of God's tool of dominion. They also don't recognize the state of disarray of Satan's forces—lawless, covetous, innately rebellious, without a philosophy of life, and without hope of long-run success. They are not effective ambassadors, for they don't recognize the imminence of God's kingdom—not the Second Coming of Christ in power, but the nearness of power available to them for the task of dominion.

Strategy

God revealed His strategy in Christ's final words with His disciples. "Go ye therefore, and teach all nations, baptizing them in the name of the Father, and of the Son, and of the Holy Ghost: teaching them to observe all things whatsoever I have commanded you: and, lo, I am with you alway, even unto the end of the world. Amen." (Matthew 28:19-20). The New English Bible translates the first sentence as: "Go forth therefore and make all nations my disciples." We are to put the nations under **discipline**. Discipline implies a set of rules. It also implies a system of law enforcement, a chain of authority. And, as we have seen again and again, it involves first and foremost the idea of **self-discipline under God** by means of God's law.

Teaching is a form of discipline. A teaching method without a rule, and without discipline, especially self-discipline, will not succeed. **We are to teach the nations, which inevitably means that we are to put them under the rule of God**. If any person or culture refuses to discipline its actions by the law of God, then that person or nation will be judged by God. **The law will crush you or elevate**

you, but it cannot be avoided. It is part of God's creation-order. It is basic to man's very being, for it is basic to the dominion assignment.

This assignment by Christ is simply a recapitulation of the dominion assignment given to Adam and Noah by God. It is the same assignment. Now Christ announces His power over history, for He has suffered in history: "And Jesus came and spoke unto them, saying, All power is given unto me in heaven and in earth" (Matthew 28:18). This is the historical foundation for His recapitulation of the original dominion assignment. The Incarnated Christ announced His absolute power—**all** power—over history. No longer must men look forward to His sacrifice; it is now behind us. No longer must the visible sign of God's victory over Satan be foreshadowed in the sacrifices of the tabernacle of the Temple (Hebrews 8:5). We have seen the victory. It is before us forever. **Now we have no further excuses for delaying the discipling of the nations.** The land of Canaan in Palestine is no longer the training ground—boot camp—for Christ's troops. We have been called to invade Satan's kingdom, the nations. Satan is now bound in history, as he had not been prior to the resurrection; this is what the meaning of the chain is in Revelation 20, where we are told that Satan is chained for a thousand years. He is restricted, for his kingdom is under attack. Only at the end will he be loosed for a little time, only to be crushed on the final day (Revelation 20:7-9). His last attempt to escape his doom, when he surrounds the camp of the faithful—which is the world itself—is immediately defeated, without a shot being fired, or so the text indicates. He cannot reclaim his lost kingdom from the victorious troops under God. His counterattack is immediately burned up by the final discontinuity in history: judgment (Revelation 20:10).

It is discouraging to realize how many Christians refuse to acknowledge the enormous significance the **resurrection of Christ** had in human history. They see that it will have personal significance for them at the time of death and at the last judgment, but this individualism neglects the significance of the resurrection for the history of the human race, in time and on earth. Christ made it very plain: it served as the basis of a **massive transfer of visible sovereignty.** He now has all power, in heaven and on earth. God always did have this power, but now this power has been manifested in history. God entered the processes of history through His Incarnation. The Second Person of the Trinity came to earth as a perfect man, lived a perfect life, met the terms of the law, and died as a substitutionary sacrifice. Yet modern Christians act as though all of this historical activity has meaning primarily in transhistorical affairs: in the soul, in heaven, at the final judgment, and in the new heavens and new earth beyond that final judgment. They act as though the supreme drama in all of history has very little significance **for** history.

Christ sent His troops out into the world, invading Satan's nations from that initial base in Palestine. God had brought them out of bondage into Palestine 1500 years before Christ's sacrifice. Now He was using Palestine as the initial base of operations for a worldwide invasion. Having taken all power **over** history by means of His sacrifice **in** history, Christ was then **delegating new authority to His subordinates.** Did this Supreme Allied Commander lack power? No. Did He possess all power? Absolutely. Do His troops lack permission to draw upon these reserves of power? Not since Pentecost, when the Comforter came. "But ye shall receive power, after that the Holy Ghost is come upon you: and ye shall be witnesses unto me both in Jerusalem, and in all Judea, and in Samaria, and unto the uttermost part of the earth. And when he had spoken these things, while they beheld, he was taken up: and a cloud received him out of their sight" (Acts 1:8-9).

How much plainer could Christ have spoken? He told them He has all power. He told them they would receive power. Then He was carried away from them into the heavens, demonstrating in the most graphic way conceivable that **He was delegating power to them,** and that they should not expect Him to exercise dominion, in time and on earth, in His physical body.

The early disciples got the message. They became His ambassadors across the face of the earth. So successful were the early disciples in their spreading of the gospel that Paul could write to the church at Colossae concerning "the hope of the gospel, which ye have heard, and which was preached to every creature which is under heaven" (Colossians 1:23b). He meant, presumably, that the gospel had been delivered throughout Satan's kingdom, that no area had been designated as "off limits" by God for His disciples. What is so disturbing in the latter decades of the 20th century is that so few of His disciples today recognize what the early disciples did: that it is the church, and not some coming discontinuous event in history, which will disciple the nations. They knew where their territory was: the whole world. They knew what they had to do: **disciple the nations**. They understood the dominion assignment: **to subdue the earth**.

What is the message we are to bring to the nations? To believe in Jesus, but not to conform themselves to His image? To accept Jesus as savior, but not as Lord? To offer a concept of Lordship which doesn't involve total obedience as the standard of performance? Of course not. Our task is to teach all nations "to observe all things whatsoever I have commanded you" (Matthew 28:20). **He told them that he came to confirm the law of God, not to abrogate or annul it** (Matthew 5:17). He gave His disciples a completed copy of His law, so that they, as His ambassadors, might announce the **terms of surrender** to Satan's troops. The terms of peace are the terms of surrender. They are also the tool of dominion.

When Rahab gave her commitment to the spies of Israel, was she a citizen of Jericho any longer? Obviously not. She was making a **covenant** with the God of Israel, through the spies (Joshua 2:12-13). She became treasonous against the kingdom of Jericho, although for a time she remained in the city as if her citizenship were still in Jericho. The point is this: **you belong to one kingdom or the other**. There is no third kingdom to which anyone can flee. You have citizenship papers in heaven or hell. You are recorded in the book of life or you aren't (Exodus 32:32; Revelation 21:27).

Every king requires obedience. Every kingdom has laws. Men are always under the law of some kingdom. The standard phrase, "We're under grace, not law," is utter nonsense. **We are always under law**. The question is: **Whose** law? God's law or Satan's? To be under Satan's law is to be a citizen of his kingdom. Then his law will condemn you, for the **work** of the law is written on every human heart (Romans 2:15). Everything valuable that Satan holds, he holds because he stole it. All good gifts come from God (James 1:17). Satan is a thief. Therefore, to command his kingdom, he needs law, and he relies on the twisted remnants of the law of God—the **work** of the law—to whip his troops into submission. Anyone who relies on his own moral strength as an obeyer of God's law is under the curse of God's law. Anyone who looks into his conscience and says that this will be his guide is under the curse of God's law. Even the work of the law in his heart is close enough to God's law to condemn him. We are always under law. The law of God always condemns sinners. The question is: will we **live** by the law or **die** by the law? Will we escape the curse of the law by God's grace through our faith in Christ's atoning sacrifice, or will we present ourselves as a spotted sacrifice, to be salted and burned forever? Will we use the law to conform ourselves to the image of God, or will we use the law to elevate ourselves above the grace of God, in a desperate attempt to become holier than God?

The **political question** facing the citizens of any nation is this: Is it better to be under the rule of God's revealed law or some satanic imitation of that law? Is it better to be under God's law or Satan's crude, twisted imitations? You would think that the answer is obvious. Why, then, have Christian leaders and theologians in this century answered the question incorrectly? Why have they proclaimed that we are no longer bound by God's law? If we are not bound by God's law on earth, then we are bound by that law in eternity, in the lake of fire. **The law is binding on every creature**: in heaven, on earth, in hell, and (finally) in the lake of fire. The question is: **Will it bind a man to life or to death**? Will Jesus Christ wrap you in His arms, as the confirmer of the law, or will Satan wrap you in his arms, as the rebel against the law, so that both you and Satan will be bound by the curse of the law for eternity? Without Christ, you are already in Satan's arms.

The **preaching of the gospel** to every person, and the **teaching of the law** to every person, is the basis of **discipling the nations**. The ambassadors come to a new people and instruct them in righteousness. There are standards of righteous behavior. These are revealed to us in God's law. The ambassadors make disciples out of the former citizens in Satan's kingdom. He delegates authority to them when they have begun to master the law of God in their particular area of life. Then they act as new ambassadors, carrying the message of the gospel to new people, with new areas of influence to capture.

No institution is exempt: church, state, family, economy, school, farm, etc. Every institution has a structure of responsibility and standards of performance. What Christ demands is a disciplining of men and institutions by means of His standards of righteous performance. If the civil government bears the sword, then it should bear the sword in terms of God's law. If a corporation makes a profit, then it should make a profit in terms of God's law. If a farm plants a crop, then it should plant it in terms of God's requirements for agriculture. In short, as long as you have to operate institutions in terms of **some** standards, you should operate them in terms of **God's** standards. It's never a question of "no standards vs. God's standards." It's always a question of **whose** standards.

Tactics

The strategy of discipling through preaching the whole counsel of God is the universally valid strategy. The question of tactics must always be local and historically bounded. Every culture, every institution, every aspect of life must be subdued, so it's the responsibility of local people to fit God's strategy into their historical and cultural circumstances. The strategy provides us with the **unified program**; the tactics provide us with the **multiple applications**.

Whatever the local tactics, every available institution should be used. The institutional church must be the focus for assembling families together, but the family is the first institution. Teaching materials for fathers are extremely important, so that the father can re-establish himself as a household priest. He must begin to rule over the family, training his children in the Bible, and making ready another generation of ambassadors.

The church will normally screen such materials, since the pastors and elders are devoting their time to this sort of work. The church is not the sole authority, but in most situations it will be the source of the preliminary written and taped resources. The church should work with heads of households to establish regular family programs of training. **The church must learn to decentralize its teaching ministries, and the first place to begin is with the families**.

Financial resources are always limited, especially in new ventures. The **tape recorder**, because of the cassette tape, provides the preliminary mechanical instructional tool, for the church can produce as many tapes as it can sell, but not tie up a lot of capital in original production, unlike books and pamphlets.

Printed materials are important, beginning with tracts for members to use as evangelism tools, and going to newsletters. A newsletter should be informative, and not just a place for weekly notices. A newsletter should probably include a smaller insert with timely notices of events that are soon forgotten. Newsletters are not that expensive to produce. Even a mimeograph machine is acceptable in the initial stages of a publishing ministry.

Pamphlets, reproductions of sermons, reprints of contemporary articles, and similar materials can be produced inexpensively, when a church or other group wants to target a special audience for evangelism. "Bread and butter evangelism," with specific materials aimed at specific audiences with specific problems to solve is probably the best way to introduce the gospel to new people. **They want to know what difference Christianity makes.** If the evangelist can demonstrate that Christian principles do apply in the specific problem areas facing the potential converts, he has made considerable inroads. Evangelism that is not geared to providing **specific biblical answers to real problems faced by real people** is weak, and it tends to produce converts who don't understand the comprehensive claims of Christ's kingdom responsibilities.

Special meetings dealing with problems faced by people in the local community are especially useful as an evangelism tool. Problems centering in family life are always a burden, so specific answers here are in demand. Other areas of life can be covered at different meetings: business, community crime, alcohol, drug abuse, and so forth. This kind of evangelism involves careful planning and speakers who have something uniquely Christian to present.

Each individual can provide his circle of associates with materials that deal with problems that he knows faces these people. People want help. They may not want to admit that they need help in their spiritual lives, or they may not grasp the magnitude of the eternal threat facing them, but they know that they have problems in more mundane areas. Christianity presents comprehensive claims on a man's life, and consistent Christianity presents comprehensive answers.

This is **dominion-oriented evangelism**. It is more than the typical "feel good" evangelism of the modern world. "Feel good evangelism" is used successfully by Satan: "If it feels good, do it." Christians have imitated this approach: "Get high on Jesus" was a familiar slogan in America in the late 1960's. "Maximum Sex" was another popular American campus evangelism program in the mid-1970's. But slogans are not much good if the content of the faith is missing. Sitting around in groups working up overwhelming emotional feelings goes only so far. An emotional binge may make people feel better temporarily, but the same old worldly problems persist when the participants float down from their mountain-top experience.

Books on a multitude of topics are needed. Without books, no movement ever succeeds. Books are what makes Christianity and Judaism unique. "The religion of the book" is a real phenomenon. The care which the ancient Hebrews took to preserve accurate copies of the Bible should testify to the centrality of the written word. Books on personal problems, books on practical issues, books on theology, books on every aspect of life: here is a program that can make a difference. Christians who have not disciplined themselves to read continually are at the mercy of their environment. They will quote those ideas that float around in our humanistic society. We need to be the people providing the popular ideas that float through a society, not a bunch of amateur distributors of used ideas developed by humanists and demonists.

Training programs are basic to any successful business organization. They are basic to any military organization. They are, of course, central to any educational organization. That's why continual training for every member of every Christian organization is absolutely fundamental. If no training is going on inside a Christian organization, it is safe to say that it won't survive for long. An institution without training—training that relies on the development of personal self-discipline—is a suicidal institution. We need **teaching**, and we need **practice**.

Newsletter networks must be built up. Translating services will eventually become mandatory. The international Christian community must build up alternative systems of communication. The international division of labor must be applied to the spreading of the gospel. We don't know when some new idea, some new technique for conquest, will come out of some obscure corner of the world. No stone should be left unturned in the quest for better teaching and training techniques.

Evangelism should be issues-oriented. What problems are bothering a particular individual? What answers does the Bible provide him? The messenger must search the Bible to find out what answers there are to people's problems. But this takes work, intelligence, and a willingness to master the law of God. This is what ancient Israel required of illiterate citizens of the kingdom. What excuses can literate, media-conscious Christians come up with to let them off the hook? None that God will listen to.

Christian schools are absolutely fundamental to any successful strategy. I will go farther than this. Any program which does not advocate the creation of Christian schools is automatically doomed. These schools should be fully independent, fully parent-financed (except for scholarships), and preferably profit-seeking. This increases the parents' control of the schools, and it gives the headmaster a financial incentive to conform to the parents' wishes. But any Christian school—profit-seeking, full-cost tuition though nonprofit, or church-operated—is better than no Christian school at all. All education is intensely religious. No education can ever be neutral. Therefore, all Christian children should be trained by Christian teachers who are using a fully consistent Christian curriculum. Any Christian who allows his children to learn the fundamentals of knowledge in a government-financed, secular humanist school has betrayed his children. Period. No qualifications, no exceptions, no excuses.

Specialists and Generalists

The God of the Bible is one and many. The Christian community is a unity, but it is also diverse. There are **unifying themes** that every Christian and every Christian community must acknowledge as fundamental. There are also **applications** of basic principle that only a few people may be aware of or concerned with. What we need is a generation of Christians who dedicate themselves to getting an intellectual and practical grasp of the general truths of the faith, yet who at the same time devote time, resources, and prayer to mastering at least one specialized area in order to bring it under the rule of Christ. Every Christian should be called upon to give serious consideration to God's standards in his own sphere of influence. The community as a whole should have these specialists on tap at any time, so that they can contribute their expertise to the dominion assignment.

Military organizations understand this principle. There are dedicated specialists in every military organization who can be relied on to supply detailed and accurate knowledge to troop commanders whenever conditions call for it. A good commander knows enough about the various fields under his command so that he knows when to call for assistance, whom to call to give it, and how to integrate it into the overall operations of the army.

Commanders like this are rare. They must be widely read. They must understand the whole picture. They must be able to spot productive subordinates. They need to be able to sift through the irrelevant details to locate the relevant details. They have to act fast. They have to act decisively. They have to bear full responsibility for their decisions. Without people like these, no army can be victorious.

Our overwhelming advantage as Christians is that we have such a Supreme Allied Commander. **God has knowledge of the whole and the details**. He knows where every subordinate is, what he can accomplish, and how he can be used best. God knows both the whole and the particulars. Satan, though a powerful creature, cannot know the whole and the particulars. Satan is like a juggler who is having an increasing number of oranges tossed at him. He is juggling furiously, but God keeps tossing in more and more oranges. Satan doesn't have the ability to match God on the battlefield. Besides, he is suffering from the effects of a mortal blow. He is a bleeding, overworked juggler.

What we need to do as subordinate officers is **to prepare ourselves for the upcoming battles**. We need to be fit servants. We need to spend time mastering at least one area, while maintaining at least a passing knowledge with both the fundamentals of the faith and the general drift of the two kingdoms. We need to be able to apply our knowledge to specific situations. As Peter told us: "But sanctify the Lord God in your hearts: and be ready to give an answer to every man that asketh you a reason of the hope that is in you with meekness and fear" (I Peter 3:15). Meekness and fear are toward God, not men; because men are meek before God, they can be confident in the face of the challenges the world directs at them. **And the sign of a man who is meek before God is his knowledge of God's requirements for him**. As Peter went on, "Having a good conscience; that, whereas they speak evil of you, as of evildoers, they may be ashamed that falsely accuse your good conversation in Christ" (I Peter 3:16). When we know what God wants from us, we can discipline ourselves so that we will be able to provide whatever it is, whenever He calls for it.

There is no earthly Supreme Allied Commander. There is no absolutely sovereign human institution. Yet there is also no supreme **demonic** commander on earth. He, too, is limited by people who are not quite sure what their job is, or how to get it done. Both commanders are limited by their troops: God by choice, and

Satan by necessity. Christians spend too much time worrying about the strength of Satan when compared to themselves, but the problem is not in man's weakness. God is absolutely sovereign. He has no problem. He has plenty of time. He can bide his time. Satan can't. **We should compare the strengths of the two supreme commanders.** Then we will get the proper perspective.

God bided His time with the Canaanites. He gave them some extra rope to hang themselves with. He let them fill up the cup of their iniquity. Then He smashed them. The Amorites are gone. The Jebusites are gone. The Hittites are gone. The Egyptians are almost all gone; mostly Arabs now live in Egypt. The Israelites persist in their influence, although many, if not most, of those calling themselves Israelites today are really descendants of caucasian converts, the Khazar kingdom of the medieval period, before the Russians conquered them. Only the Israelites persist in influence. God will deal with them as a people again (Romans 11). The rest of the ancient kingdoms are gone. God can afford to bide his time. Satan's kingdoms rise and fall, but God's people persist, increasing their numbers, and preparing (though few seem to realize it) for the establishment of God's comprehensive, universal kingdom, in time and on earth.

Conclusion

The international kingdom of God must be **decentralized**. No new tower of Babel will do Christians any good. We recognize the permanence of national distinctions, although this or that nation is impermanent. We can have no Supreme Allied Commander on earth, giving directions, and promoting us in a literal army or bureaucracy. But person by person, church by church, occupation by occupation, nation by nation, the world is to be brought under the dominion of God.

The **program of conquest** must be primarily **educational**. "So faith cometh by hearing, and hearing by the word of God" (Romans 10:17). But hearing is not enough. "But be ye doers of the word, and not hearers only, deceiving your own selves. For if any be a hearer of the word, and not a doer, he is like unto a man beholding his natural face in a glass [mirror]: for he beholdeth himself, and goeth his way, and straightway forgetteth what manner of man he was. But whoso looketh into the perfect law of liberty, and continueth therein, he being not a forgetful hearer, but a doer of the work, this man shall be blessed indeed" (James 1:22-25).

The message of dominion is **self-government under God's law**, by the grace of God, through faith in Jesus Christ, and Him crucified. Nothing less will suffice. We need organizations. They must be **hierarchical** in structure, but not primarily bureaucratic. They must be more like courts of law, with rules on top, and supervisors who issue judgments in a hierarchical chain, but the rulers are only to **manage by exception**. They are to handle the problems that arise from below, not impose a command system from the top. Isn't this God's way? Don't we face a day of final judgment? Doesn't God give us spheres of influence, for which we are fully responsible? Isn't the **development of maturity** based on the progress of **self-mastery over time**, through trials and tribulations?

Then let us stop longing for a cosmic miracle to bail us out. The blessed hope we should have is Christ's return in power and glory, as the capstone of history, when He will deliver up a **completed** kingdom to His father, after He has put down all His opponents (I Corinthians 15:24-26). He will not deliver up an unleavened loaf as a peace offering to God, but a fine loaf, fully leavened, fully risen (Leviticus 7:13), ready for that final baking. The satanic leaven, Satan's kingdom, He has reserved for burning. Satan's kingdom is being replaced by God's leavened dough.

Let us eat no more unleavened bread. The sacrifice is over. Let us eat no more bitter herbs. Let us drink the wine of celebration. Christ is our Passover. We no longer look for an overnight deliverance from bondage, as the Hebrews did. We are free men, ambassadors of Christ, bringing to the kingdom of Satan God's peace treaty, and its terms are simple: **unconditional surrender**. The victory, in principle, is over. "And I appoint unto you a kingdom, as my Father hath appointed unto me; that ye may eat and drink at my table in my kingdom, and sit on thrones judging the twelve tribes of Israel" (Luke 22:29-30).

We are the judges. We shall judge the angels (I Corinthians 6:3). Why should we continue to sit quietly, huddled in our tiny congregational fortresses, as if Satan were about to sound his trumpet, and we were defending the last outpost? The next time Satan tries that stunt will be the day of judgment for him. Until then, he is in a defensive battle. Let us make it hot for **him**. Let him get a foretaste of things to come. Let us get the signatures of the bulk of his followers on the peace treaty which God offers to all people who will surrender unconditionally.

SUMMARY OF PART III

Get to work.

CONCLUSION

CONCLUSION

What is Christianity? That's a tough question. You might want to answer it **historically**. What has it been, and what is it today? That approach will take a lifetime of work, and it will make a pessimist out of almost anyone who attempts to answer it. Christianity is a lot of things historically. But it has generally been a religion of **this** world—a religion based on conquest, to one extent or another, a religion of exploration and dominion. It has also been a religion of the written word, of creeds and tracts and theological treatises. It has been a religion that has stressed commitment to a sovereign God who intervenes in the processes of time.

What is Christianity? This question can also be answered **theologically**. That's what I've tried to do in this little book. I have looked at important questions that Christianity has answers for: What is God? What is man? What is law? And what do our answers have implications for: family, church, state, economy? What does the Bible tell us about these aspects of human thought and culture? In other words, what **difference** can Christianity make in this world?

Here are a few of the important themes of this book. If my arguments are generally faithful to the Bible, then these themes are biblical themes:

The Trinity (One and Many simultaneously)
The Trinity (ontological and economical)
The sovereignty of God: predestination and providence
The personalism of creation (cosmic personalism)
The image of God in man
Man's subordination to God (personal and legal)
Nature's subordination to man

233

Man's ethical rebellion: total depravity
The two sonships: natural and ethical (adoption)
The curse of nature (scarcity)
Holiness (set apart-ness): God and man
Salvation: definitive, progressive, final
Salvation: justification, sanctification, dominion
Biblical law: judicial, moral, dominical
Nature's restoration under law
God's peace treaty: surrender and conquer
The impossibility of neutrality
Restitution
Decentralization (anti-pyramid)
Self-government under biblical law (responsibility)
Courts of appeal (hierarchies)
Multiple sovereignties (competition and cooperation)
God's law and God's love: correlative
Covenants and sacraments
Bureaucracy vs. responsibility
Delegated authority and dominion
God's laws vs. Satan's laws
God's law and economic growth
Satan's laws and poverty
Kingdoms as leaven: growth and maturity
Evangelists as ambassadors
Evangelists as educators
Strategy and tactics (God's omniscience)
The last outpost: God's or Satan's

The basic theme, as it applies to man, is **redeemed** man's dominion over creation, in time and on earth. It is not the victory of
Satan, in time and on earth.

My hope is that a growing number of Christians will begin to
take seriously God's dominion assignment. They will take seriously
His law. They will take seriously the biblical teaching of the continuity of victory, in time and on earth. They will then begin to
train themselves for the battle. They will start reading more, and
getting involved in the battles confronting the kingdom of God.
They will begin to take personal responsibility for applying God's
law to their area of personal influence.

There are **four kinds of sheep** in this world: rams that lead, ewes that follow, wandering sheep that get sheared, and lost sheep that get roasted. What I'm recommending to all of God's sheep is that they either become rams or follow rams. I'm convinced that the overwhelming majority of Christ's sheep in this century are wandering sheep who are following equally lost sheep, and they are certain to get shorn by the enemy. We have adopted a **theology of inevitable shearing** and a **psychology of the about-to-be-shorn**. Until we adopt a theology of victorious head-butting, making rams of our herd rather than drifting sheep, we will not escape our plight. God will allow this generation to be sheared.

I intend to do my best to butt my head against the satanic goat and his kingdom. I suggest that you do the same. If I didn't have complete confidence in the Good Shepherd, I wouldn't risk the headaches. If I weren't convinced that He has delegated head-butting responsibilities to His sheep, I wouldn't advocate the effort. But He is trustworthy, He did delegate the assignment, and He did promise victory to His sheep. I figure the best way not to get sheared is to butt heads with the enemy, not run wildly into the enemy's pens. It's a shame that so many professional wandering sheep have adopted a theology which tells them that being sheared is inevitable, or even more improbably, that Christ will secretly sneak down and unlock the gate of the pen to let His sheep out, when nobody else is looking. The best advice I can give you is to **stay out of the pen in the first place**. Let's build a pen for the goats. They belong in the pen, not us.

One of the aspects of modern Christianity that most discourages me is the unwillingness of Christians to discipline themselves to read. This is true even of pastors, who should be the leaders in any program of Christian reconstruction. Judaism has emphasized the importance of education and life-long reading, and the result has been the influence of Jews in modern life way out of proportion to their numbers. But this is precisely what we should expect: blessings in terms of God's requirements.

Christians seldom read. They read simple things when they read at all. This is slowly beginning to change as the Christian school movement grows, but it is like moving an iceberg. Ill-informed people cannot take effective leadership positions. Until we are willing to read, as a people, we will be the followers rather than the leaders. Until we are ready and willing to offer systematic alternatives to the world of humanism—workable, well-thought-out alternatives—we will remain captives, just as surely as the Hebrews were captives in Egypt, Assyria, Babylon, and Medo-Persia. The price of our deliverance is our willingness to master the Bible, which in turn means mastering the world, for the Bible is an all-encompassing document calling men to a program of comprehensive dominion.

The books and materials are available. Each Christian should at least be willing to master his own calling, meaning the published materials in his profession. He should be reading steadily to see what the Bible has to say to him concerning his work. That's the minimum requirement. But the task is broader than this. We must be specialists and generalists simultaneously. He who reads can usually teach. He who teaches gains influence. The teacher, if he has prepared himself, has taken Peter's words seriously: "But sanctify the Lord God in your hearts: and be ready always to give an answer to every man that asketh you a reason of the hope that is in you with meekness and fear" (I Peter 3:15).

I have provided you with a bibliography. That's all I can do. The rest is up to you.

BIBLIOGRAPHY

BIBLIOGRAPHY

This book is based on the findings of a lot of other authors. Readers who are convinced that there is merit to the perspective of this book owe it to themselves to continue their investigation of these topics. They cannot expect to be able to master the whole field by rereading this little introductory book.

There are several areas that may interest readers. There is **theology proper.** Questions of the nature of salvation, the reliability of the Bible, the history of Christian doctrine, and so forth may be of interest. There are several books I can recommend that are written in modern English and that deal with contemporary problems. Then there is the question of **biblical law.** Several good books are available in this field. The question of **eschatology**—the "last things"—is important too. The same is true of **education.**

What about the Bible itself? Aren't there several translations available? Aren't there a lot of different Bible commentaries, Bible study aids, and other materials? There are tons of material, most of it not very good. But there are some useful, reliable, and even valuable items. There are books every serious Christian has to own.

So let's make a brief survey of the field. What are the basic materials that serve as foundations for the kind of Christianity found in this book's outline?

Bibles and Bible Study:

Your basic tool is a King James Version edition of the Bible. The American Bible Society makes available many inexpensive editions, but the best study Bible is unquestionably the *Thompson Chain Reference Bible*, published by the B. B. Kirkbride Bible Co. Most Bible book stores sell it. If you were to limit yourself to only one Bible, this would be the one to buy.

Modern translations have advantages and problems. Anything

done by committee has problems, including the King James Version. The *New American Standard Bible* is reliable. The *Modern Language Bible*, also known as the Berkeley Version, is readable, although it contains some of the silliest footnotes on the Bible ever published.

For careful study, I'm a great fan of *The Bible Self-Explained*, published by Moody Press. It gives you a King James Version translation, but in between almost every verse are small type parallel or related verses from other parts of the Bible. When you're trying to study a verse or a chapter, this saves a great deal of time, since you don't have to look up parallel verses and go flipping through the Bible. It has done at least the preliminary groundwork for you.

You need a Bible concordance. There are two good ones that are keyed to the King James Version (which is why you memorize the King James Version, so you can find missing verses that have slipped your memory): Strong's and Young's. Both are good. For Bible study, which involves word studies, Young's is better. For locating missing verses, Strong's is better. A short concordance, like Cruden's, isn't very useful. A less expensive edition of *Strong's Exhaustive Concordance* is sold by Puritan Reformed Discount Books, 1319 Newport Gap Pike, Plaza 41, Wilmington, DE 19804.

An adequate one-volume Bible commentary is *The New Bible Commentary: Revised*, published by Eerdmans. Multi-volume commentaries that are good include Keil & Delitzsch, *Commentary on the Old Testament*, published by Eerdmans; Matthew Henry's *Commentary on Whole Bible*, published by Revell, and also by MacDonald Pub. Co., in McLean, Virginia; and Charles Ellicott, *Bible Commentary*, published by Zondervan, 4444 52nd St., S.E., Grand Rapids, MI 49505.

Biblical Law:

The simplest introduction to the topic is R. J. Rushdoony's book, *Law and Liberty*, published by Thoburn Press, 11121 Pope's Head Rd., Fairfax, VA 22030. His comprehensive book, *Institutes of Biblical Law*, Vol. I, was published in 1973 by Craig Press, and a second volume is scheduled for publication soon by Thoburn Press. *The Institutes* is a detailed study of the Ten Commandments, with the other laws of the Bible catalogued under one or more of the Ten Commandments. The first volume is almost 900 pages long. You cannot say you understand the Bible if you haven't read this book. Craig Press, P.O. Box 817, Phillipsburg, NJ 08865.

Another lengthy defense of the idea of biblical law is Greg Bahnsen's *Theonomy in Christian Ethics*, published by Craig Press. He has also written a brief book on one aspect of biblical law, *Homosexuality: A Biblical View*, published by Baker Book House. His next book, a lengthy defense of *Theonomy* against all its critics, is scheduled for publication by the Geneva Press, 708 Hamvassy, Tyler, TX 75701. Bahnsen has also written a short defense of biblical law, *The Authority of God's Law,* shortly to be published by Geneva Press.

The first volume of my own economic commentary on the Bible, which is a specific application of Biblical law in an academic discipline, has been published: *The Dominion Covenant: Genesis.* It was published by the Institute for Christian Economics, P.O. Box 6116, Tyler, TX 75711. A second volume on Exodus is scheduled for publication soon. A simplified verse-by-verse version appears each month in the *Chalcedon Report*, which is available by request from Chalcedon, P.O. Box 158, Vallecito, CA 95251. Chalcedon also published a book-length study on biblical law in *The Journal of Christian Reconstruction*, Vol. II, No. 2 (Winter, 1975-76): $5.00.

Eschatology:

A simple introduction is J. M. Kik's book, *An Eschatology of Victory*, published by Presbyterian & Reformed Publishing Co. Also important is the exegesis of Romans, chapter 11, in John Murray's fine commentary, *The Epistle to the Romans*, published by Eerdmans. Also good is Charles Hodge's late-19th-century book, *Commentary on the Epistle to the Romans*, also published by Eerdmans. Romans 11 deals with the conversion of the Jews as the prelude to a long period of external, international blessings. Roderick Campbell's fine book, *Israel and the New Covenant*, is available from Geneva Press.

A book-length study of the millennium was published in *The Journal of Christian Reconstruction*, Vol. III, No. 2, (Winter, 1976-77). It is available for $5.00 from Chalcedon, P.O. Box 158, Vallecito, CA 95251.

An important essay is Benjamin B. Warfield's "Are There Few That Be Saved" (1915), which appears in his book, *Biblical and Theological Studies*, published by Presbyterian & Reformed. This is a very valuable book to own on theology in general.

Iain Murray's book, *The Puritan Hope*, provides an introduction to the beliefs concerning the future of Christ's kingdom that were held in 17th-century England and America. It is published by the Banner of Truth Trust, and sold by Puritan Reformed, 1319 Newport Gap Pike, Plaza 41, Wilmington, DE 19804.

Education:

The best book is R. J. Rushdoony's classic, *The Messianic Character of American Education* (1963), published by Thoburn Press. It's a book exposing the religious impulse of the humanists who founded the American public education system. Another of his books, *Intellectual Schizophrenia*, shows the conflict between Christianity and so-called "neutral" education. It is also published by Thoburn Press. *The Philosophy of the Christian Curriculum*, his third book on education, is published by Ross House Books, P.O. Box 67, Vallecito, CA 95251.

The Purpose of a Christ-Centered Education, edited by David Cummings, is a good introduction to the philosophy of Christian education. It was published by Presbyterian & Reformed, P.O. Box 817, Phillipsburg, NJ 08865

The Journal of Christian Reconstruction, Vol. IV, No. 1 (Summer, 1977) is devoted to a report on education. Available from Chalcedon, P.O. Box 158, Vallecito, CA 95251, for $5.00.

Essays on Christian Education by Cornelius Van Til is an advanced book, but absolutely necessary for providing a proper philosophical foundation for all education. It is published by Presbyterian & Reformed.

For an introduction to university education, and what the Christian view is in contrast to the secular view, in education, psychology, economics, mathematics, politics, sociology, and philosophy, see *Foundations of Christian Scholarship*, published by Ross House Books, P.O. Box 67, Vallecito, CA 95251: $7.50.

Rebirth of a Nation, by Donald Howard, shows what can be done by means of Christian education; published by Accelerated Christian Education, Rt. 1, Box 114, Lewisville, TX 75067. On the legal war against independent Christian education by State bureaucrats and humanists, see Alan Grover's book, *Ohio's Trojan Horse*, published by Bob Jones University Press, Greenville, South Carolina.

A free monthly newsletter for Christian teachers is available from *The Biblical Educator*, P.O. Box 6116, Tyler, TX 75711. Others besides teachers may subscribe.

Economics:

Tom Rose's book, *Economics: Principles and Policies from a Christian Perspective* is the only textbook on Christian economics. It is published by Mott Media, P.O. Box 236, Milford, MI 48042. He is also the author of *How to Succeed in Business*, available from the author c/o Economics Dept., Grove City College, Grove City, PA.

My book, *An Introduction to Christian Economics*, is available from the Institute for Christian Economics, P.O. Box 6116, Tyler, TX 75711. Also good is E. L. Hebden Taylor, *Economics, Money, and Banking*, published by Craig Press. More exegetical than the others is my economic commentary on the Bible, *The Dominion Covenant: Genesis*, also published by the Institute for Christian Economics.

Two issues of *The Journal of Christian Reconstruction* deal with Christian economics: Vol. II, No. 1 (Summer, 1975), and Vol. VII, No. 1 (Summer, 1980). Available from Chalcedon, P.O. Box 158, Vallecito, CA 95251; $5.00 each.

A free newsletter, *Biblical Economics Today*, is available from the Institute for Christian Economics, P.O. Box 6116, Tyler, TX 75711.

Politics:

The most important books are written by R. J. Rushdoony. The most important one is *Foundations of Social Order: Studies in the Creeds and Councils of the Early Church*, published by Thoburn Press, as are all of the following books. This book shows the warfare between Christianity and the Roman Empire, as well as between Christianity and heresies of the early church. The political implications are spelled out in detail, something which no other book on the creeds attempts. Then comes *The One and the Many*, Rushdoony's history of political philosophy from early paganism to modern humanism. It deals with the war between the decentralized Christian political order and the centralized humanistic State.

Politics of Guilt and Pity provides specific applications of biblical principles to political and economic topics. His two studies of American political history are also important: *This Independent Republic*, a study of early American history, and *The Nature of the American System*, essays on the conflict between Christian political principles and Unitarian and humanist political principles.

Two issues of *The Journal of Christian Reconstruction* are relevant: the one on politics (Vol. V, No. 1, [Summer, 1978]) and the one on the American Revolution (Vol. III, No. 1, [Summer, 1976]). Both sell for $5.00 from Chalcedon, P.O. Box 158, Vallecito, CA 95251. The issue on biblical law also applies.

E. L. Hebden Taylor has written *Reformation or Revolution*, published by Craig Press. It deals with society as a whole, but also with politics.

R. L. Dabney's *Discussions*, Vol. IV, *Secular*, is an important 19th-century work, published by Ross House Books, P.O. Box 67, Vallecito, CA 95251.

John Robbins' book, *Answer to Ayn Rand*, counters the secular humanist philosophy of anarchism: The Trinity Foundation, P.O. Box 169, Jefferson, MD 21755; $2.50.

Theology:

Two books by R. J. Rushdoony are good: *Infallibility: An Inescapable Concept* and *The Necessity for Systematic Theology*, published by Ross House Books, P.O. Box 67, Vallecito, CA 95251. His little book on retreatism is important: *The Flight from Humanity*, published by Thoburn Press, 11121 Pope's Head Rd., Fairfax, VA 22030.

Benjamin B. Warfield's books are all very good. The ten-volume set of his collected works is available from Baker Book House, and an abridged five-volume set from Presbyterian & Reformed. Presbyterian & Reformed also publishes a two-volume set of shorter essays, available nowhere else. Books of sermons and theology are also available, which are not included in the sets of Warfield's collected works. All can be obtained from Puritan Reformed Books.

John Murray's little book, *Redemption Accomplished and Applied*, is good on the order of salvation. It is also published by Eerdmans and distributed by Puritan Reformed Books, 1319

Newport Gap Pike, Plaza 41, Wilmington, DE 19804.

J. Gresham Machen's books, written in the 1920's and 1930's are all good: *What is Faith?*, *Christianity and Liberalism*, *Christian Faith in the Modern World*, and *The Origin of Paul's Religion*. Eerdmans keeps these books in print.

Herman Bavinck's books are all very good. Strongly recommended is *Our Reasonable Faith: A Survey of Christian Doctrine*, published by Baker Book House in Grand Rapids, Michigan.

Perhaps the most important works from the Protestant Reformation are Martin Luther's *The Bondage of the Will*, published by Revell, and John Calvin's *Institutes of the Christian Religion*, published by Westminster Press.

Gordon Clark, *Biblical Predestination*, published by Presbyterian & Reformed, is a readable introduction to the question of the sovereignty of God.

Philosophy:

The one philosopher whose works should be mastered by serious Christians is Cornelius Van Til. His works are not easy to read, but they can be read by people without degrees in philosophy. An easy introduction to his thought is Richard Pratt's book, *Every Thought Captive*, published by Presbyterian & Reformed. More difficult but still popular is R. J. Rushdoony's *By What Standard?*, published by Thoburn Press.

Van Til's general approach, called biblical presuppositionalism, is defended in George Marston's simple little book, *The Voice of Authority*, published by Ross House Books, P.O. Box 67, Vallecito, CA 95251.

Booklets by Van Til that are good introductions are: *Who Do You Say that I Am?*, *My Credo*, and *Why I Believe in God*. He also wrote *The Intellectual Challenge of the Gospel*, *Paul at Athens*, and *Is God Dead?*

His books include *The Defense of the Faith*, *A Christian Theory of Knowledge*, *A Survey of Christian Epistemology* (which I think is one of his best), *The Doctrine of Scripture*, *Christ and the Jews*, and his classic, *Christianity and Barthianism*. *The New Modernism: An Appraisal of the Theology of Barth and Brunner* (1947), is still worth reading. He also wrote several syllabi, including *An Introduction to Systematic Theology*, which is very good, and *Christian Theistic-Evidences*, which is important for understanding how

not to argue for God's existence. His *Psychology of Religion* is also very useful.

Two books contain essays on his work, some critical (in the first book), as well as favorable ones: *Jerusalem and Athens*, edited by E. R. Geehan, published by Presbyterian & Reformed, and *Foundations of Christian Scholarship*, edited by Gary North, published by Ross House Books. The latter book contains an important essay on Van Til's theology written by John Frame.

Most of Van Til's books are published by Presbyterian & Reformed, P.O. Box 817, Phillipsburg, PA.

History:

S. G. De Graff, *Promise and Deliverance*, a four-volume Bible history, is distributed by Presbyterian & Reformed.

Alfred Edersheim's books are lengthy but excellent: *Old Testament Bible History* and *The Life and Times of Jesus the Messiah*, both published by Eerdmans. Also very good are *The Temple: Its Ministry and Services* and *Sketches of Jewish Social Life*, published by Eerdmans.

A standard multi-volume history of the church is Philip Schaff's *History of the Christian Church*, published by Eerdmans. A less expensive set is sold by Puritan Reformed. Another is Kenneth Scott Latourette, *A History of Christianity*, published by Harper & Row (2 vols.), and his longer sets, *A History of the Expansion of Christianity* (7 vols.), published by Zondervan, and *Christianity in a Revolutionary Age* (5 vols.), published by Zondervan (paperback) and Greenwood (hardback). Eerdmans publishes a series edited by F. F. Bruce, *The Advance of Christianity Through the Centuries*.

On the premises of history, see R. J. Rushdoony, *The Biblical Philosophy of History*, published by Thoburn Press, and Gordon H. Clark, *Historiography: Secular and Religious*, published by the Craig Press.

On the fact that the bulk of those who call themselves Jews today are really the descendants of a medieval nation located in what is now southern Russia, the Khazar kingdom, see Arthur Koestler's book, *The Thirteenth Tribe* (Random House, 1976). For a thoroughly documented study of modern Israel's history, see Alfred M. Lilienthal, *The Zionist Connection: What Price Peace?* (Dodd, Mead & Co., 1978).

Newsletters:

Christian Reconstruction (bi-monthly)

Biblical Economics Today (bi-monthly)

Biblical Educator (monthly)

Occupy! (monthly)

Tentmakers (pastors, church officers only;
bi-monthly)

Published by: The Institute for Christian Economics
P.O. Box 6116
Tyler, TX 75711

Temple Times (weekly)

Published by: Calvary Temple
2560 Sylvan Rd.
East Point, GA 30344

Chalcedon Report (monthly)

Published by: Chalcedon
P.O. Box 158
Vallecito, CA 95251

Calvin Speaks (monthly)

Published by: Geneva Divinity School
708 Hamvassy
Tyler, TX 75701

All of these newsletters are sent free of charge on request. They are wholly supported by voluntary donations.

Publishers:

Baker Book House
1019 Wealthy St., S.E.
Grand Rapids, MI 49506

Banner of Truth Trust
(British)
Distributed By:
Puritan Reformed Books
1319 Newport Gap Pike
Plaza 41
Wilmington, DE 19804
($5.00 annual membership fee)

Craig Press
(See Presbyterian & Reformed)

Eerdmans
255 Jefferson Ave., S.E.
Grand Rapids, MI 49503

Presbyterian & Reformed
P.O. Box 817
Phillipsburg, NJ 08865

Puritan Reformed
(see Banner of Truth)

Ross House Books
P.O. Box 67
Vallecito, CA 95251

Thoburn Press
11121 Pope's Head Rd.
Fairfax, VA 22030

SCRIPTURE INDEX

OLD TESTAMENT

Genesis

1	83
1:2	18
1:3	10
1:11-12	11
1:24	95
1:24-25	55, 72
1:26	18, 24
1:26-28	23, 91, 196, 201
2:7	23
2:10-14	25
2:15	25
2:17	26, 55
2:19-20	91
2:20	25
3:4	26
3:5	13, 26
3:8	18
3:12	33
3:13	34
3:15	27
3:17-19	34, 147
3:21	36
3:22	40
3:24	201
4	39
4:4	17
7:5	24
9:1-7	84, 91, 196
9:15-17	181
11	143
11:7	18
12:1-3	99
15:2-3	99
15:13-16	208
15:16	211
15:18	99

Genesis

17:1	15
17:23	114
18:32	72
19:26	196
25:23	198, 204
25:29-34	198
27:1-7	204
31:1	165
31:36-42	165
32:24-30	111
34	115
39:6	198
39:22	198
41	167
41:34	131
41:38-43	165
41:40-43	198
47:24	131

Exodus

5	22
8:7	195
8:18	195
12:8	183
12:11	118
12:13	118
12:15	125, 184
12:26-27	107, 120
16:15	211
16:31-35	211
18:20	140
18:21-22	140
18:25-26	140
19:6	107
20:1-17	216
20:5	16

Exodus

20:11	160
20:12	95, 162
21:15, 17	76
21:19	75
21:22-25	204
21:24-25	75
21:30	75
22:5-6	159
22:18-20	76
23:10-11	72
23:25-26	162
23:26	99
23:29-30	69f
32:32	220

Leviticus

3	107, 120
7:13	183, 228
13	134f
13:3-44	134f
13:45-46	135
13:57	135
14	134f
14:35	135
19:1-2	14, 15
19:29	160
19:36	160
20:7	15
20:10	76, 160
20:26	15
23:17	183
25:8-17	198

Numbers

14	80
14:6-10	207
14:24	207
20:7-11	121

Deuteronomy

4:5-8	58, 64, 78 198, 199
6	99f
6:4	19
6:6-7	94, 140
7:6-8	73
8	65f, 97, 112, 161

Deuteronomy

8:10-17	163
8:10-20	38
8:11	68
8:11-20	199
8:17-18	68
8:19-20	66
10:17-19	109f
14:26	121
14:28-29	97f
19:15	123-124
20:10-11	198
20:10-13	63
20:10-15	210
20:12-15	198
21:17	97
22:8	159
22:23-24	76
24:5	170
28	65f, 112, 161, 197
28:15-68	38, 66
28:20	163
31:10-13	140
32:21	199
34	202

Joshua

2	64
2:9-11	211, 213
2:12-13	220
5:12	211

Judges

1	208
1:2	70
2:34	202
9:45	196

I Samuel

8:5	131
8:11-12	130
8:13-18	131
8:20	131
16:15-23	166
17	165f
18:10-11	166
24:20	166

II Samuel
12:14   59, 65

II Kings
6:15-20   194

I Chronicles
26:16-19   136
26:21   136
29:14   145

Ezra
1:3   72
36:24-27   117
36:26-27   43

Job
1   215
1:6-12   29
28:28   139
38-41   41, 83, 210
42   41

Psalms
24:1   145, 197
24:1-2   11
51:5   62
90:1-2   12
94:12   48
119:9-12   57
127:3-5   93, 162
139:7-8   12

Proverbs
1:7   139
11:14   203
13:22   197
19:18   48
21:1   13

Proverbs
22:6   94

Ecclesiastes
12:13   139

Isaiah
6:9-10   180
28:13   74
43:13   13
53:4-5   16
55:9   11-12
57:15   12
64:6   18
65   162
65:17   199f
65:20   200

Jeremiah
17:9   63
17:18   63
31:32-34   112
31:34   140
50:34   72

Daniel
3   22
5   67
6   67

Amos
3:2   16

Jonah
3:5-10   72, 115

Malachi
3:6   55

NEW TESTAMENT

Matthew
3:13-36   114
4   35, 56
4:8-9   126
5:5   65

5:13   196
5:14   199
5:14-16   144
5:15-16   199
5:17   220

Matthew			*Matthew*	
5:17-18	55		28:19-20	217
5:48	15		28:20	220
6:11	184			
6:24	31		*Mark*	
6:32	127		2:22	70
6:33	127, 162		9:48	196
7:12	168		9:49	196, 212
7:15-20	58		13:31-32	20
7:16	71		14:36	120
10:34-36	79		14:61-64	19
12:30	79			
12:38-41	118		*Luke*	
13:3-8	105		1:36	114
13:3-23	179		2:2-4	145
13:11	180		3:38	49
13:15	180		10:33-35	96
13:24-30	179ff		12:42-48	145
13:30	65		12:45-48	145f
13:31-32	179, 183		14:20-30	155
13:33	183		16:1-8	145
13:34-35	179f		22:12	118
13:37-42	180		22:26	111
13:43	180		22:29-30	118, 228
13:44	179		24:46-47	45
13:45-46	179			
16:18	27, 53, 191		*John*	
16:25-26	5, 6		1:1-5	39
18:15	123		1:10-12	39
18:16	123		1:13	45
18:17	124		2	121
18:18	128		3:3	43
18:23-35	179		3:6-8	43
20:27-28	165		6:44	20
21:33-41	197		10	206
22:14	42		13-17	118
22:30	56, 103		14:2	105
24:6	185		14:6	20
24:35	55		14:26	18-19
24:37-39	181		15:12	108
25:14-30	179, 197		15:17	108
25:15-16	157		16:7	19, 89
25:20-23	158		16:13	89
25:41	27		21:15-17	207
26:11	161			
28:18	218		*Acts*	
28:18-20	177, 192, 212		1:8-9	219

Acts

2:41-42	119
5:26-29	132
6	207
6:2	106
8:36	116
8:38	106
13:48	45
16:33	114, 116
17:26-27	40
25:11	76
28:27	180

Romans

1:18	38
1:18-20	59, 62
1:18-25	31-32
2:14-15	63, 78
2:15	220
3:20	47
3:23	30
3:24	47
3:31	60
4:11-12	115
5:6-8	16-17
5:12	30
6:1-2	60
6:23	30
7	197
7:9-12	59-60
7:22-23	71
7:23-25	122
8:7	57
8:13-15	40
8:19-23	52
8:26	19
8:29	46
8:30	47
8:33	47
8:38-41	42
9	210
9:7-8	115f
9:11	116
9:11-13	61
9:14-15	61
10:8-10	41
10:17	227

Romans

10:19	199
11	227
11:11	199
11:25	199
11:36	12-13
12:18	132
12:19	129
13:1	129
13:2	129, 141
13:3	129f
13:4-7	130
13:5	132
13:7	132
13:10	109

I Corinthians

1:18	44
1:26	42
1:29	43
2:14	43f, 45
5:17	118
6:2-3	123
6:3	193, 228
6:5	123
6:6-7	123
6:14	58
7:2	103
7:8	103
7:14	115
7:29	103
7:32-33	103
9:24	46
10:12-14	121
11:8-9	91
11:11-12	91
11:21	119
12	110
12:12-14	121
14:34-35	107
15:24-26	127
15:45	75
15:50	191
15:52	187, 191

II Corinthians

3:17	89

II Corinthians

5:17	43
5:21	49
6:14	101
9	111

Galatians

3:10	60
3:13	60
3:16	116
3:16-18	99
3:16-19	208
3:24	57, 71
6:16	112

Ephesians

1:3-6	29
1:4	105
1:4-5	40, 42
2:1-10	41
2:5	45
2:8-9	196
2:10	48
2:11-12	112
4:11	106
4:14-16	108f
5:11	58
5:22-28	92
6:11	197
6:14-17	197
6:19-20	64

Philipians

2:5-8	21
2:12	52, 146, 150
3:14	46
3:20	12

Colossians

1:23	219
3:18-20	92

II Thessalonians

3:10	111

I Timothy

1:4	145

I Timothy

2:12-14	107
2:14	32, 92
3:2, 12	93
3:4-5, 12	93
3:10	106
3:11	106
5	111
5:3-13	98
5:8	98
5:14	103
6:10	109

II Timothy

1:9	29
4:7-8	46

Hebrews

1:10-12	13
8:5	218
8:8-10	112
8:10	118
8:11	140
10:10	74
10:12-14	74
12:1	46, 72
12:6	48

James

1:17	220
1:22-24	4
1:22-25	227
2:10	44
2:17-18	71

I Peter

1:3-5	46
1:22	108
2:9	107, 121
3:1	91
3:6	91
3:7	91, 92
3:15	226
3:16	226, 236

II Peter

2:1-2	105

II Peter

3:10-14	191

I John

1:5	9
1:6-10	17
3:4	17
3:14	108
3:16	108
4:8	9

Revelation

1:18	191
6:10	194

Revelation

9:1-6	195
12:4	194
12:5-9	126
12:9	13
12:10-12	127
20	67
20:7-9	218
20:7-10	186, 200, 218
20:14	17, 126, 201
21	56
21:24, 26	74
21:27	220
22:2	74, 201

INDEX

Abel, 17, 37, 39
Abortion, 204
Abraham, 72, 97, 98, 99, 208
  Circumcision, 114, 115
Abram, 98, 100, 111
Abundance, 38
Accounting, 158
Adam, 38, 70, 107
  Assignment, 34, 111, 169
  Basic training, 36
  Calling, 25, 34, 91
  Curse, 33ff., 40
  Intelligence, 36
  Originial sin, 16, 30, 48
  Priest, 169
  Testing God's Word, 13, 67
  Treaty, 62
Adoption, 29, 39, 40, 50, 52, 53, 68, 110, 198
Adultery, 76, 160, 170
Africa, 188
Air, 147f
Allocation, 148
Ambassadors, 64f, 69, 70, 113, 118, 127, 210, 217, 221
Amorites, 202
Anarchy, 142, 151, 159, 160, 211
Angels, 33, 36, 180, 193, 194, 201, 228
Animals, 55
Answers, 4
Antinomianism, 138f, 150
Aristotle, 10
Army, 192ff, 207
Athens, 40
Athlete, 46
Atonement, 16, 32, 85, 59
Auction, 156
Authority, 203ff

Delegated, 204f, 219
  Structure of, 150
Autonomy, 132, 141, 215

Babel, 143f
Babylon, 67, 72, 79, 184
Balance, 170, 176
Baptism, 113ff
Basic training, 36
Bathsheba, 59
Beastiality, 160
Belshazzar, 67
Bible
  Inspiration, iii
Bitter herbs, 183
Blessings, 177, 197, 199, 200
Bloomsbury Group, 161
Boot camp, 218
Brotherhood of man, 39
Bureaucracy, 102, 106, 122, 136f, 205, 206, 209
Bystanders, 159

Cain, 37
Caleb, 80, 178, 207f, 213
Calling, 42, 43, 150
Calvary 71
Canaan, 15, 69, 184, 178, 198, 203, 208
Canaanites, 147, 164, 193, 211, 227
Capital, 148, 197, 198
  Growth, 100
  Preservation, 99
Capital punishment, 76, 77, 141f
Carnival, 149
Celebration, 119, 121
Centralization, 136, 143, 188
Chaos festivals, 149
Charities, 100

Charity, 111, 136
Children
  Dominion, 100
  Lord's Supper, 120f
  Tool of dominion, 94
Choice, 148, 175
Christ
  Commander 215
  Law and, 55f
  Law of God, 49
  Perfect man, 45, 47
  Restitution, 80
  Substitution, 85
Christian reconstruction, 7, 235
Christian Socialism, 98
Church, 27
  Agency of dominion, 122
  Bureaucracy, 106
  Christ's love, 92
  Community 108
  Division of labor, 110
  Doctrine, 108f
  Eschatological, 105
  Excommunication, 124f
  Hierarchy, 106
  Historical, 105
  Impotence, 176
  Infallible, 133
  Institutional, 105
  Invisible, 105
  Kingdom and, 126, 128
  Leadership, 111
  Offices, 106
  Sacraments, 113ff
  Social club, 125
  Women officers, 107
Circumcision, 115
Citizenship, 12
City on hill, 58, 144, 199
Civil government, 171
Clean slate, 62
Clock, 11
Coercion, 153
Collective, 110
Collectives, 72f
Commander-in-Chief, 26, 34-35
Commanders, 226f

Communion, 18; see Lord's Supper
Communism, 6
Communist Party, 133
Competition, 156
Complexity, 143
Compound interest, 100
Confession, 17
Conquest, 69f
Conscience, 132
Consumer, 152, 154, 158
Continuity, 190
  History, 216
  Victory, 211, 213, 216
Continuity in history, 187, 200
Continuity of defeat, 202
Continuity of history, 180f, 185
Control, 56
Co-operation, 37, 169
Cosmic chess, 27
Cosmic egg, 10
Cosmic personalism, 83
Costs, 155, 156, 159, 167
Court of law, 47
Courts, 204
Covenant, 111ff
  Church, 126
  Family, 114
  Sign, 116
Covenantalism, 90
Creation, 10, 24
  Personal, 24
Creator, 9ff
Creator-Creature, 83
Creator-Creature distinction, 11ff
Cross, 70, 110
Curse, 137, 148, 163
  Of law, 60
  Removal of, 52
Curse of ground, 37
Curses, 73

Darius, 67
David, 59, 166
Day, 10, 11
Day of judgment, 125
Death, 29, 49
Decapitalization, 197

Decentralization, 89, 140, 143, 149, 204
  Church teaching, 222
Defeat, 216
Defections 195
Definitive sanctification, 45
Deism, 12
Delegation, 203ff, 219
Depravity, 44, 169
Depression, 164f
Despair, 205, 206
Devil, 13
Devolution, 36
Dinah, 115
Discipline, 122, 217
  Market, 157, 167
Discontinuity, 181, 182, 184, 205f, 209
Disinheritance, 40, 54, 62
Divine right, 151, 161
Division of labor, 102, 110, 138, 140, 150, 158, 175
Doctrine, 108
Dominion, 23, 50, 158
  Assignment, 37, 91, 201, 209, 210
  Delegation, 204f
  Evangelism, 223f
  Image of God, 24
  Impulse, 208
  Law and, 73, 196, 213
  Lord's Supper, 119
  Marriage, 102f
  Population and, 162
  Service and, 166
  Subordination, 31, 198, 215
  Whose?, 184
Dominion assignment, 37, 53, 80, 84, 191
Dominion Covenant, 23, 84, 111, 113, 125
Dominion man, 31, 50, 189, 190, 207
Double portion, 97
Dough, 184f, 189, 190
Dr. God, 13
Drunkenness, 119

Economic commentary, i

Economic good, 148
Economic growth, 162, 163
Economic justice, 164
Eden, 37, 148, 169, 188, 201
Education, 94f, 235
Egypt, 67, 79, 80, 131, 183f, 184, 195
Egyptians, 14, 22
Election 39, 42f, 62
Emperor, 5
Enemies of God, 63
Entrepreneurs, 157, 166
Environmentalism, 34, 35
Envy, 154, 167
Esau, 61, 97, 116, 198, 204
Eschatology, 210, 216
Ethics, 15, 28, 30, 33, 54, 195, 208
Ethiopian eunuch, 116
Evangelism, 77, 78, 223
Eve, 13, 25
Evil, 181
Evolution, 14, 21, 36
Excommunication, 124f, 128
Exploitation, 153, 157
Eye for eye, 75f

Factory, 158
Facts, 24
Faith, 41, 45, 51, 71 99, 101
Fall, 26ff, 138
False teachers, 105
Family
  Capital, 99
  Capital punishment, 76
  Christ divides, 79
  Church office, 93f
  Dominion, 102, 103
  Fellowship, 101f
  Future-orientation, 99
  Hierarchy, 91f, 92
  Judgment, 93
  Lord's Supper, 118
  Mutual obligations, 95
  Name, 101
  Self-government, 98
  Training, 93
  Trustee, 98ff
  War against, 169

Welfare, 96, 98
Fatherhood of God, 39
Fear of God, 139, 140
Feeney, 124
Fellowship, 17
Fire, 185, 191
Firstborn, 118
First-fruits, 184
Flood, 84, 181, 200
Forgiveness, 17
Foreign aid, 164
Four G's, i
Franklin, 197
Freedom, 167, 170, 211
Free market, 151, see Market
Fruit, 58
Fruits, 71
Funeral, 119
Future, 157, 167
Future orientation, 99

Gambling, 101
Gates of hell, 27, 53, 80, 214
Goat, 235
God
  Army of, 172f, 188, 207
  Character and law, 80
  Court of law, 47
  Creator, 10-11
  "Dr.", 13
  Enemies of, 63
  Fatherhood of, 39
  Fear of, 139, 140
  Forgiveness, 17
  Holiness, 56
  Holy Spirit, 18-19, 20, 89
  Image of, 23, 39, 42, 54, 84
  Jealous, 16
  Justice, 175
  Kingdom of, 67
  Law of, 43, 47, 49, 113
  Love, 108
  Mercy, 63, 175
  Mercy of, 63
  One-many, 110, 203
  Ownership, 145
  Personal, 18, 24

Persons, 18, 19
Promise, 99
Promises, 100
Property, 15, 23
Providence, 11, 21
Sovereignty, 11, 23, 25, 41, 90, 93
  147, 169, 204, 210
Trinity, 18ff, 72, 106
Unity, 19

Gold, 165
Good Samaritan, 96
Gospel, 59, 70
Government
  Civil, 171
Grace, 41, 45, 68
Grape juice, 120
Great commission, 177, 192, 212, 217
Growth, 175, 182, 183ff, 189
Guilt, 163

Hagar, 116
Haran, 99
Harmony 168
Heart, 43, 45, 117, 180, 220
Heaven, 12, 53
Hebrews, 15, 70, 72
Hell, 27, 33, 50, 60, 61, 192, 193, 196,
  see also Gates of hell
Helpmeet, 25
Heroin, 160
Hierarchy, 91, 106, 130, 140, 144, 150,
  151f, 158, 167f, 204, 206, 228
High priest, 19, 132
History, 7, 46, 74
  Continuity, 216
  Dynamic, 213, 216
Hivites, 115
Holiness, 14ff, 56, 58, 115
Holy Spirit, 18-19, 20, 89
Homosexuality, 160, 161
Households, 115, 119
Humanism, 94, 138
Humility, 12
Hypocrisy, 59, 60

Idols, 117

Image, 32, 33
  Twisted, 42
Image of God, 23ff, 37, 54, 84
  Hatred of, 39
Incest, 160
Institute of Christian Economics, i
Institutions
  Sovereignty, 89
Investment, 100
Isaac, 204
Ishmael, 97, 116
Islam, 213
Israel, 73, 111, 118, 198

Jacob, 61, 97, 111
Jealousy, 199
Jericho, 164, 210
Jethro, 140
Jews, 101, 177, 199
Job, 201
Jonah, 115, 118
Jordan, James, i
Jordan River, 208
Joseph, 67, 198
Joshua, 80, 207f, 213
Jubilee, 198
Judge, 28
Judges, 57, 118, 123, 228
Judgment, 57, 217
  Final, 182, 187
  National, 160
Justice, 122, 164, 175
Justification, 47ff

Keynes, J. M., 148, 161
Kingdom, 53, 64, 118
  Bureaucratic?, 206
  Centralized, 188
  Church and, 126, 128
  Internal, 209
  International, 127
  Man's, 131
  Satan's, 80
  Visible, 127
  Whole world, 199f
Kingdom of God, 67
  Bureaucracy?, 206, 207

Comprehensive, 212
  Decentralized, 227
  Whole earth, 191
Kingdom of Satan, 27

Labor unions, 152ff
Last outpost, 192ff
Law, 68, 138f, 216
  Confirmation, 220
  Curse, 86, 212
  Discipling, 221
  Equality under, 158
  God's, 38
  Love, 109
  New Testament, 124
  Read to all, 140
  Schoolmaster, 86
  Sin and, 17
  Tool of dominion, 80, 85, 113,
    189, 196, 203, 213, 216
Law of God, 43
  Christ and, 55ff
  Christ's conformity to, 47
  Control, 56
  Curse, 60
  Dominion, 73
  Gospel, 59
  Holiness, 59
  Love, 110
  Permanent, 56
  Power, 56f
  Schoolmaster, 57, 59
  Social order, 89
  Three uses, 49
  Tool of dominion, 100
  Treaty, 113
  Universal, 99
  Work of, 78
Leadership, 207f, 211, 213
Lease, 197
Leaven, 183, 184, 189, 190, 228
Leprosy, 134, 159
Lewis, C. S., ii
Life span, 200
Light, 9
London, 100
Lord

Trinity, 175
Lord's Supper, 118
  Children, 120f
  Dominion, 119
  Household, 119ff
  Victory, 119
Lot, 72
Love, 9, 108, 109, 110
Lamennais, 143

Man
  Brotherhood, 39
  Creature, 24ff
  Depravity, 44, 169
  Dominion, 24ff, 31
  Image, 32, 33, 84
  Image of God, 24ff, 37
  Judge, 28
  Perfect, 45, 47
  Pseudo-creator, 13f
  Responsible, 33
  Steward, 26
  Subordinate, 26, 28, 30, 31, 35, 85
Manager, 151f
Managers, 168
Manna, 211
Mardi Gras, 149
Market
  Discipline, 157
  Sovereignty, 159
Market process, 156
Marxism, 148f, 163, 213, 216
Maturity, 95, 108, 228
Meaning, 46, 83
Meekness, 210, 226
Mercy, 29, 63, 175
Messiah, 16, 21
Middle Ages, 101
Millennium, 187
Miracles, 211
Mistakes, 157
Money, 110
Money calculation, 167
Monopoly, 152
Moses
  Judgment, 140
Motivation, 176

Murder, 37, 76, 204
Mustard seed, 183
Mustard tree, 190
Myths, 10

Nathan, 59
Nations, 217
Natural law, 38, 69, 78
Natural men, 44
Nature
  Curse, 35, 85
  Cursed, 37, 52
  Incomplete, 24
  Rebellion, 34
Nebuchadnezzar, 21f, 67
Neighbor, 96
Nero, 103
Neutrality, 35, 69, 79, 83
New heavens, 199f
Newsletter, 222f
Newsletters, i
Nineveh, 72, 115
Noah, 84, 182, 192

One-many 72, 102, 110, 175, 203, 226
Optimism, 100, 207, 213f
Oven, 185-186
Ownership, 145, 146ff

Palestine, 70f, 77, 187, 219
Pantheism, 12
Parables, 179, 189
Paradox of Deuteronomy Eight, 66
Passover, 118, 119, 120, 123, 187
Peace, 142, 186
Pentecost, 119, 182
Perfection, 142
Personalism, 147
Pessimism, 165, 205f, 208, 211
Philip, 116
Pied Pipers, 113
Pietism, 217
Poor, 161f
Population, 162
Potiphar, 198
Poverty, 38, 50, 53, 98, 137, 163, 164
Power, 33, 52, 56f, 198

Service, 111
Powers, 129
Prayer, 51
Predestination, 214
Price, 156f, 168
Priest, 169
Priests, 107
Profit, 166
Progress, 53, 200
Property, 11, 23
    God's 15
Prosperity, 66, 68, 163
Prostitution, 160
Providence, 11, 21, 83
Publican, 124
Publishing, 222f
Puritans, 100
Pyramid, 36, 90, 143, 170

Quarantine, 134
Questions, 3f

Rahab, 64, 113,
Rapture, 186
Rebekkah, 204
Rebellion, 32, 34, 67, 169
Red Sea, 121
Reformation, 100
Regeneration, 43ff
Religion, 3, 5
Responsibility, 33, 85, 146, 147, 150,
    188, 204
Restitution, 74ff, 80, 125, 142, 159
Restoration, 41, 51ff
Return of Christ, 181, 186
Revelation, 38, 78
Revolution, 85
Rhodesia, 164
Robot, 189
Roman Empire, 5, 106

Sacraments, 113ff
Sacrifice, 74, 80, 100, 196, 211, 218
Salt, 196, 211
Salvation, 38ff
    By man, 133, 144
    State, 137, 138

Sanctification, 43ff, 71f, 73, 74, 86,
    114, 115
Sanhedrin, 19-20
Satan, 26, 53
    Autonomy, 215
    Bureaucrat, 206
    Capitulation to, 209f
    Decapitalization, 197
    Defeated, 70
    Defeats God?, 188f
    Defections, 195
    Eviction, 126
    Family revolution, 92
    Kingdom, 64f, 67, 80
    Last outpost, 194, 214
    Last rebellion, 200
    Last stand, 127
    Leaven, 190
    Lies, 112, 186, 194
    Powerless, 33
    Rebellion, 67
    Society of, 90
    Squatter, 198
    Tempter, 126
    Thief, 220
Saul, 166
Scale of being, 12
Scarcity, 37, 38, 137, 147f, 148
School, 225
Schoolmaster, 57, 59, 86
Science, 11
Second death, 17, 33, 52, 125
Second Lieutenant, 24f, 26, 31, 34
Seeds, 180f
Self-government, 86, **98**, 105, **122**,
    124, **140**, 141, 142, 143, 150,
    169, 204, **206**, 211f, 212, 217,
    228
    Law-order, 139
Sellers, 156
Separation, 15
Service, 111, 165, 166, 177
Sheep, 234f
Silas, 116
Sin, 17, 26, 33, 46, 49, 72, 122, 123,
    161
Sinners, 61

Slaves, 211, 213
Soaring Twenties, 164f
Socialism, 98, 151
Social action, 7
Social order, 89, 170, 176
Society of Satan, 79
Sodom, 72
Sonship, 40
Sovereignty, 23, 25, 41, 90, 137, 158, 214
  Final, 132f, 142
  Legal, 155
  Of God, 11, 93, 147, 169, 204, 210
  Of institutions, 89
  Visible, 218
Spark of divinity, 10, 14, 25
Specialists, 225
Stability, 175
Standards, 15, 16, 57, 71, 112, 222
State
  Caretaker, 160
  Divine, 14
  Education, 94
  Fear of, 14
  God's law, 78, 79
  Infallible, 133
  Legitimate functions, 134, 138
  Magician, 148
  Messianic, 94, 132, 134, 136, 137, 138, 148, 168
  Ministerial, 130, 142
  Negative, 134f, 150
  Night watchmen, 160
  Priesthood, 134
  Pseudo-family, 95, 97, 100f
  Punishment, 75
  Savior, 21, 32
  Vengeance, 129
  Welfare, 96
Steward, 145, 155
Stewards, 166
Stewardship, 26, 38, 158
Strachey, Lytton, 161
Strangers, 112
Strategy, 222ff
  One-many, 226
Strong drink, 121

Subordination, 20, 26, 28, 30, 31, 69, 85, 93, 200
Substitute, 16, 17, 49, 75, 76, 85
Suffering, 111
Sunday School, 108
Superiority, 93
Surrender, 195, 210, 220
Sword, 192

Talent, 157f
Tares, 179ff, 187
Tariffs, 152
Tax collector, 124
Taxes, 101, 130, 131, 132, 164
Temptation, 13, 35, 67, 126
Ten Commandments, 216
Third World, 163
Tickets, 157
Time, 30, 36, 48, 67, 100, 101, 148, 158, 183, 185, 227
Tithe, 121, 163f
Tompkins, Peter, 36, 143
Treaty, 61ff, 69, 74, 86, 112, 113, 117, 187, 192, 210
  Universal knowledge, 140
Tree, 26, 30
Tree of knowledge, 56, 84
Tree of life, 40
Trinity, 18ff, 72, 83, 106, 147, 150, 175
  Economical, 20
  Ontological, 20
Trustee, 98ff
Tunisia, 161

Uncertainty, 157, 167
Unconditional surrender, 69, 74
Unequal yokes, 101
Unions, 152ff
Unleavened bread, 125
Upper room, 118
Uzziah, 136

Vengeance, 75, 129
Victim, 74
Victory, 27, 74, 84, 111, 127, 140, 176
  Continuity, 26, 178

Eschatology of, 210
Internal, 202, 209
Lord's Supper, 119
Scenario, 177
Spiritual, 202
Voluntarism, 150

War, 62, 194
Wars, 185, 186, 187
Way of life, 3
Wealth, 167, 175
Welfare, 96, 135, 136, 137, 161

Welfare state, 161
Wheat, 179ff, 189
Wilderness, 113, 211, 213, 217
Wine, 70, 121
Wineskins, 70f
Witchcraft, 76
Wives
  Husbands and, 92
World War I, 165
Worm, 196

Zimbabwe, 164

ORDER BLANKS

I am including several pages of order blanks that you can use to get on mailing lists, find out about important programs, and buy materials. These organizations are hard working, geared to Christian reconstruction, and aimed at intelligent laymen. They all deserve your consideration. I strongly recommend that you cut out or tear out these pages and mail them to the various addresses that appear on each sheet. Nothing appears on the back sides of the sheets.

Gary North

Geneva Divinity School
708 Hamvassy
Tyler, TX 75701

Gentlemen:

I read about your school in Gary North's book *Unconditional Surrender*. I would like to find out more about the school. I understand that you sell audiotapes, workbooks, and textbooks that are part of a home-study course leading to various degrees in theology. Please send further information. I am especially interested in the following program:

☐ One-year course for high school graduates (no degree)

☐ Two-year course for college graduates (M.A. in theology)

☐ Three-year course for pastors (Th.B)

☐ Four-year course in theology (Th.M)

I would like to receive your monthly newsletter, *Calvin Speaks.*

_____ name

_____ number & street

_____ city, state, zip

☐ I'm enclosing a tax-deductible donation to help defray expenses.

Institute for Christian Economics
P.O. Box 6116
Tyler, TX 75711

Gentlemen:

I read about your organization in Gary North's book, *Unconditional Surrender*. I understand that you publish several newsletters that are sent out for one year free of charge. I would be interested in receiving the following:

☐ *Biblical Economics Today* and *Christian Reconstruction*

☐ *Occupy!*

☐ *The Biblical Educator*

☐ *Tentmakers* (church officers and seminarians only, please)

Please send any other information you have concerning your program.

_____ name

_____ number & street

_____ city, state, zip

☐ I'm enclosing a tax-deductible donation to help defray expenses.

Chalcedon
P. O. Box 158
Vallecito, CA 95251

Gentlemen:

I read about your organization in Gary North's book, *Unconditional Surrender.* I understand that you publish a monthly newsletter, the *Chalcedon Report,* and that this includes Dr. North's column, "An Economic Commentary on the Bible." Please add my name to your mailing list.

Also, I would like to receive any other materials you make available concerning books and other services, including *The Journal of Christian Reconstruction.*

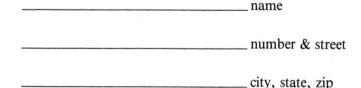

_____ name

_____ number & street

_____ city, state, zip

☐ I'm enclosing a tax-deductible donation to help defray expenses.

The American Vision
P. O. Box 720515
Atlanta, GA 30328

Gentlemen:

I read about your organization in Gary North's book, *Unconditional Surrender*. I understand that you publish a reading list dealing with the Christian history of America. I'd like to receive a copy. Also, I understand that you produce other educational materials. Please send me additional information.

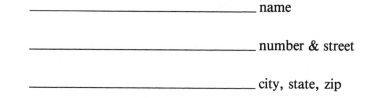

_____ name

_____ number & street

_____ city, state, zip

☐ I'm enclosing a tax-deductible donation to help defray expenses.

Foundation for American Christian Education
2946 Twenty-fifth Ave.
San Francisco, CA 94132

Gentlemen:

I read about your organization in Gary North's book, *Unconditional Surrender*. I understand that you publish materials showing the relationships historically between Christianity and the American Revolution and U. S. Constitution. Please send me further information. I also understand that you offer seminars for teachers in American history. I'd like to learn more about these seminars, either for myself or for a friend.

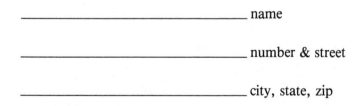

_____ name

_____ number & street

_____ city, state, zip

☐ I'm enclosing a tax-deductible donation to help defray expenses.

The Roundtable
1500 Wilson Blvd., Suite 502
Arlington, VA 22209

Gentlemen:

I read about your organization in Gary North's book *Unconditional Surrender.* I understand that you publish a monthly newsletter, *Roundtable Reports,* which sells for $15 per year. I would be interested in receiving a sample copy. Enclosed is a dollar to cover expenses. Please let me know about other aspects of your program.

_____ name

_____ number & street

_____ city, state, zip

Temple Times
2560 Sylvan Rd.
East Point, GA 30344

Gentlemen:

I read about your publication in Gary North's book, *Unconditional Surrender*. I would like to be added to your mailing list.

_____ name

_____ number & street

_____ city, state, zip

☐ I'm enclosing a tax-deductible donation to help defray expenses.

Thoburn Press
11121 Pope's Head Rd.
Fairfax, VA 22030

Gentlemen:

I learned about you in Gary North's book, *Unconditional Surrender*. Please send me a catalogue of your publications.

_____ name

_____ number & street

_____ city, state, zip

The AMERICAN SENTRY Report
P. O. Box 653
Ashland, OH 44805

Gentlemen:

I learned about your newsletter in Gary North's book *Unconditional Surrender.* I understand that you are the best source for
hard-to-get information of interest to serious Christians, and that
you are boiling down the information contained in other newsletters to make it available to us in condensed form. I understand
that the newsletter is published monthly, and costs $20.00 per year.

☐ Please send me a free sample copy.

☐ Enclosed is $20.00. Send me a year's worth.

_____ name

_____ number & street

_____ city, state, zip